CURRICULUM FOR INTEGRATED LEARNING

A Lesson-Based Approach

CURRICULUM FOR INTEGRATED LEARNING

A Lesson-Based Approach

Kent Freeland, Ph.D.
Morehead State University

Karen Hammons, M.A.
Morehead State University

Delmar Publishers

I(T)P® International Thomson Publishing

Albany • Bonn • Boston • Cincinnati • Detroit • London • Madrid
Melbourne • Mexico City • New York • Pacific Grove • Paris • San Francisco
Singapore • Tokyo • Toronto • Washington

NOTICE TO THE READER

Cover Illustration: Laurent Linn
Cover Design: Kristina Almquist

Delmar Staff
Publisher: William Brottmiller
Acquisitions Editor: Jay Whitney
Associate Editor: Erin O'Connor Traylor
Project Editor: Marah Bellegarde
Production Coordinator: Sandra Woods
Art and Design Coordinator: Carol Keohane
Editorial Assistants: Ellen Smith/Mara Berman

Copyright © 1998
By Delmar Publishers
a division of International Thomson Publishing

The ITP log is a trademark under license

Printed in the United States of America

For more information, contact:

Delmar Publishers
3 Columbia Circle, Box 15015
Albany, New York 12212-5015

International Thomson Publishing Europe
Berkshire House 168–173
High Holborn
London WC1V 7AA
England

Thomas Nelson Australia
102 Dodds Street
South Melbourne, 3205
Victoria, Australia

Nelson Canada
1120 Birchmont Road
Scarborough, Ontario
Canada M1K 5G4

International Thomson Editores
Campos Eliseos 385, Piso 7
Col Polanco
11560 Mexico D F Mexico

International Thomson Publishing GmbH
Konigswinterer Strasse 418
53227 Bonn
Germany

International Thomson Publishing Asia
221 Henderson Road
#05-10 Henderson Building
Singapore 0315

International Thomson Publishing—Japan
Hirakawacho Kyowa Building, 3F
2-2-1 Hirakawacho
Chiyoda-ku, Toyko 102
Japan

1 2 3 4 5 6 7 8 9 10 XXX 03 02 01 00 99 98 97

Library of Congress Cataloging-in-Publication Data
Freeland, Kent
    Curriculum for integrated learning : a lesson-based approach /
Kent Freeland, Karen Hammons.
      p.   cm.
    Includes bibliographical references and index.
    ISBN 0-8273-8176-X
    1. Education, Elementary—United States—Curricula. 2. Lesson
planning—United States.   3. Interdisciplinary approach in
education—United States.   I. Hammons, Karen. II. Title.
LB1570.F695   1998
372.13'028—dc21
                        97-18974
                        CIP

CONTENTS

CHAPTER

16

Learning Centers, Activity Cards, and Movement   223

PREFACE

We envision this book will be used as a textbook for a college course on methods for teaching or elementary/middle school curriculum. We wrote it from the viewpoint that teachers need information about integrating the various curriculum areas. It can be used primarily at the preservice, undergraduate level, although it should prove beneficial for the practicing experienced teacher, too. Undergraduates who use this book already may have completed a foundations of education course, introduction to education, and a course in human growth and development.

We chose as our title *Curriculum for Integrated Learning: A Lesson-Based Approach* because we focused our book on a practical approach, using actual lesson plans to illustrate major points. We designed some of the lesson plans to show how objectives can be established and taught to adults—those who are taking a college course—while others illustrate activities that actually can be implemented when teaching elementary-age students.

Our purpose is to encompass early elementary, elementary, and middle school education, taking into consideration the beginning of schooling for a young child through the end of the middle grades. Essentially, this book discusses integrated education from kindergarten through eighth grade. Although the integrative character of education is seen frequently in the early school years, we feel that middle school still exhibits integration, especially when teachers on a team work together to create units of study.

Good reading skills are vital to a student's success in school and good literature is important if learners are going to enjoy reading. We have included many book references in our chapters and have woven them into the lesson plans. Knowing that a classroom contains many reading levels, we have suggested a variety of books. Some of the books relevant to the chapter topics are easy books, while others are more difficult to read. A person who wants to find children's or adolescents' books should use one of the many search options to look up a topic.

Although the term *elementary* is used as a generic designation for the years that come before middle school, we use other words frequently to designate the educational range. *Early **elementary grades*** (K–3) occur before the *later elementary grades* (4–6), and both occur before **middle school** (5–8). *Early primary* (K–2) generally indicates the first few years of a child's schooling, while *later primary* (3–4) suggests the years that follow. Naturally, the years overlap when the terms **early elementary**, **later elementary**, *early primary*, *later primary*, *intermediate grades*, and *middle school* are used.

This book contains sixteen chapters that cover many different themes, including fingerprints, shelter, museums, technology, and the curriculum. It also contains five appendixes, including a directory of resources and materials, curriculum guidelines for professional organizations, and three matrices that show the organization of the lesson plans by content area, teaching/learning strategies, and grade level.

We have consolidated the three matrices into one comprehensive matrix that appears in the front matter. This matrix offers the reader a quick reference to a lesson plan's content and organization.

In order to ensure a consistent flow of information, all figures depicting lesson plans appear at the end of the lesson plan in chapters 3 through 16.

We have worked with integrated education at Morehead State University for several years, and much of the results of this effort are reflected in this book. Lesson plan formats, tips on how to get integrated methods started, and caveats about potential problems stem from the experiences gained from teaching this course to undergraduate students.

Many books on the market that address integrated curriculum contain information that paradoxically contradicts their purpose. By that, we mean there is a separate chapter on methods, a separate chapter on assessment, a separate chapter on reading, a separate one on social studies, a separate one on art, and so on. This text indicates true integration. Our book uses lesson plans as its backbone. Each plan contains several curriculum areas that are taught and assessed. This realistic presentation conforms to the way that education in an integrated setting actually occurs. We also juxtaposed the research evidence for the way a lesson is taught with that lesson. Therefore, the reader can easily read why the lesson is supported by sound learning principles.

ACKNOWLEDGMENTS

We would like to thank the following reviewers for their valuable input.

Jerri Carroll, Ph.D.
Wichita State University
Wichita, KS

Linda S. Estes, Ed.D.
Lindenwood College
St. Charles, MO

Jann James, Ed.D.
Troy State University
Goshen, AL

James R. Kerr, Ph.D.
Edward Waters College
Jacksonville, FL

Steven F. Reuter
Mankato State University
Mankato, MN

Legend

- Art
- Health
- Mathematics
- Arts & Architecture
- Music
- Visual Arts
- Reading
- History
- Science
- Anthropology
- Language Arts
- Writing
- Social Studies
- Geography
- Vocational Studies & Practical Living
- Industrial Technology
- Physical Education & Movement

Lesson Plans
For Teaching/Learning Strategies

for Chapters 3–9 by Grade Level and Content Area

CHAPTER:							
GRADE LEVEL:	3	4	5	6	7	8	9
CHAPTER	A B	B C	A B / C	A B / C	A B / C	C	C
CONTENT AREA							

TEACHING/LEARNING STRATEGIES

	3	4	5	6	7	8	9
Computer work							
Creative thinking	✓	✓	✓	✓	✓	✓	✓
Critical thinking	✓		✓	✓	✓	✓	✓
Data collecting			✓	✓	✓		
Decision making	✓	✓	✓	✓	✓	✓	✓
Deductive thinking	✓	✓	✓	✓	✓	✓	✓
Discussion	✓	✓	✓				
Dramatic activities		✓					

A   Early Elementary

B   Later Elementary

C   Middle School

TEACHING/LEARNING STRATEGIES

Exhibits	✓					
Experimenting			✓		✓	
Field trip					✓	
Games		✓				
Graphic representation		✓		✓	✓	
Inductive thinking		✓	✓	✓	✓	✓
Inquiry		✓	✓	✓	✓	✓
Interviewing				✓	✓	✓
Large group work	✓			✓	✓	
Learning centers						
Lecture	✓				✓	
Manipulatives	✓	✓		✓	✓	✓
Maps/globes					✓	
Modeling/demonstrating						
Multimedia materials	✓				✓	✓
Problem solving		✓		✓	✓	
Puppets						
Questioning	✓	✓		✓	✓	✓
Recitation						
Reflective Thinking	✓	✓		✓	✓	✓
Research			✓	✓	✓	
Role playing		✓				
Seatwork						
Simulation		✓	✓			
Skill development/practice		✓	✓	✓		✓
Small group work		✓	✓	✓	✓	✓

Legend

- Art
- Health
- Mathematics / Arts & Architecture
- Music / Visual Arts
- Reading / History
- Science / Anthropology
- Language Arts / Writing
- Social Studies / Geography
- Vocational Studies & Practical Living / Industrial Technology
- Physical Education & Movement

Lesson Plans For Teaching/Learning Strategies

for Chapters 10–15 by Grade Level and Content Area

TEACHING/LEARNING STRATEGIES	10	11	12	13	14	15
GRADE LEVEL:	C	BC	BC	ABC	BC	AB C
Computer work	✓	✓	✓		✓	✓
Creative thinking	✓	✓	✓		✓	✓
Critical thinking	✓	✓	✓	✓	✓	✓
Data collecting	✓	✓	✓	✓		✓
Decision making	✓	✓	✓	✓	✓	✓
Deductive thinking	✓	✓	✓	✓	✓	✓
Discussion	✓	✓		✓	✓	✓
Dramatic activities						

A Early Elementary
B Later Elementary
C Middle School

TEACHING/LEARNING STRATEGIES					
Exhibits					
Experimenting				✓	
Field trip			✓		
Games		✓			
Graphic representation				✓	
Inductive thinking	✓	✓	✓	✓	✓
Inquiry	✓	✓	✓	✓	✓
Interviewing	✓				
Large group work	✓	✓	✓	✓	✓
Learning centers					
Lecture					
Manipulatives		✓	✓	✓	✓
Maps/globes			✓	✓	
Modeling/demonstrating					
Multimedia materials		✓	✓	✓	✓
Problem solving	✓				✓
Puppets					
Questioning	✓		✓	✓	
Recitation					
Reflective Thinking	✓	✓	✓	✓	✓
Research	✓	✓	✓		✓
Role playing					
Seatwork					
Simulation					
Skill development/practice	✓	✓	✓	✓	✓
Small group work		✓	✓	✓	✓

THEMES: MAKING MEANING

KEY IDEAS

- Developing thematic teaching units enables a teacher to integrate content areas.
- Blocking of courses facilitates unit teaching and subject matter integration.
- Making an assessment to evaluate performance.

INTRODUCTION

Teacher education institutions must provide their undergraduate students with **field experiences** in elementary and middle schools. By the same token, undergraduate students desire (and sometimes feel anxious about) opportunities to meet, work with, and teach these youngsters. Although methods courses typically are taken separately, a growing number of teacher education institutions have elected to block **methods courses** and provide students with a shared field experience practicum (Lanier & Little, 1986). The intent of chapter 1 is to provide undergraduate students who are assigned to off-campus field experiences with some ideas about how to teach integrated units in classrooms.

THEMATIC TEACHING UNITS

Part of the daily routine in many classrooms involves studying a topic organized into a **thematic teaching unit** or concept **theme**. Because there is no single "right" way to introduce a **unit** of study to children, preservice teachers must learn many ways to choose, initiate, and carry out these units. They must understand that a unit of study can begin from an individual child's interest or from curricular goals and objectives the teacher considers important. Sometimes a unit of study will emerge naturally from a previous unit of study or a special unexpected event. The Different Ways of Knowing (DWoK) program (1994, pp. 13, 14) urges teachers to organize their **curriculum** into four phases: (1) students should explore what they already know about the theme; (2) students explore and research the topic; (3) students collaborate with each other to become more knowledgeable about the theme; and (4) students relate—or connect—what they learn.

After World War II, primary schools in England moved toward a child-centered curriculum (Parker, 1979) characterized by active exploration on the part of the students. The city of Reggio Emilia, Italy, also developed a new approach to schooling its young children after the war, emphasizing the creativeness of the child, a **constructivist approach** to a student's learning, the importance of a **whole language** orientation in the classroom, and the involvement of parents in schools (Bredekamp, 1993). School systems throughout the world have borrowed ideas from these two locations during the last five decades, so **integrated curriculum** and thematic unit instruction in the United States in the 1990s have precedents in practices found in schools in England and Reggio Emilia.

There seems to be a movement in the United States toward meaningful thematic teaching units (Allen & Piersma, 1995), with the teachers working together to actively involve students of different ages and abilities. By the end of the 1994–95 school year in Kentucky, 200,000 students and 8,500 teachers representing 837 schools were participating in what is called the primary school in that state (*Kentucky Teacher*, 1995). One of the main thrusts of this primary school is thematic unit instruction.

What Is a Thematic Teaching Unit?

A thematic teaching unit is a collection of materials, activities, and techniques organized around a concept or theme. It is an organizational tool that allows a teacher to relate subjects to one another, thereby avoiding a program that is highly fragmented by isolated daily lessons. A thematic teaching unit also enables the learner to make connections among understandings, attitudes, and skills as well as among curricular areas. Figure 1.1 contains a bare bones type of unit from which a teacher could construct many days of instruction.

The term **unit** may be considered the generic term for instruction on a general topic. Katz and Chard (1991) write that some educators often refine the term and reword it with slightly different meanings. They feel some educators design a thematic unit to be presented over time, usually for a week or two. Many or all of the components of the curriculum are included, for example, music, movement, mathematics, social studies, language arts, science, etc. Some units have a strong language- and vocabulary-building

---

FIGURE 1.1

Unit on Mexico

The following represents a "bare bones" thematic unit. A minimum number of items are used as examples, just to illustrate how the different parts fit together. For example, part I would contain more than one short paragraph; part II would have more than three concepts, more than one generalization to go with each concept, and more than three facts to accompany each generalization. This would then apply to the remaining parts III–VIII.

I. **Overview**

This unit is a study about the country of Mexico. We share not just a border with our neighbor to the south, but we have ties through customs, economics, and language.

II. **Concepts, Generalizations, and Facts**

   A. Currency
   1. People use money to buy things.
      a. Mexico uses the peso for its unit of money.
      b. There are 2,800 pesos to the U.S. dollar.
      c. Americans from border towns go to Mexico to shop for bargains.

   B. Population
   1. Rapid population growth presents problems.
      a. Mexico's population is growing at an annual rate of 3 to 4%.
      b. There are 90 million people living in Mexico.
      c. Unemployment in Mexico is high because of the large number of people looking for jobs.

   C. Living Accommodations
   1. Homes differ according to the geography of a country.
      a. Adobe houses are made of mud/clay that is found in the native soil of Mexico.
      b. Houses on large ranches are known as *haciendas*.
      c. In the tourist areas, such as Acapulco, there are expensive condominiums.

Continued

FIGURE 1.1 *Continued*

III. Understandings, Attitudes, and Skills
  A. Understandings
     1. Students will specify the rate of exchange between Mexican and United States currency.
     2. Students will know how fast Mexico's population is growing.
     3. Students will understand that there are a variety of residences in Mexico.
  B. Attitudes
     1. Students will appreciate the stability of the United States dollar compared to Mexican currency.
     2. Students will show sympathy for other people who live in crowded and cramped conditions.
     3. Students will take pride in their own homes.
  C. Skills
     1. Students will be able to make change with Mexican money.
     2. Students will be able to locate the largest cities in Mexico on a map.
     3. Students will be able to make a model of a hacienda.

IV. Motivational Activities
On the first day of the unit, the teacher will have a large outline map of Mexico attached to the bulletin board. Only a few of the largest cities will be shown on the map: Mexico City, Juarez, Acapulco, and Merida. The teacher will have some pictures cut out depicting an oil well, a mountain, a desert scene, a city, a cattle ranch, and a seaside resort. At the beginning of the day's lesson, the teacher will place each of these pictures at the top of the map, telling the class that each one shows an area of the country they are about to study. It will be up to the students—as the unit progresses—to be able to place the pictures in the proper location on the map. This activity will give the students a purpose for the unit and motivate them to learn about the various aspects of the country of Mexico.

V. Developmental Activities
To teach about the rapidly increasing population in some parts of Mexico, the teacher will have the students push their desks to the perimeter of the room and they will stand in a circle near their desks. The teacher will put strips of masking tape on the floor so that a large square—with sides that are roughly eight feet long—is created in the center of the room. The teacher will then ask a student to walk into the square. This solitary student represents a county with very sparse population; that is, there is plenty of room for this person to move around. Ask another student to enter the square. Continue to do this until students can't be added without bumping into someone who is already in the circle. At this point the teacher should ask the students in the circle how they feel about having this number of people "in their country." This activity will demonstrate the increasing feeling of cramped conditions as people are gradually added to a limited area.

VI. Self-Evaluation Checklist
As students work in small groups to build haciendas, they will be asked to evaluate their own efforts. When the project is completed, each member of the groups will complete the checklist as shown:

Continued

FIGURE 1.1 *Continued*

> ## Self-Evaluation Checklist for
> ## Understandings, Attitudes, and Skills
>
> Date: _____   Name: _____
>
> | *In this unit I did the following* | **Always** | **Usually** | **Sometimes** | **Very Seldom** |
> |---|---|---|---|---|
> | I contributed my share of effort to the group project | | | | |
> | I cooperated with the rest of the group | | | | |
> | I gave help or encouragement to others in my group | | | | |
> | I cleaned up the area at the end of the day | | | | |

At the end of the unit, each student will write a pen pal letter to a child in Mexico. The students will make a list of the things they learned about Mexico during the unit and then will include information about these items that correspond to their own area. For example, the students will need to mention the following information:

1. Population: Give the number of people who live in their hometown and home state.
2. Homes: Tell about the kind of homes they live in. They should tell what the house is made of, how many rooms it has, if it has a garage, if the child has a room of his/her own, etc.
3. Money: Write about the way they get spending money and the things they buy with it.
4. Climate: Explain how the climate of parts of Mexico compare to the climate where the student lives.

This concluding activity will allow the students to apply the concepts of the unit to their own surroundings. A connection can be made between the Mexican and United States examples for these concepts.

VII. Bibliography

For the students:

Orozco, J. L. *De colores and other Latin American folk songs for children.*
Shannon. T. *A trip to Mexico.*
Pope, B. N. *Your world: Let's visit Mexico.*
Epstein, S. *The first book of Mexico.*
Koch, S. *Mexico.*
Ross, P. *Mexico.*
Johnson, W. W. *Life, Mexico.*
Grossman, R. *Mexico: The land, the art, the people.*
Tosi, F. *New guide to Mexico.*

Continued

FIGURE 1.1 *Continued*

For the teacher:
    Riding, A. *Distant neighbors: A portrait of the Mexicans.*
    Montgomery, T. S. *Mexico today.*
    Hofstadter, D. *Mexico 1946–73.*
    Hodges, D. and Gandy, R. *Mexico 1910–1976: Reform or revolution.*
    Greeleaf, R. and Meyer, M. *Research in Mexican history.*
    Dominquez, J. I. and Lindenberg, M. *Central America: Current crises and future prospects.*
    Cumberland, C. C. *Mexico: The struggle for modernity.*
    Quirk, R. E. *Mexico.*
    Brand, D. *Mexico, land of sunshine and shadow.*
    Heusinkveld, P. R. *Inside Mexico.*
    Franz, C. *The people's guide to Mexico.*
    Michener, J. *My lost Mexico.*

VIII. Other Sources
    Videos
        Way of Life: Mexico, AIMS Media
        Mexico: Our Neighbor to the South, United Learning
    Videodisc
        STV: Maya, National Geographic
    CD-ROMs
        Legends of the Americas, Troll
        3D Atlas CD, Educational Resources
    Transparencies
        Mexico, CS Hammond
    Records
        Spotlight on Latin America, Hy Zaret and Lou Singer
    Kits
        Mexican Revolution of 1910, Multi Media Productions
        Conflicts of Culture, Multi Media Production
        Seeing Mexico Series, Coronet Films
        Mexican Arts and Crafts, Encore Visual Education, Inc.
        Mexico: Our Dynamic Neighbor, Teaching Resources Films
    Filmstrips
        Mexico: Landforms, Climate, Vegetation, Budek Films and Slides, Inc.
        The Course of Mexico's Culture, Multi Media Productions
        Exploring Ancient Mexico, Imperial Film Co.
        Seeing Mexico, Coronet Instruction Films
    Films
        Mexico: Four Views, Coronet Instructional Media
        Crowded City: Mexico City, Lucerne Films

basis and secondhand rather than firsthand information gathering. Breadth rather than depth of study is typical, as one can see from these examples:

- Woodland Indians
- Oceans
- Our Earth
- Transportation
- Community Helpers

Still other educators speak of a theme as being merely a focus, having no clear connection to a concept or idea; they consider it as being disconnected from concrete materials. Some examples of this approach include letters of the day, D is for dinosaur, color of the day, shape for Saturday, or number of the day.

Figure 1.2 shows what one elementary school created with its primary, fourth, and fifth graders as a six-week thematic unit on fairy tales, fables, and legends. This use of the term may conform to the way Katz and Chard perceive themes.

Katz and Chard explain their view about the **project approach** as being an extended study over time by individuals and small and/or large groups. Investigation is emphasized; children act as ethnographers, anthropologists, and data collectors. This approach is similar to the inquiry method of learning, which solicits students' feelings, choices, and selections. A wide variety of skills are embedded into the project, for example, writing, reading, building, calculating, problem solving, analyzing, observing, and experimenting. Children choose the focus, tasks, level of performance, and the length of time the project is studied. Projects have **horizontal relevance** rather than vertical relevance; that is, the work undertaken by the children is meaningful the same day rather than later and has direct relation to their life experiences. Their examples of projects are

- Study of Balls
- Shadows and Light
- School Buses
- Homes
- Water in Our Town

- Baskets
- Shoes
- Drinking Vessels
- Chairs
- Hats

It may be helpful to consider Katz and Chard's three terms in this relationship: (1) themes are names given to a broad topic and give rise to units on

FIGURE 1.2

Fairy Tales, Fables, and Legends

Mathematics

- Primary students made graphs to compare classmates' costumes (the number with hoods, with jackets, with ruffles).
- "The Shoemaker and the Elves" story encouraged counting by 2's.
  Many tales involved counting by 3's: three bears, three pigs, three wishes, three billy goats gruff.
- Older students kept lists of their readings, then determined the proportion of legends to fables read.
- Students learned how many years must pass before a character becomes a legend, then calculated how many more years must pass before people now living can be considered legends.
- Students compared the number of heroes to the number of villains in the books they read.
- Students in grade 4 conducted a survey to identify their classmates' favorite fable characters; they graphed the results.
- After reading about Johnny Appleseed, students measured apples and compared circumferences, diameters, weights.

Language Arts

- Readers of "The Lion and the Mouse" wrote all the words they could think of that had the long "i" sound in "lion" and the "ou" sound in "mouse."
- Students made red books and wrote about red things (apples, cherries).
- Older children audiotaped their parents telling or reading stories.
- Finding and writing about common themes in fairy tales became a portfolio project.
- Older students rewrote "Hansel and Gretel" from the witch's point of view; "The Three Little Pigs" from the wolf's point of view; and "The Three Bears" from the bears' point of view (Goldilocks was a vandal!). They read their original stories to the younger students.
- Students researched authors (such as the Brothers Grimm, Mother Goose).

FIGURE 1.2 *Continued*

Music

◆ Students learned ballads and songs about the fables, legends and characters they studied.
◆ Students used familiar melodies and changed the lyrics to fit thematic characters.

Geography

◆ Students identified on maps the Great Lakes, the Mississippi River, the Appalachian mountain range, the Grand Canyon and other "creations" of Paul Bunyon.
◆ Primary students made illustrated maps for Red Riding Hood and the Gingerbread Man adventures.

Science

◆ Students studied their characters' environments (coniferous and deciduous forests, tundra, mountains).
◆ They studied the health and nutritional value of Johnny Appleseed's apples; they learned about growing conditions and the effects of weather on apple production.
◆ In lessons about the human body and wellness, students learned to "be friends" to themselves (just as the fabled mouse was a friend to the lion) by taking care of their bodies.

Social Studies

◆ Johnny Appleseed readers researched the nation's most productive apple-growing regions and the impact of the crop on local economies and ways of life.
◆ After reading "The Mouse and the Lion," students assumed the roles of mouse and lion to learn skills for making and being friends.
◆ Students used maps to trace routes taken by Daniel Boone.
◆ Betsy Ross researchers created a play about her visit from George Washington and the creation of the first American flag.

Courtesy of the Kentucky Department of Education. To order information, contact the Kentucky Department of Education Publications Center, 500 Mero Street. Frankfort, KY 40601.

the topic; (2) thematic units are a series of preplanned lessons; and (3) each lesson could contain a project in which students can be engaged.

Pappas, Kiefer, and Levstik (1995) have a more liberal approach to a unit because they believe it can have either a broad approach or a narrow focus:

> Cumulative stories or information books on a particular topic (such as a country) or the study could focus on a specific kind of literature (such as poetry), the works of one author or illustrator, or even a single book. Whatever the topic or length of study, the aim of any thematic unit is to choose a topic worth knowing about that will provide a supportive context for meaning making (p. 50).

Some states have prepared a configuration of a unit so that teachers in that state have a guide as they prepare classroom units. This is called a **curriculum planning map** (see fig. 1.3).

A brief explanation of the boxed terms appears as follows:

- Level: Ages or grade levels

- Course Unit Title: Name of unit

- Approximate Time: How long unit will take

- Organizers: Connects the unit to life

- Goals/Selected Outcomes: Statements of objectives or purposes

- **Culminating Performance:** The way to end the unit

- Scoring Guide: A guide to determine how well the unit, or activities within the unit, have been accomplished

- Knowledge: What the students should be able to know, or understand

- Instructional/Assessment Activities: Activities in which students are engaged on a day-to-day basis, along with specified ways to evaluate the students

- Skills/Abilities/Attitudes: Statements indicating what students will actually be able to do, perform, or feel

- Critical Resources: Materials that will support the learning process

In a classroom where students are engrossed in thematic unit work, a visitor can detect certain qualities. Harmin (1994) terms these as active learning characteristics: (1) students are confident and ready to learn; (2) students are busy, engaged, and involved; (3) students are self-managing; (4) students work with each other in the room as a community; and (5) students are aware of what is happening around them in the classroom.

FIGURE 1.3

Curriculum Planning Map

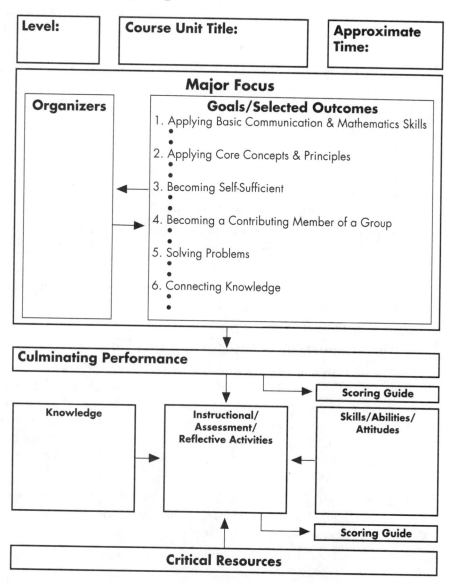

Courtesy of the Kentucky Department of Education. To order information, contact the Kentucky Department of Education Publications Center, 500 Mero Street. Frankfort, KY 40601.

How Do I Choose a Topic?

This is a very fundamental question for a teacher to address in the initial stages of planning. If the organization of the school is such that teachers are teaming, then the possibilities of themes become all that richer. The group—whether it is two, three, or more teachers—needs to consider the following in order to make a wise decision:

- What are the interests of the students? [After a survey, a teacher may find that a class is especially interested in pets.]
- What are the interests of the teachers? [Some of the teachers may have a particular interest in a foreign country.]
- What do the school's/district's curriculum guides require? [The district may have a scope and sequence already in place.]
- What is developmentally appropriate for the students? [Will it build upon previous knowledge? Will it be engaging?]
- Will there be enough resources to teach this unit? [Books, speakers, manipulatives, and primary source material need to be available.]
- Does the topic lend itself to incorporation of learning experiences from many curricular areas? [It's not a thematic unit if only one curriculum area is represented.]

How Important Is Integration to a Unit?

The final bulleted question from the preceding list can best be answered if several teachers who are teaming can sit down and create a webbing brainstorming (sometimes called *themestorming*). Webbing will be discussed in chapter 2. Integration is desirable because life is integrated. The problems people face daily are not only problems in mathematics or problems in geography, they are also problems requiring answers that involve knowledge and skills from many areas.

Integration can be visualized quite easily through a **Venn diagram** (fig. 1.4), which is used to organize information. It is composed of overlapping circles, usually two, that help show how things are alike and different.

When studying the topic of patterns, social studies can be taught by studying how quilts had different patterns and designs representing the culture of communities in such regions as New England and Appalachia as well as in other parts of the world. Good themes incorporate a basic organizing, conceptual question, which supplies a reason for studying it. In the instance of quilt making, for example, it would be important for students to have a

---

FIGURE 1.4

Venn Diagrams

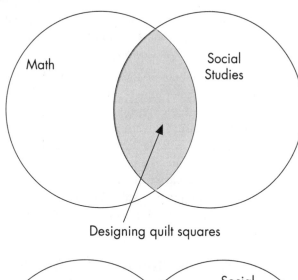

Designing quilt squares

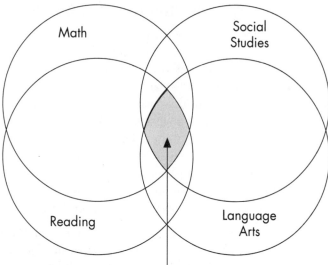

Designing quilt squares and a book extension activity

---

question in mind. One such organizing question may be: How are the lives of people reflected in their handicrafts? The organizing question is certainly open-ended. The question challenges the student to think about possible answers throughout the unit.

Continuing with the example about quilts, mathematics is brought in when the class makes quilt pieces from various geometric designs and calculates the size of the pieces that can be sewn into a large display. Reading and language arts are included when students select books, transforming them through play, art, drama, music, and language. Several examples that could lead to book extensions are Flournay's *The Patchwork Quilt* (1985) and Kinsey-Warnock's *The Canada Geese Quilt* (1989).

Integration should not be forced, however. If a group is studying the topic of elephants, a teacher must not feel compelled to have the students do activities on this topic during the entire day. What true mathematical value is there if a student writes the numbers one through five on paper outlines of five elephants? What is the benefit of having students use a gray crayon to color the shape of an elephant? What worth is there to having a cutout of an elephant hanging above a table, calling it the Elephant Writing Center? Theme connection to content subjects should not be artificially constructed; themes should "allow for a deeper examination of ideas" (Shanahan, 1995).

Can a Topic Be Too Broad or Too Narrow?

Sometimes a topic seems as though it would make an excellent unit, only to come to nothing when the students tackle it. The reason for this failure often can be attributed to lack of manageable focus. For example, many teachers believe the solar system is a great theme for students to study; however, the effort and work to truly understand our solar system is as great as the name suggests. Could a ten-year-old or a thirteen-year-old genuinely understand the solar system with the range of activities that are commonly available in a classroom? Would it be sufficient for a student to look at hand-drawn pictures of planets? Would it be adequate for a student to draw pictures of the planets on a sheet of paper? Could a student really experience the solar system from his or her desk?

Perhaps it would be better to decrease the enormity of the topic. The following list contains some unit titles that may be more appropriate yet still retain some connection to the topic of the solar system:

• Telescopes/binoculars

• Sizes—big and small

• Magnification

• Things far away

• Things close up

Students could even study about the topic of perspective in art, the art technique of pointillism, or the scientific effects of round objects that spin. By narrowing the huge and unrelated topic of the solar system, children can develop a curiosity about more relevant questions. They could attempt to find answers to

- What happens if I put two magnifying lenses on top of each other?

- What will the door look like if I view it through the other end of the telescope?

- Why does the window turn upside down when I look at it through a magnifying lens?

- How is it that this painting by Monet appears to be just a bunch of bumpy, colored dots when I hold it up close, but when I stand back it looks much more like a painting?

- How long will it take this spinning basketball to stop spinning?

- Do I really need to know this?

When Do I Teach Themes?

Thematic instruction does not occur in neat, one-hour, thirty-minute, or forty-five-minute blocks of time. On the other hand, very few teachers operate with thematic instruction the entire day, for time must be set aside for specific skill instruction. Teaching students about place value in mathematics is an example of skill instruction that is taught independently of any theme—it is taught for its own sake. Then, of course, there are contributions made by teachers of **special classes**. For example, the music teacher can add songs to a theme, the physical education teacher can include dances, and the art teacher can incorporate paintings. Although there are many opportunities for these special subjects to be integrated into themes, there are still times when they must be taught independently to offer instruction on specific skills, such as learning a tune in three-four time, arranging cutouts to form a **collage**, or kicking a soccer ball to develop eye-foot coordination.

Commonly, a large block of time is devoted to theme work either in the morning, the afternoon, or both. A two-hour period allowing students to work uninterruptedly on a thematic project or activity is an example of restructuring the day to allow for various students' interests, their learning styles, and the rate at which students assimilate information. A teacher may organize a day in the following manner:

8:00 AM–9:00 AM	Students arrive at school; attendance and other administrative matters are taken care of; news of the day is explored; a chapter from a book is read to the class; the learning centers in the room are explained
9:00 AM–10:00 AM	Students work on activities related to the theme topic at the learning centers; teacher and aide monitor/take anecdotal assessment notes on students; teacher holds skill sessions with various students
10:00 AM–10:20 AM	Physical education
10:20 AM–10:50 AM	Art teacher comes to the room
10:50 AM–11:20 AM	Buddy reading
11:20 AM–12:15 PM	Lunch
12:15 PM–1:00 PM	Journal writing
1:00 PM–3:00 PM	Students work on theme projects/activities while teacher and aide monitor, assess, and conduct skill sessions

How Do I Introduce a Unit?

Here are some different ways to introduce a unit.

1. The K-W-L activity (Roberts, 1996) is one technique a teacher could use to introduce a unit. K stands for "what I know about the topic," W is "what I want to know about the topic," and L is "what I learned from the unit." Additionally, some educators ask children to consider "How will I learn this?"—computers, books, interviews, etc.—and this modifies the technique into a K-W-H-L. K and W should be done at the outset, whereas L cannot be done until the unit has been completed. If a unit on moving around has been selected, then twelve-year-old students may feel they already know the following:

   • The fastest vehicle on land is a racing car.

   • A plane travels faster than cars or trains.

   • Electricity travels along wires.

   • People move from city to city during their lives.

   • A microwave causes molecules to move around and bump into each other.

The students may want to know the answers to these questions:

- Why are fish able to move so quickly in water?

- How can movies be made to work in slow motion?

- Why does Jell-O pudding get thick when I shake it up?

- Can a big truck move a load that weighs more than the truck does?

2. If a class is studying a unit on how people earn money, perhaps a guest speaker from the bank could come in to speak to the students about how a bank keeps customers' money and earns interest for them.

3. A very simple way to begin a unit is to read a story to the class. *Strega Nona* may be a good selection to begin a unit on eating.

4. Show pictures or a videotape to begin a unit. If the topic is voices, a collage of photographs could be displayed on a bulletin board showing various examples of people and machines capable of speaking or conveying messages.

5. Play a record or tape. If the topic is friendship, then one of Hap Palmer's songs could be played with the students analyzing the lyrics that convey acts of kindness.

6. Have the students learn a poem. If the theme is animals, a selection from Jack Prelusky's *A Gopher in the Garden and Other Animal Poems* would be an entertaining choice.

7. Have the students do an observation activity either in the classroom or outdoors. If the theme is light and dark, the class could take prisms outdoors and observe how light is refracted (bent) to display the rainbow colors.

8. Bring a visual representing something relative to the theme, for example, a piece of coral. The class could discuss where it came from, is it alive, what use does it have, etc.

ASSESSMENT

The purpose of student **assessment** is to find out what pupils have learned, and it needs to be attuned to the students' needs—especially those of younger students. Assessment is not something a teacher "does" on isolated occasions during the semester or grading period; rather, it is an ongoing process (Goodman, Goodman, & Hood, 1989). A teacher's observations are the mainstay of the kid-watching technique of assessing (Goodman, 1986). Some helpful tips on assessing students are given by Hohmann, Banet, &

Weikart (1979, p. 124): try out different evaluation forms; have a specific focus; and state a problem to solve and generate strategies for dealing with it. Hohmann, Banet, and Weikart have additional suggestions for teachers working in teams: set aside a regular time each day for evaluating and planning; share the recording tasks—have one member record the evaluation, for example, while another records plans and another keeps notes about individual children; and periodically look at how effectively the team works together.

A number of assessment strategies have been used frequently in the classroom over the years. One of the most common is observation. Figure 1.5 shows a form that can be used to record information that can be divided into *narrative* (data and facts) and *notes* (subsequent actions by the teacher).

Other assessment techniques include

- Teacher observing a student's behavior

- Teacher conferencing with a student

- Teacher reading a student's reflections written in a log or diary

- Teacher leading a group discussion

FIGURE 1.5

Narrative and Notes Observation Form

Observer _____   Observee _____

Site of Observation _____   Date _____

Beginning Time _____ AM PM   Ending Time _____ AM PM

NARRATIVE (data, facts)	**NOTES** (actions the teacher could take to meet child's needs)
[Write what you see and hear on this side. Give an objective account of what the child does, and write the words that come out of his or her mouth. Include facsimiles of the work, the drawings, the writings. Draw a diagram of the room and trace the child's movements, for example. This side includes only data. No opinions! No generalizations! No labeling! Note who the child interacts with. Count behaviors. Time performances. Get the facts without interpreting. Do not use names of teachers or children. Use code names.]	[Since you have already been taught how to observe children, write ideas for how you would support this child's continuing growth. What materials would help this child? What verbal and/or non-verbal support might you provide? How will you respond to meet the physical, emotional, social, cognitive, and aesthetic developmental needs of this child? In short, what will you do to help this child move toward the academic expectations/goals? What is your next step, based on the data you have collected?]

- Teacher listening to a student's experience summary (a recapitulation of his/her learning experience)
- Teacher keeping **anecdotal records** on a student
- Teacher examining student's work samples
- Teacher perusing a questionnaire a student has filled out to indicate his/her opinions/views on a topic
- Teacher viewing the student-completed check list that reflects how he/she has done on certain indicators
- Teacher administering and inspecting a sociogram to address a student's affective experiences
- Teacher preparing, administering, and scoring objective questions, such as matching, multiple choice, short answer, alternate choice
- Teacher constructing, administering, and grading subjective essay questions

Performance-Based Assessment

More recently, **performance-based assessment**, another approach to assessment, has been successfully used whereby actual products and performances of students are evaluated. For example, if an elementary student is studying the Constitution, he/she could create a wall poster to show how the First Amendment rights apply to one's life. If a middle school student is working with the impact of advertising, he/she could write a slogan to entice people to buy a product. Tasks or projects are more successful when they are related to real life, meaningful, and open to many solutions. Students are more enthusiastic if they are asked to approach the assignment with authenticity; that is, as though it may be a job a person in the real world may perform. A student could pretend to be (1) a commercial artist and design a display; (2) an advisor to a mayor and make recommendations about the use of a piece of city land; (3) a scientist and write regulations about using animals in experiments; (4) a historian and prepare a slide demonstration of famous Americans; or (5) a store clerk and write a letter to a supervisor about how to display a new product.

Portfolio

Students can showcase their work so their best results can be assessed. This is accomplished when a **portfolio** is compiled by the students—with input from the teacher. Portfolios are a type of performance assessment that reflects revisions of assignments and projects, showing growth over time. Students can integrate subject matter and skills easily from various content areas. Any of the following could represent a portfolio:

1. A videotape created by a group of students (technology and visual arts)

2. A copy of a letter a student received for writing an award-winning newspaper essay contest (language arts)

3. A photograph showing the neighborhood that the student had adopted in a litter cleanup campaign (science and visual arts)

4. A sketch showing a project the student had entered in a science fair competition (science and math)

5. A computer slide show

6. A computer spreadsheet or data-based printout

7. An audiotape the student had recorded when interviewing a local senior citizen (social studies and language arts)

8. Draft copies, along with the final copy, of a paper the student had written for a class assignment (reading and writing)

9. A chart showing the time it took the student to run a mile at various dates during the year (physical education and math)

10. Evidence to show self-assessment

Using portfolios allows the teacher to see how the student's work matured throughout the construction process. Teacher, student, and parents can have something tangible to discuss at conference time, enabling the student to reflect on the manner in which he/she chose the item and developed it.

Both areas of performance assessment and portfolios are consistent with the fact that children have various strengths when it comes to learning. Gardner's theory of multiple intelligences (1983) encourages teachers to consider the different ways students can exhibit what they know and are able to do.

REFERENCES

Allen, D. D., & Piersma, M. L. (1995). *Developing thematic units: Process and product*. Albany, NY: Delmar.

Barclay, K., Benelli, C., Campbell, P., & Kleine, L. (1995, Summer). Dream or nightmare? Planning for a year without textbooks. *Childhood Education*, pp. 205–211.

Bredekamp, S. (1993, November). Reflections on Reggio Emilia. *Young Children, 49*(1), 13–17.

Carroll, J. H., Ahuna-Ka'Ai'Ai, J., Chang, K., & Wong-Kam, J. (1993, April). Integrated language arts instruction: Reviews and reflections. *Language Arts, 70*(4), 310–315.

Crosser, S. (1990, November). Making the most of water play. *Young Children, 46*(1), 28–32.

deFina, A. (1992). *Portfolio assessment: Getting started.* New York: Scholastic.

Different ways of knowing: Institute discovery journal. (1994). Los Angeles: The Galef Institute.

Edwards, C. P., & Springate, K. (1993, Fall). Inviting children into project work. *Dimensions of Early Childhood, 22*(1), 9–12, 40.

Elkind, D. (1989). Developmentally appropriate practice. *Phi Delta Kappan, 71*(2), 113–117.

Farivar, S. (1993, Winter). Continuity and change: Planning an integrated history-social science/English-language arts unit. *Social Studies Review, 32*(2), 17–24.

Farr, R., & Tone, B. (1994). *Portfolio and performance assessment.* Orlando, FL: Harcourt Brace and Company.

Flournoy, V. (1985). *The patchwork quilt.* New York: Dial.

Fogarty, R. (1994, March). Thinking about themes: Hundreds of themes. *Middle School Journal*, pp. 30, 31.

Fogarty, R. (1991). *How to integrate the curricula.* Palatine, IL: Skylight.

Gardner, H. (1983). *Frames of mind: The theory of multiple intelligences.* New York: Basic Books.

Goetz, E. (1985). In defense of curriculum themes. *Day Care and Early Education, 13*(1), 12, 13.

Goodman, K. (1986). *What's whole in whole language?* Portsmouth, NH: Heinemann.

Goodman, K., Goodman, Y., & Hood, W. (Eds.). (1989). *The whole language evaluation book.* Portsmouth, NH: Heinemann.

Graves, D. (1993, Spring). Let's rethink children's entry points into literacy. *Dimensions: Journal of the Southern Early Childhood Association, 21*(3), 8–10, 39.

Harmin, M. (1994). *Inspiring active learning: A handbook for teachers.* Alexandria, VA: Association for Supervision and Curriculum Development.

Hohmann, M., Banet, B., & Weikart, D. (1979). *Young children in action.* Ypsilanti, MI: High/Scope Press.

Jasmine, J. (1993). *Portfolios and other assessments.* Huntington Beach, CA: Teacher Created Materials, Inc.

Katz, L. G., & Chard, S. C. (1991). *Engaging children's minds: The project approach.* Norwood, NJ: Ablex.

Kentucky Teacher (1995, Summer). Frankfort, KY: Kentucky Department of Education, p. A-15.

Kinsey-Warnock, N. (1989). *The Canada geese quilt*. New York: E. P. Dutton.

Lanier, J., & Little, J. (1986). Research on teacher education. *Handbook of research on teaching*. (M. Wittrock, Ed.). New York: Macmillan, pp. 527–569.

Maehr, J. M. (1991). *High/scope K–3 curriculum series: Language and literacy*. Ypsilanti, MI: High/Scope Press.

Nunnelley, J. C. (1990). Beyond turkeys, Santas, snowmen, and hearts: How to plan innovative curriculum themes. *Young Children, 46*(1), 24–29.

Pappas, C. C., Kiefer, B., & Levstik, L. (1995). *An integrated language perspective in the elementary school: Theory into action* (2nd ed.). White Plains, NY: Longman.

Parker, F. (1979). *British schools and ours*, PDK Fastback 122. Bloomington, IN: Phi Delta Kappa.

Peters, T., Schubeck, K., & Hupkins, K. (1995, April). A thematic approach: Theory and practice at the Aleknagik school. *Phi Delta Kappan*, pp. 633–636.

Prelusky, J. (1966). *A gopher in the garden and other animal poems*. New York: Macmillan.

Roberts, P. L., & Kellough, R. D. (1996). *A guide for developing an interdisciplinary thematic unit*. Englewood Cliffs, NJ: Prentice-Hall.

Roberts, P. L. (1996). *Integrating language arts and social studies for kindergarten and primary children*. Englewood Cliffs, NJ: Prentice-Hall.

Salyers, F. (1993, October). Fairy tales, fables and legends: How Drakesboro Elementary applied one theme to many subject areas. *Kentucky Teacher*. Frankfort, KY: Kentucky Department of Education, pp. 7–9.

Seely, A. E. (1995). *Integrated thematic units*. Westminster, CA: Teacher Created Materials, Inc.

Seif, E. (1993, Summer). Integrating skill development across the curriculum. *Schools in the Middle, 2*(4), 15–19.

Shanahan, T. (1995, May). Integrating curriculum: Avoiding some of the pitfalls. *The Reading Teacher, 48*(8), 718, 719.

Thompson, G. (1991). *Teaching through themes*. New York: Scholastic.

Wassermann, S. (1990). *Serious players in the primary classroom: Empowering children through active learning experiences*. New York: Teachers College Press.

Weaver, C., Chaston, J., & Peterson, S. (1993). *Theme explorations: A voyage of discovery*. Portsmouth, NH: Heinemann.

Wilson, L. (1991). *An integrated approach to learning*. Portsmouth, NH: Heinemann.

TIME

KEY IDEAS

- Time is relative: the younger the student, the less able he/she is to grasp the meaning of time.
- Because time is an abstract concept, children need experiences to build their understanding of the elements of time.
- **Webbing** with the concept of time results in a wide variety of topics.

INTRODUCTION

The activities described in this chapter will acquaint preservice teachers with several ways to introduce a unit on understanding, using, and measuring time. The **lesson plan** in this chapter differs from all the others in this book because it is designed for a group of college method students. As in all the other lesson plans in this book, the final step is for you to reflect upon and assess your planning and teaching. After working through the directions given to you in this chapter, you will have an opportunity to practice designing a lesson plan that conforms to the format in figure 2.1 and can be taught to a group of early elementary students.

FIGURE 2.1

LESSON PLAN FORMAT

Students'
Names: Date:

Title of
Lesson:

Ages/Grades:

Length of
Time:

Content
Areas: History, Reading

                   Writing

Materials:

Objectives:

Beginning:

Middle:

End:

Assessment
of Student
Learning:

LESSON PLAN

TITLE: **WAYS TO INTRODUCE A UNIT ON UNDERSTANDING, USING, AND MEASURING TIME**

Ages/Grades: College students

Time: Two hours

Content Areas:

 History, Reading

 Writing

Materials: Time-related books

Lesson plan format

Paper and pencil

References such as those by Piaget, Wasserman, Vygotsky, Elkind, and Hohmann

Objectives:
- Students will construct meaning from a variety of print materials for a variety of purposes through reading.

- Students will communicate ideas and information to a variety of audiences for a variety of purposes in a variety of modes through writing.

- Students will distinguish among the past, present, and future.

- Students will describe relationships among objects, ideas, and actions.

- Students investigate the manner in which scientific principles operate.

- Students explore a web and derive some observations from it about planning a unit about time.

- Students read/skim books to decide and describe the relationship between the books and time-related key experiences.

- Students (referring to the web, curriculum resource guides, and books) write and develop a draft form of a lesson plan for a unit on time.

Beginning: Can you recall any movies you have seen that dealt with the concept of time, for example, *Back to the Future*? How did the plot or events in the movie show the passage of time?

Middle: Today's work includes drafting a plan from which you can later create a lesson on the topic of time that you can teach to a group of early elementary children. Think of all the many different areas of the curriculum that can be brought into action. One way to summon the curriculum areas is to use the technique of webbing. Examine figure 2.2, which details how the topic of *community* is presented as a central focus with many curriculum areas webbed to it.

Pair yourself with another student in class and choose one of the books in figure 2.3 that relates to the topic of time. Use the experiences about time from your own lives and the information about time from the books to create a web diagram on time. Assume that you are preparing a lesson on time for a group of early elementary children who have already read this book. Refer to figure 2.4, which is a listing of high/scope experiences that deal with the past, present, and future characteristics of time. The lesson plan should conform to the format described in figure 2.1.

Think broadly of all the topics related to the concept of time. For example, time can refer to a grandfather clock, which can lead into the investigation of how such a mechanical object operates; time can be associated with music, and this can lead to understanding the tempo of a musical selection; or time can refer to chronology, causing students to reflect on changes occurring during their own lifetimes.

End: After all of the pairs in your class have had a chance to create a web and then a draft of a lesson plan, rearrange yourselves into groups of six (three pairs) so you can share what you have done with others.

Assessment of Student Learning: Have one of the pair of students from the class who feel confident that they have completed the task explain their web and lesson plan draft to the entire class. Through self-reflection, this pair should "think aloud" to the group, informing the rest of the class how their lesson plan contains elements of time from the book they used. Have the methods professors in the room give their opinions as to how well the pairs' plan conforms to the lesson plan format and how well it contains elements of time.

Return to the group of six you had earlier and have each of the three pairs go through a **debriefing**, telling the others how they would evaluate their plan, now that they have heard the professors' comments on the plan that was shared with the entire class. By reading articles and books on child development and learning theories—connected to the topic of children's understanding of time—each pair should expand and modify their ideas so that they could be used to teach a time-related lesson at a later date.

FIGURE 2.2

Web

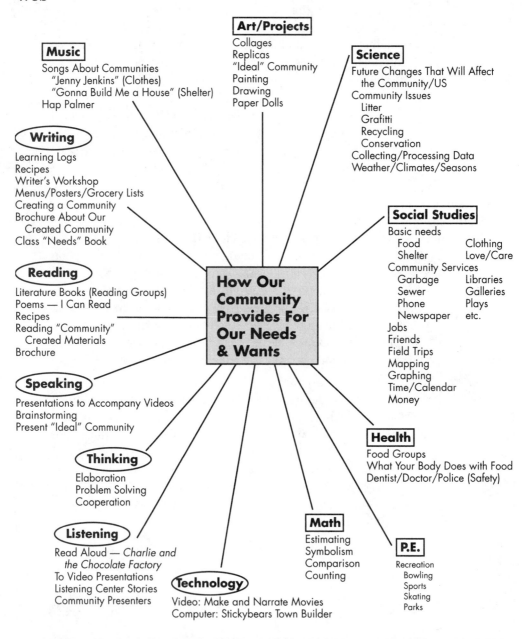

Music
Songs About Communities
  "Jenny Jenkins" (Clothes)
  "Gonna Build Me a House" (Shelter)
Hap Palmer

Writing
Learning Logs
Recipes
Writer's Workshop
Menus/Posters/Grocery Lists
Creating a Community
Brochure About Our
  Created Community
Class "Needs" Book

Reading
Literature Books (Reading Groups)
Poems — I Can Read
Recipes
Reading "Community"
  Created Materials
Brochure

Speaking
Presentations to Accompany Videos
Brainstorming
Present "Ideal" Community

Thinking
Elaboration
Problem Solving
Cooperation

Listening
Read Aloud — *Charlie and
  the Chocolate Factory*
To Video Presentations
Listening Center Stories
Community Presenters

Technology
Video: Make and Narrate Movies
Computer: Stickybears Town Builder

Art/Projects
Collages
Replicas
"Ideal" Community
Painting
Drawing
Paper Dolls

Science
Future Changes That Will Affect
  the Community/US
Community Issues
  Litter
  Grafitti
  Recycling
  Conservation
Collecting/Processing Data
Weather/Climates/Seasons

Social Studies
Basic needs
  Food   Clothing
  Shelter   Love/Care
Community Services
  Garbage   Libraries
  Sewer   Galleries
  Phone   Plays
  Newspaper   etc.
Jobs
Friends
Field Trips
Mapping
Graphing
Time/Calendar
Money

Health
Food Groups
What Your Body Does with Food
Dentist/Doctor/Police (Safety)

Math
Estimating
Symbolism
Comparison
Counting

P.E.
Recreation
Bowling
Sports
Skating
Parks

How Our Community Provides For Our Needs & Wants

FIGURE 2.3

Books Dealing with Time

Alexander, Lloyd. *The Fortune Tellers.*
Begley, Evelyn. *The Little Red Hen.*
Bryan, Ashley. *All Night All Day.*
Duke, Kate. *Bedtime.*
Fleischman, Paul. *Time Train.*
Hall, Donald. *Ox-cart Man.*
Havill, Juanita. *Leroy and the Clock.*
Heide, Florence, and Heide, Judith. *The Day of Ahmed's Secret.*
Houston, Gloria. *My Great-Aunt Arizona.*
Johnston, Tony. *Yonder.*
Lindbergh, Reeve. *The Day the Goose Got Loose.*
Lobel, Arnold. *Frog and Toad All Year.*
McCloskey, Robert. *Time of Wonder.*
Merriam, Eve. *Train Leaves the Station.*
Noble, Trinka Hakes. *The Day Jimmy's Boa Ate the Wash.*
Rylant, Cynthia. *Night in the Country.*
Viorst, Judith. *Alexander and the Terrible, Horrible, No Good, Very Bad Day.*
Wiesner, David. *June 29, 1999.*

FIGURE 2.4

High/Scope Key Experiences on Time

The High/Scope Key Experiences (Hohmann, 1979) are central to young children's development. They occur most often in active learning situations where children have opportunities to make choices and decisions, manipulate materials, use language in personally meaningful ways, and receive appropriate verbal and nonverbal adult support.

1. Starting and stopping an action on signal
2. Experiencing and describing different rates of movement
3. Experiencing and comparing time intervals
4. Experiencing and representing changes over time
5. Recalling events
6. Anticipating events
7. Representing the order of events
8. Using conventional time units and observing that clocks and calendars mark the passage of time

REFERENCES

Clay, M. (1991). *Becoming literate: The construction of inner control.* Portsmouth, NH: Heinemann.

Elkind, D. (1970, October 11). Of time and the child. *New York Times Magazine*, pp. 90, 91.

Elkind, D. (1989). Developmentally appropriate practice. *Phi Delta Kappa, 71*(2), 113–17.

Graves, D. H. (1993, Spring). Let's rethink children's entry points into literacy. *Dimensions: Journal of the Southern Early Childhood Association, 21*(3), 8–10, 39.

Hohmann, M., & Weikert, D. (1995). *Educating young children.* Ypsilanti, MI: High Scope Press.

Maehr, J. M. (1991). *High/Scope K–3 curriculum series: Language and literacy.* Ypsilanti, MI: High/Scope Press.

Pappas, C. C., Kiefer, B. Z., & Levstik, L. S. (1994). *An integrated language perspective in the elementary school: Theory into action* (2nd ed.). White Plains, NY: Longman.

Piaget, J. (1929). *The child's conception of the world.* New York: Harcourt Brace.

Piaget, J. (1930). *The child's conception of physical causality.* London: Kegan Paul.

Piaget, J. (1969). *The child's conception of time.* London: Routledge & Kegan Paul.

Vygotsky, L. (1978). *Mind in society: The development of higher psychological functions.* Cambridge, MA: Harvard University Press.

Wassermann, S. (1990). *Serious players in the primary classroom: Empowering children through active learning experiences.* New York: Teachers College Press.

BOOK SUGGESTIONS FOR CHILDREN

Alexander, L. (1992). *The fortune tellers.* New York: Dutton Children's Books.

Anderson, M. (1979). *In the circle of time.* New York: Alfred A. Knopf, Inc.

Anderson, M. (1979). *In the keep of time.* New York: Alfred A. Knopf, Inc.

Anderson, M. (1984). *The mists of time.* New York: Alfred A. Knopf, Inc.

Babbit, N. (1975). *Tuck everlasting.* New York: Farrar, Straus, & Giroux, Inc.

Begley, E. (1966). *The little red hen.* Racine, WI: Whitman Pub. Co.

Behn, H. (1950). *All kinds of time*. New York: Harcourt, Brace.

Bond, N. (1976). *A string in the harp*. New York: Atheneum.

Boston, L. (1955). *The children of Green Knowe*. New York: Harcourt, Brace.

Branley, F. (1961). *What makes day and night*. New York: Crowell.

Brindze, R. (1949). *The story of our calendar*. New York: Vanguard Press.

Bryan, A. (1991). *All night all day*. New York: Atheneum.

Burns, M. (1978). *This book is about time*. Boston: Little, Brown.

Byars, B. (1980). *The night swimmers*. New York: Delacorte

Comden, B., and Green, A. (1967). *Good morning, good night*. New York: Holt, Rinehart & Winston.

dePaola, T. (1979). *When everyone was fast asleep*. New York: Puffin Books.

Duke, K. (1986). *Bedtime*. New York: E. P. Dutton.

Duran, C. (1971). *Hildilid's night*. New York: Macmillan.

Fleischman, P. (1988). *Time train*. New York: Greenwillow Books.

Fox, M. (1989). *Night noises*. San Diego, CA: Harcourt Brace & Jovanovich, Inc.

Greenfield, E., and Little, L. (1979). *Childtimes: A three-generation memoir*. New York: Crowell

Greenfield, E. (1991). *Night on neighborhood street*. New York: Dial Books for Young Readers.

Griffin, P. (1991). *A dig in time*. New York: Macmillan.

Hall, D. (1979). *Ox-cart man*. New York: Viking Press.

Harvey, B. (1988). *Cassie's journey: Going West in the 1860s*. New York: Holiday House.

Havill, J. (1988). *Leroy and the clock*. Boston: Houghton Mifflin.

Heide, F., and Heide, J. (1990). *The day of Ahmed's secret*. New York: Lothrop, Lee & Shepard Books.

Horwitz, E. (1975). *When the sky is like lace*. Philadelphia: Lippincott.

Houston, G. (1992). *My great-aunt Arizona*. New York: Harper Collins Publishers.

Howe, J. (1983). *The celery stalks at midnight*. New York: Atheneum Publishers.

Hurmence, B. (1982). *A girl called Boy*. New York: Tickner & Fields.

Johnston, T. (1988). *Yonder*. New York: Dutton.

Lasky, K. (1983). *Sugaring time*. New York: Macmillan.

L'Engle, M. (1973). *A wrinkle in time*. New York: Dell Pub. Co.

Lindbergh, R. (1990). *The day the goose got loose*. New York: Dial Books for Young Readers.

Lobel, A. (1976). *Frog and Toad all year*. New York: Harper & Row Publishers, Inc.

Lucht, I. (1993). *In this night*. Westport, CT: Hyperion.

Lunn, J. (1983). *The root cellar*. New York: Scribner.

Major, B. (1982). *Porcupine stew*. New York: W. Morrow.

McCloskey, R. (1957). *Time of wonder*. New York: Viking Press.

McPhail, D. (1985). *Farm morning*. San Diego, CA: Harcourt Brace Jovanovich, Inc.

Merriam, E. (1992). *Train leaves the station*. New York: Henry Holt.

Miles, M. (1971). *Annie and the old one*. Boston: Little, Brown.

Mitchell, M. (1993). *Uncle Jed's barbershop*. New York: Simon & Schuster Books for Young Readers.

Nichols, P., and Nichols, B. (1988). *Archaeology: A study of the past*. Austin, TX: Eakin Press.

Noble, T. (1980). *The day Jimmy's boa ate the wash*. New York: Dial Books for Young Readers.

Norton, A. (1972). *Breed to come*. New York: Ace Books.

Ormondroyd, E. (1963). *Time at the top*. Berkeley, CA: Parnassus Press.

Pearce, P. (1953). *Tom's midnight garden*. Philadelphia: J.B. Lippincott.

Rohmann, E. (1994). *Time flies*. New York: Crown.

Rylant, C. (1986). *Night in the country*. New York: Bradbury Press.

Sauer, J. (1943). *Fog magic*. New York: Viking Press.

Shapiro, A. (1981). *Mr. Cuckoo's clock shop*. Los Angeles: Intervisual Communications, Inc.

Silverstein, S. (1964). *The giving tree*. New York: Harper & Row.

Skofield, J. (1981). *Nightdances*. New York: Harper & Row Publishers, Inc.

Tudor, T. (1990). *A time to keep*. New York: Macmillan.

Uttley, A. (1964). *A traveler in time*. New York: Viking Press.

Viorst, J. (1972). *Alexander and the terrible, horrible, no good, very bad day*. New York: Atheneum Publishers.

Wiesner, D. (1991). *Tuesday*. New York: Clarion Books.

Wiesner, D. (1992). *June 29, 1999*. New York: Clarion Books.

Willard, N. (1986). *Night story*. San Diego, CA: Harcourt Brace Jovanovich, Inc.

Wiseman, D. (1982). *Thimbles*. Boston: MA: Houghton Mifflin Co.

Ziner, F. (1956). *The true book of time*. Chicago: Children's Press.

DIVERSITY

KEY IDEAS

- **Multiculturalism** can be approached by learning about oneself, people in far away lands, or people closer to home.

- **Artifacts** are objects that tell something about the people who owned them.

- People need to be more aware of varying social groupings, institutions, and world views as they relate to diversity.

- Beliefs, customs, norms, roles, **equity**, order, and change are important concepts associated with multiculturalism.

INTRODUCTION

This chapter presents a lesson on the topic of **multicultural education**. Multicultural education is not simply learning about people of other races; rather, it encompasses learning about our near and far neighbors who represent various ages, ethnicities, religions, and lifestyles, as well as both sexes. This chapter plan can be used with a group of students of any age to help them realize the multiplicity of backgrounds among themselves.

35

LESSON PLAN

TITLE: RECOGNIZING, DESCRIBING, AND GENERALIZING ABOUT CULTURAL SIMILARITIES AND DIFFERENCES BY COLLECTING, GROUPING, LABELING, AND TALKING ABOUT ARTIFACTS

Ages/Grades: Early and Later Elementary

Time: One hour

Content Areas:

 Language Arts

 Reading

 Mathematics

 Social Studies

Materials: Students' self-selected artifacts from home

Transparencies

Overhead projector

Labels: Families, Work, Housing, Individualizing Item, Clothing, Food, Fine Arts, and/or markers and paper for other labels

Objectives: • Students recognize varying social groupings and institutions and address issues of importance to their members, including beliefs, customs, norms, roles, equity, order, and change

- Students associate the terms listed above with families, work, housing, clothing, food, fine arts, and personal items
- Students demonstrate understanding of, appreciation for, and sensitivity to a multicultural and world view
- Students practice the following skills:

Locating resources

Reading

Listening

Classifying

Writing

Speaking

Productive team membership

Open mind to alternative perspectives

Critical thinking

Multiple perspectives

Observing

Make connections among pieces of knowledge

Beginning: The teacher says, *A few days ago I asked you to collect some items, in other words* artifacts, *which represent you. You were to collect between five and ten items that portray you. Let's get out our items now and display them around the room.*

All the students exhibit artifacts they have brought from home that represent information about themselves. Then, for a few minutes, they walk around the room visiting their classmates' display areas, examining what the others have brought. Each person observes and converses with classmates about the artifacts, which are intended to represent truly valued possessions.

Middle: Allow approximately ten minutes for students to finish their wandering around the room—visiting, observing, and conversing about the artifacts. The teacher then says, *Now that we have observed and discussed the artifacts each of you has brought,* *we are going to group these artifacts. Think about the many aspects to a person's life to create the groups.*

The teacher places a transparency on the overhead projector to guide them in this task, asking, *As one example of a category, what would you suggest we come up with as a group name for some of the items you saw in the displays?*

A student may volunteer that five of the objects (family Bible, letters from family members, and photographs of family members) fall into the category of *families*. The teacher writes this term at the top of the transparency. Distribute materials so that students can work in small groups and decide on words or phrases to describe the various categories of displayed objects. Allow about fifteen minutes for the students to work and arrive at labels for the categories. Following are some labels (McCracken, 1993) that may be suggested by the class members:

1. Families

2. Work

3. Housing

4. Clothing

5. Food

6. Fine arts

7. Items that individualize you (in a group)

On separate transparencies the teacher writes all the category labels the students have generated.

End: The teacher gives the following debriefing instruction: *Share with someone sitting next to you some of your observations about each of the categories of items.*

Allow time for several students to share their observations with the entire class. The teacher listens to, paraphrases, extends, causes students to analyze, or challenges students' observations or comments. Then the question is asked: *What generalizations about each of the categories can be made based on our collection of artifacts for each of the categories? For example, what generalizations can be made about "families" of people in this room?*

As students respond, the teacher writes the generalization beneath the label on the transparency. Figure 3.1 shows some generalizations the students might think of.

Assessment of Student Learning: Ask the students to consider what the implications of this activity are for teaching young children about multicultural education. How may this activity enable a person to understand others? Have the class, as a large group, formulate a list of *to do's* that a teacher may follow in order to promote multiculturalism in the classroom. Figure 3.2 contains some potential implications.

FIGURE 3.1

Generalizations That Incorporate Diversity into the Curriculum

Families
- People live in many kinds of families.
- Every family has a history.
- People use written and spoken language to communicate.
- Families teach their children what they value.
- Families help each other.

Work
- People work together at home.
- People work with each other in many places.
- People do many kinds of work.
- Some people work for fairness so others may have better lives.

Housing
- People live in a variety of homes.
- Types of homes are affected by the weather, available building materials, local history, and many other factors.

Continued

FIGURE 3.1 *Continued*

Clothing
- People dress in ways that vary by culture.
- A culture's resources, religions, gender values, social activities, economic system influence dress.
- Dress changes over time.
- Dress is part of every culture.

Food
- Food helps us grow and stay healthy.
- Cultures and families have different food preferences and eating habits.
- Foods grow in different climates.
- Foods are prepared in many ways.
- Food is a precious natural resource.

Fine Arts
- Cultural and individual expressions are found in movement, dance, music, poetry, literature, and many types of art.
- People create their own art.
- People enjoy each other's art.

Individual and Group Similarities
- People all need food, clothing, shelter, and each other.
- Physical features vary among individuals and between ethnic and racial groups.
- People eat, dress, work, and live in ways that vary by culture.

Reprinted, with permission, from Janet B. McCracken (1993). Valuing Diversity: The Primary Years. *National Association for the Education of Young Children: Washington, DC.*

FIGURE 3.2

Implications for Including Multicultural Education in the Classroom

To Do's
1. Connect culture activities to individual children and their families.
2. Remember that while cultural patterns are real and affect all members of an ethnic group, families live their culture in their own individual ways.
3. Connect cultural activities to concrete, daily life.
4. Explore cultural diversity within the principle that everyone has a culture.
5. Have cultural diversity permeate the daily life of the classroom through frequent, concrete, hands-on experiences related to young children's interests.
6. Avoid the editorial we when talking with children because such an approach may lead to our making assumptions about homogeneity that may not be true.
7. Explore the similarities among people through their differences.
8. Begin with the cultural diversity among the children and staff in your classroom.

REFERENCES

Banks, J. (1994). *An introduction to multicultural education*. Boston: Allyn & Bacon.

Derman-Sparks, L. and the A.B.C. Task Force. (1989). *Anti-bias curriculum: Tools for empowering young children*. Washington, DC: National Association for the Education of Young Children.

Gillespie, C., Powell, J., Clements, N., & Swearingen, R. (1994, September). A look at the Newberry Medal books from a multicultural perspective. *The Reading Teacher, 48*(1), 40–48.

Kentucky Department of Education (Ed.). (1993). *Transformations: Kentucky's curriculum framework*. Frankfort, KY: KDE.

McCracken, J. B. (1993). *Valuing diversity: The primary years*. Washington, DC: National Association for the Education of Young Children.

NAEYC. (1996, January). Position statement: Responding to linguistic and cultural diversity—recommendations for effective early childhood education. *Young Children, 51*, 4–12.

Tiedt, I. (1994). *Multi-cultural teaching: A handbook of activities, information and resources*. Needham Heights, MA: Allyn & Bacon.

BOOK SUGGESTIONS FOR CHILDREN

Carlstrom, N. (1992). *Northern lullaby*. New York: Philomel.

Dorros. A. (1991). *Abuela*. New York: Trumpet Club.

Franklin, C. (1994). *The shepherd boy*. New York: Atheneum.

Heide, F., & Gilliland, J. (1990). *The day of Ahmed's secret*. New York: Lothrop, Lee, & Shepard.

Hoffman, M. (1991). *Amazing grace*. New York: Dial.

Hopkinson, D. (1993). *Sweet Clara and the freedom quilt*. New York: Knopf.

Howard, E. (1989). *Chita's Christmas tree*. New York: Bradbury Press.

Howard, E. (1991). *Aunt Flossie's hats and crab cakes later*. New York: Clarion Books.

James. B. (1991). *The dream stair*. New York: Harper Collins.

Johnson, A. (1990). *Do like Kyla*. New York: Orchard.

Jones, R. (1991). *Mathew and Tilly*. New York: Dutton.

Larrabee, L. (1993). *Grandmother Five Baskets*. Tucson, AZ: Harbinger.

Lowry, J. (1989). *Number the stars*. Boston: Houghton Mifflin.

Nicholas, E. (1994). *A feather for her hair*. Cleveland: Modern Curriculum Press.

Pinkney, A. (1993). *Seven candles for Kwanzaa*. New York: Dial.

Reed, D. (1995). *The kraken*. Honesdale, PA: Boyds Mills.

Ringgold, F. (1991). *Tar beach*. New York: Crown.

Roe, E. (1991). *Con mi hermano/With my brother*. New York: Bradbury Press.

Roessell, M. (1993). *Kinaalia: A Navaho girl grows up*. Minneapolis, MN: Lerner.

Say, A. (1993). *Grandfather's journey*. Boston: Houghton Mifflin.

Soto, G. (1993). *Too many tamales*. New York: Putnam.

Spinelli, J. (1990). *Maniac Magee*. Boston: Little, Brown.

Walter, M. (1990). *Two and too much*. New York: Bradbury.

Yashima, T. (1958). *Umbrella*. New York: Viking.

BARBARA FRIETCHIE

KEY IDEAS

- Students usually find it enjoyable to learn about social history through literary books.
- Oral expression by students can easily accompany the reading of stories.
- Events in a story can be visualized with a **time line**.
- Events in a story can be illustrated on a map.

INTRODUCTION

This chapter combines the curriculum areas of history, geography, and language arts. The lesson in this chapter is associated with a historical character of the nineteenth century—a woman named Barbara Frietchie who was immortalized in a poem by John Greenleaf Whittier. The lesson can be taught to later elementary or middle school students.

HISTORY THROUGH LITERATURE

The concept of history is difficult for many children to acquire. Some educators such as Hallam (1972) and Zaccaria (1978) believe that a student's ability to comprehend history in a meaningful way does not occur until the late teen years (Piaget's formal operations stage).

Other educators, however, encourage teachers to present historical lessons to young children so they can develop a sense of chronology, time, and history. Freeland (1990, 66) calls this engaging students in "history readiness." Vukelich and Thornton (1994, p. 22) describe students' abilities by different ages:

Ages 3–5	They are capable of sequencing daily events and can rank order family members by age.
Ages 6–8	They can develop the ability to use "historical numbers" to represent the past; they can sometimes match dates with major events, e.g., Christmas is December 25.
Ages 9–11	They can become capable of matching persons and events with textbook descriptions, e.g., colonial period.
Ages 12–14	They are able to use time classifications with increasing ease, e.g., decade.

Lamme (1994) describes how stories from the past can make history come alive for children. Egan (1982) feels that children are impulsively drawn to the exotic and fantastic, which supports the belief by Freeman and Levstik (1988) that historical content can be added to the curriculum by historical literature. Drake and Drake (1990) read historical literature to third and fourth graders, finding out not only that the children gained information from the books, but they had an interest in the past.

ORAL EXPRESSION

Allowing students to express themselves orally not only provides students with opportunities to think out loud, it also enables them to enjoy language. Choral reading, drama, pantomime, puppetry, readers' theater, plays, and creative dramatics (Petty, Petty, & Salzer, 1994) are some of the practices whereby children in groups can engage in oral expression. The lesson on Barbara Frietchie utilizes several of these practices: unison choral reading requires students to all say the same words; pantomime is communication without speech.

TIME LINES

Time lines are graphic representations of historical events to depict their order. Figure 4.1 shows a simple time line encompassing a span of 100 years. Following are some basic principles that students should use in constructing a time line:

1. Decide the form for the time line; that is, will it be arranged horizontally with the oldest date to the left and the most recent to the right? Will it be portrayed as a vertical line with the oldest event at the bottom and the most recent at the top? Possibly some other form could be used, for example, a curved line to characterize the order of events.

FIGURE 4.1

American History Time Line

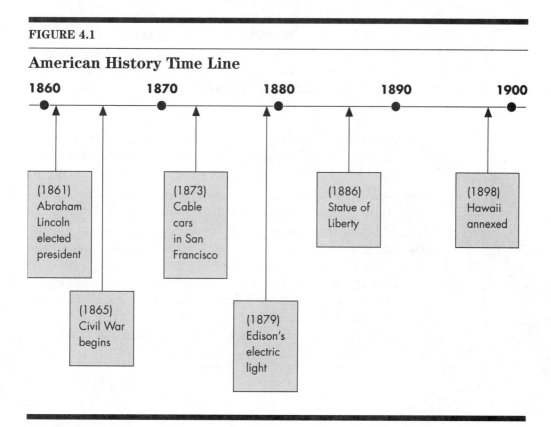

2. Decide how large the time intervals will be and the length that will be used on the time line to represent this interval. For example, will a time line from 1860 to 1900 be divided into four ten-year periods, with each ten-year period shown as two inches wide?

3. Decide on which events are important and how they will be indicated. One way is simply to write the name of the event on the time line. Perhaps the event could be drawn; or a three-dimensional object could be constructed to represent the event and then placed on the time line.

4. Select a title for the time line.

MAP MAKING

Maps are used to communicate ideas, data, and relationships in spatial form. Because they are very abstract, it often helps if students relate them to a photograph (i.e., maps are two-dimensional representations of real, three-dimensional things just as photographs are representations of live people and real objects). Blocks and building materials can be a great way to enable children to construct streets, buildings, and trees, etc., that they experience in the world around them. Cameras with quick developing film can be used to take pictures of places inside the classroom so students can see the relationship between the actual objects and a flat object.

Sandra Pritchard (1989) used the children's story *Katy and the Big Snow* to have students engage in activities related to the story, such as determining in which direction Katy went from the school to the railroad station and describing a walk along First Street. One teacher read the story *Jack Jouett's Ride* to his class and then had the students draw a map of the events. Jack Jouett was a Revolutionary War hero who—in Paul Revere fashion—left his Virginia home and rode to Monticello to warn Thomas Jefferson and other Colonial patriots that a troop of British soldiers were on their way to arrest Jefferson and other local insurgents. Figure 4.2 is a map one student drew after listening to the story.

FIGURE 4.2

Map of Story

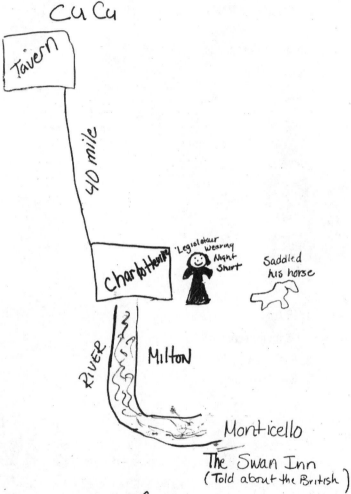

Cu Cu

Tavern

40 mile

Charlottsville   "Legislatour wearing Night Shirt"   Saddled his horse

River   Milton

Monticello

The Swan Inn
(Told about the British)

Gen. Stevens was wounded and he and Jack switched places.

Jack led the British on a chase & Gen. Stevens slipped away.

LESSON PLAN

TITLE: **BARBARA FRIETCHIE**

Ages/Grade: Later elementary or middle school

Time: one hour

Content Areas:

 Geography

 History

 Language Arts

Materials:
1. *Barbara Frietchie*, a poem by John Greenleaf Whittier
2. Transparencies
3. Overhead projector
4. Marking pens

Objectives:
- Students will explore temporal relationships of historical events
- Students will distinguish among the past, present, and future
- Students will explain the influence of geographic factors on human movement
- Students will develop listening skills by recognizing meaning from verbal cues (e.g., tone of voice, pitch, volume)
- Students will demonstrate verbal skills (e.g., voice variety, rate, pitch) and nonverbal skills (e.g., gestures, movement)

Beginning: Distribute the handout on oral response technique (fig. 4.3), which explains how students can react to stories read aloud to them. Then set the stage for the story by informing the class that Barbara Frietchie was a ninety-five-year-old widow who lived in Frederick, Maryland, where people were divided in their loyalties to the North and South during the Civil War. In 1862 Stonewall Jackson marched his Confederate troops through the city as he made his way to the Battle of Antietam at Sharpsburg. Barbara Frietchie was a supporter of the North and defiantly waved a Union flag from a window of her house at General Jackson's troops as they trudged beneath her along the street.

Middle: The class listens as the teacher reads the story of Barbara Frietchie's boldness during the United States Civil War in the nineteenth century. If enough copies of the poem or book are available, students can be divided into small groups in which someone is selected to read aloud by the group or teacher. Students jot down words or events that occur in the story. The story is read again; this time the students act out or mimic sounds that could be part of the story. For example, they may whinny like one of the horses ridden by a Confederate soldier; they might pantomime Barbara Frietchie waving the flag from her upstairs window; or they might stomp their feet on the floor to imitate the sounds of troops marching along the street.

End: Next students work with a partner to draw a time line on an overhead transparency and place some of the events they selected from the story in the order in which they occurred. Some of the students may have Frederick in the center of their map with cornfields on all sides of the city. Various symbols could be located to indicate trees, cornfields, and roads. Some other students may decide to make a map of just the town of Frederick, showing various buildings on the street where the troops passed by. Symbols in this case would be a church, house, store, street, tree, etc. In all cases, students should pay attention to showing the four cardinal directions on their maps and drawing a map key to display the symbols they have chosen.

**Assessment
of Student
Learning:**   Students will take turns placing their map/time line on the
overhead projector and explaining what they have created. Have
students look at other books dealing with history. See if they can
identify parts of the stories—which would lead to good oral
responses or gestures by children—and events that could be
placed on a time line. A few books (full reference citations
appear at the end of this chapter) that could be webbed with the
topic of the Revolutionary War or the Civil War in our country's
history include:

Felicity Saves the Day by Valerie Tripp

Sybil Rides for Independence by Drollene Brown

And Then What Happened, Paul Revere? by Jean Fritz

Sheridan's Ride by Thomas Buchanan Read

George the Drummer Boy by Nathaniel Benchley

Why Don't You Get a Horse, Sam Adams? by Jean Fritz

Uncle Sam's 200th Birthday Parade by Irwin Shapiro

Pink and Say by Patricia Polacco

The selections below are not related to war, but are stories that
provide good opportunities for students to carry out oral
response or map-making activities.

Feliciana Feydra Leroux: A Cajun Tall Tale by Tynia
Thomassie

Lupe and Me by Elizabeth Spurr

Grandfather's Journey by Allen Say

Ben and Me by Robert Lawson

George Washington's Cows by David Small

Rover and Coo Coo by John Hay

Susanna of the Alamo by John Jakes

My Great-Aunt Arizona by Gloria Houston

The Boy Who Loved Music by David Lasker

Who Came Down that Road by George Ella Lyon

Watch the Stars Come Out by Riki Levinson

Our Snowman by M. B. Goffstein

When Everyone Was Fast Asleep by Tommie de Paola

Harald and the Stag by Donald Carrick

The Favershams by Roy Gerrard

My Prairie Year by Brett Harvey

The Erie Canal by Peter Spier

Tin Lizzie by Peter Spier

Sally Ann Thunder Ann Whirlwind Crockett by Caron Lee Cohen

Going West by Jean Van Leeuwen

Grandpa Had a Windmill, Grandpa Had a Churn by Louise Jackson

A New Coat for Anna by Harriet Ziefert

Alexander and the Terrible, Horrible, No Good Very Bad Day by Judith Viorst

Mike Fink by Steven Kellogg

The Potato Man by Megan McDonald

The Watsons Go to Birmingham by Christopher Curtis

FIGURE 4.3

Oral Response Stories

Discuss the technique of oral communication with the students. Response techniques can take many forms, some of which are speaking, mime, and sound effects. To make a story into an oral response story, oral responses for certain characters are assigned to groups of students. As the book is read aloud by the teacher (or by selected student readers), she/he pauses when those characters are mentioned. As students hear their parts read, they interject with their assigned oral response. Students should be guided to speak together and use their voices to portray the feelings of the character as much as possible. A tired horse's hoofbeats would sound different than those of a fresh mount's. Notice that the parts don't have to be human and the responses don't have to be words.

REFERENCES

Curriculum Standards for Social Studies: Expectations of Excellence, Bulletin 89 (1994). Washington, D.C.: National Council for the Social Studies.

Drake, J. J., & Drake, F. D. (1990, November/December). Using children's literature to teach about the American revolution. *Social Studies and the Young Learner, 3*(2), 6–8.

Egan, K. (1982, March). Teaching history to young children. *Phi Delta Kappan, 63,* 439–441.

Freeland, K. (1990). *Managing the social studies curriculum.* Lancaster, PA: Technomic.

Freeman, E. B., and Levstik, L. (1988). Recreating the past: Historical fiction in the social studies curriculum. *The Elementary School Journal, 88,* 330–337.

Hallam, R. N. (1972). Thinking and learning in history. *Teaching History, 2,* 337–346.

Lamme, L. L. (1994, March). Stories from our past: Making history come alive for children. *Social Education, 58*(3), 159–164.

Mapping the world by heart. (n.d.). Curriculum kit. Watertown, MA: Tom Snyder Productions.

Maxim, G. W. (1995). *Social studies and the elementary school child* (5th ed.). Englewood Cliffs, NJ: Merrill-Prentice Hall.

National standards for history for grades K–4. (1994). Los Angeles, CA: National Center of History in the Schools.

Petty, W. T., Petty, D. C., & Salzer, R. T. (1994). *Experiences in language: Tools and techniques for language arts methods* (6th ed.). Needham Heights, MA: Allyn & Bacon.

Pritchard, S. (1989, July/August). Using picture books to teach geography in the primary grades. *Journal of Geography, 88*(4), 126–136.

Rubin, D. (1995). *Teaching elementary language arts* (5th ed.). Needham Heights, MA: Allyn & Bacon.

Turner, T. N. (1994). *Essentials of classroom teaching: Elementary social studies.* Needham Heights, MA: Allyn & Bacon.

Vukelich, R. & Thornton, S. J. (1994, Fall). Children's understanding of historical time: Implications for instruction. *Childhood Education, 67,* 22–25.

Zaccaria, M. A. (1978). The development of historical thinking: Implications for the teaching of history. *The History Teacher, 11*(3), 323–340.

BOOK SUGGESTIONS FOR CHILDREN

Benchley, N. (1977). *George, the drummer boy*. New York: Harper & Row.

Brown, D. (1985). *Sybil rides for independence*. Morton Grove, IL: Albert Whitman & Co.

Burton, V. L. (1943). *Katy and the big snow*. Boston: Houghton Mifflin.

Cohen, C. L. (1985). *Sally Ann Thunder Ann Whirlwind Crocket*. New York: Greenwillow.

Curtis, C. (1995). *The Watsons go to Birmingham*. New York: Delacorte.

Fritz, J. (1973). *And then what happened, Paul Revere?* New York: Coward, McCann & Geoghegan.

Fritz, J. (1974). *Why don't you get a horse, Sam Adams?* New York: Coward, McCann & Geoghegan.

Fritz, J. (1979). *Stonewall*. New York: Puffin.

Gerard, R. (1982). *The Favershams*. New York: Farrar, Straus, Giroux.

Goffstein, M. B. (1986). *Our snowman*. New York: Harper & Row.

Hailey, G. (1973). *Jack Jouett's ride*. New York: Viking Press.

Harvey, B. (1986). *My prairie year*. New York: Holiday House.

Hay, J. (1986). *Rover and Coo Coo*. La Jolla, CA: Green Tiger Press.

(1995). *Interactive geography* [CD-ROM] Portland, OR: Pieran Springs Software.

Jackson, L. (1977). *Grandpa had a windmill, Grandpa had a churn*. New York: Parents' Magazine Press.

Jakes, J. (1986). *Susanna of the Alamo*. San Diego, CA: Gulliver's Books.

Kellogg, S. (1992). *Mike Fink*. New York: Morrow Junior Books.

Lawson, R. (1939). *Ben and me*. Boston: Little, Brown.

Lyon, G. E. (1992). *Who came down that road?* New York: Orchard Books.

McDonald, M. (1991). *The potato man*. New York: Orchard Books.

(1995). *Picture Puzzle* [Computer software]. Washington, DC: National Geographic.

Polacco, P. (1994). *Pink and say*. New York: Philomel.

Read, T. B. (1993). *Sheridan's ride*. New York: Greenwillow.

Say, A. (1993). *Grandfather's journey*. Boston: Houghton Mifflin.

Shapiro, I. (1974). *Uncle Sam's 200th birthday parade*. New York: Golden Press.

Small, D. (1994). *George Washington's cows*. New York: Farrar, Straus & Giroux.

Spier, P. (1970). *The Erie Canal*. Garden City, NY: Doubleday.

Spier, P. (1975). *Tin Lizzie*. Garden City, NY: Doubleday.

Spurr, E. (1995). *Lupe and me*. New York: Gulliver Green Books.

Thomassie, T. (1995). *Feydra Leroux: A Cajun tall tale*. Boston: Little, Brown.

Tripp, V. (1992). *Felicity saves the day*. Middleton, WI: Pleasant Co.

(1995). *Trudy's time and place house* [CD-ROM]. Redmond, WA: Edmark.

Van Leeuwen, J. (1992). *Going West*. New York: Dial Press.

Viorst, J. (1972). *Alexander and the terrible, horrible, no good very bad day*. New York: Atheneum.

Whittier, J. G. (1992). *Barbara Frietchie*. New York: Greenwillow Books.

Ziefert, H. (1986). *A new coat for Anna*. New York: Knopf.

(1994). *ZipZapMap* [Computer software]. Washington, DC: National Geographic.

PETER RABBIT

KEY IDEAS

- One way a child can express or recall details of a familiar story is by creating a **graffiti wall**.

- The concept of justice can be explored through an enactment of a **mock trial**.

INTRODUCTION

This chapter integrates the curriculum areas of social studies, reading, and language arts. Although the lesson works well with students in the later elementary grades, it also can be completed by students who are in the middle grades.

GRAFFITI WALL

A graffiti wall is a "free-form space for brainstorming or communicating key words, phrases, or ideas on a topic" (Pappas, Kiefer & Levstik, 1995, p. 239). It utilizes the natural propensity young people have for scribbling, doodling, or writing. The teacher, for example, could instruct the students to write all of the words that pop into their minds in response to a topic or a particular story. Students write on a large sheet of paper taped to the wall instead of writing on the wall itself.

MOCK TRIAL

A mock trial is an enactment of a court case. It achieves the double benefit of teaching students about our legal system as well as giving them practice in performing a dramatic activity. Students act out the roles of judge, witnesses, attorneys, bailiff, etc., thereby learning essential aspects of courtroom procedure. Older students can act out historic incidents, such as the Dred Scott case, where the outcome of the case is known. They also can conduct mock trials reflecting current events so that they have to debate issues that have not been settled.

Younger students, however, need to work with more simplified situations. A classroom court could be developed to deal with students who have broken classroom rules. Another idea is to have students put a character from a book on trial—for example, the wolf in *Little Red Riding Hood* is charged with assault; Goldilocks is charged with breaking and entering.

This is an excellent opportunity for a teacher to introduce the topic of **conflict resolution**. Students encounter personal examples of conflict on the playground, in the classroom, in their homes, and in their neighborhoods. Because these incidents will not go to court where a judge decides who is right or wrong, the children need to learn that they must resolve many of the conflicts in their lives. Basic steps in conflict resolution involve checking to see if the two parties understand one another's position and realize how the other person feels. Each side needs to verbalize what he/she is thinking, try to get at the issues, and try to find a solution where both students feel good about the outcome.

Before conducting the mock trial, the teacher needs to familiarize the students with the facts of the case and help them analyze them, as well as decide what charges should be brought against the defendant and what the duties and responsibilities are for each of the participants in the trial. Norton (1992) suggests the following sequence of events in a mock trial:

1. The court clerk announces the case.

2. The prosecuting attorney and the defense attorney give opening statements to the judge/jury.

3. The prosecution case is conducted whereby the prosecuting and defense attorneys conduct the examination of witnesses.

4. The defense case is conducted whereby the defense and prosecuting attorneys conduct the examination of witnesses.

5. Closing statements are made by attorneys on both sides.

6. The judge gives instructions to the jury.

7. A decision is made on the case.

8. The court clerk adjourns the court.

LESSON PLAN

TITLE: PETER RABBIT

Ages/Grades: Early elementary, later elementary, or middle school

Time: One teacher used the following schedule when carrying out this activity:

Day 1: Read the story and discuss; investigate the author.

Day 2: Review story; review concepts of responsibility, rights, property, justice, etc.

Day 3 (day 4 if a field trip to a court house is taken on day 3): Group discussion of our court system; television program showing a court trial.

Day 4 (or day 5): Discuss roles of people from TV or field trip; introduce idea of putting Peter Rabbit on trial; establish characters and setting up room.

Day 5 (or day 6): Have a mock trial; critique it by encouraging the class to consider the strengths and weaknesses of the performance and what they might do to improve it if it were done again.

Day 6 (or day 7): Another mock trial; critique it.

Content Areas:

  Social Studies

  Art

  Reading

  Language Arts

Materials: Beatrix Potter, *The Tale of Peter Rabbit*

Posters

Markers

Dictionary

Objectives:
- Students will demonstrate democratic behavior.
- Students will recognize the existence of the need to follow rules.
- Students will identify sources of authority.
- Students will practice formal speaking presentation for a specific audience and purpose.
- Students will identify the connection between new information and prior knowledge.

Beginning: The class does a graffiti wall whereby the students move into small groups and think of items that are suggested by their recollections about the story of Peter Rabbit. They are asked to use magic markers to write words (or draw pictures), such as Mr. McGregor, the fence, the blue jacket, etc. on large sheets of butcher paper. When every group is finished with the drawings, tape the papers to the classroom walls. Each student walks around the room to view the graffiti walls.

Middle: Students are put back into their small groups and each group is given a copy of *The Tale of Peter Rabbit*. One person from each group is selected to read to the other members. Have a discussion of the story afterward, focusing on the following:

- Did Peter get away from Mr. McGregor? How? Where?
- Look at the illustrations. What words in the story match the pictures? Do you think you could retell the story using just the pictures as story clues?
- Look for these phrases in the story. What do they mean?

  "Never get in the garden again."

  "New folks in town."

  "Peter was late for supper."

• What did Peter take when he felt sick?

• Make a spelling list of adjectives you find in the story.

The class comes back to meet as a large group so that a list of participants can be made, for example, judge, jury members, court clerk, bailiff, prosecuting attorneys, defense attorneys, witnesses, etc. Charges against Peter Rabbit need to be determined. One possibility is that Peter would be charged with trespassing in Mr. McGregor's garden. Flopsy and Mopsy—his siblings—might be called as character witnesses for Peter. Each team of trial lawyers prepares a case, and the other participants (judge, Mr. McGregor, Flopsy, etc.) need to review their roles.

End: Students act out the case the way a real trial would be conducted. After all direct examination, cross examination, and closing statements have been completed, the jury decides on the case and the judge announces the verdict. One class of elementary students found Peter guilty when they conducted a mock trial, but they suggested leniency, feeling Peter should be released into his mother's custody.

Assessment of Student Learning: Students will critique their performances and respond to the following questions:

1. How is democratic behavior exhibited in a courtroom?

2. Why is it important for the members of a society to follow rules and laws?

3. The judge is an authority figure in a courtroom; who are authority figures in other situations?

4. What did you learn about the jobs of persons who work in a courtroom from this activity?

REFERENCES

Block, C. C. (1993). *Teaching the language arts: Expanding thinking through student-centered instruction.* Needham Heights, MA: Allyn & Bacon.

Choices, Choices. (1993). [Computer software.] Watertown, MA: Tom Snyder Productions.

Decision, Decisions Series. (1993). [Computer software.] Watertown, MA: Tom Snyder Productions.

Luke, J., & Myers, C. (1994/95, Winter). Toward peace: Using literature to aid conflict resolution. *Childhood Education, 71*(2), 66–69.

Mecca, J. T. (1992). *Plays that teach: Plays, activities, and songs with a message.* Nashville, TN: Incentive Publications, Inc.

Norton, J. (1992, September/October). The state vs. the big bad wolf: A study of the justice system in the elementary school. *Social Studies and the Young Learner, 5*(1), 5–9.

Pappas, C. C., Kiefer, B., & Levstik, L. S. (1995). *An integrated language perspective in the elementary school: Theory into action* (2nd ed.). White Plains, NY: Longman.

Peters, M., & Bjorklun, E. (1996, March/April). Torts and tales: Teaching about personal injury law in the primary grades. *Social Studies and the Young Learner, 8*(4), 5–8.

Tobin, J. (1993). *Finding our way: Teacher stories from the Resolving Conflict Creatively Program.* Boston: Educators for Social Responsibility.

BOOK SUGGESTIONS FOR CHILDREN

Aardema, V. (1977). *Who's in Rabbit's house?* New York: Dial.

Adoff, A. (1985). *The cabbages are chasing the rabbits.* San Diego, CA: Harcourt. Brace Jovanovich.

Alcock, V. (1990). *The trial of Anna Cotman.* New York: Delacorte.

Bate, L. (1986). *Little Rabbit's baby brother.* New York: Crown Publishers.

dePaola, T. (1989). *Too many Hopkins.* New York: Putnam.

Fisher, A. (1964). *Listen, Rabbit.* New York: HarperCollins.

Getting to the Heart of It. (1995) [Videocassette]. Watertown, MA: Tom Snyder Productions.

Han, S. (1995). *The rabbit's escape.* New York: Henry Holt.

Harris, J. C. (1986). *Jump! The adventures of Br'er Rabbit.* San Diego, CA: Harcourt Brace Jovanovich.

Harris, J. C. (1892). *Uncle Remus and his friends*. Boston: Houghton Mifflin.

Kerr, J. (1972). *When Hitler stole pink rabbit*. New York: Coward, McCann.

Lionni, L. (1982). *Let's make rabbits*. New York: Pantheon.

Little Rabbit's loose tooth. (1990) [Videocassette]. Deerfield, IL: Coronet.

McDermott, G. (1992). *Zomo the rabbit*. San Diego, CA: Harcourt Brace Jovanovich.

Oughton, J. (1992). *How the stars fell into the sky: A Navajo legend*. Boston: Houghton Mifflin.

Petry, A. (1964). *Tituba of Salem Village*. New York: HarperCollins.

Potter, B. (1902). *The tale of Peter Rabbit*. New York: Frederick Warne & Co.

Soto, G. (1994). *Too many tamales*. New York: Putnam.

Wayland, A. (1989). *To Rabbittown*. New York: Scholastic.

Wells, R. (1985). *Max's birthday*. New York: Dial.

Wilhelm, H. (1985). *Bunny trouble*. New York: Scholastic.

Williams, M. (1958). *The velveteen rabbit*. New York: Doubleday.

Zeinert, K. (1989). *The Salem witchcraft trials*. New York: Watts.

6

FINGERPRINTS

KEY IDEAS

- **Concepts** can be thought of as mental images, or names given to "ideas."
- Concepts are a number of commonly accepted methods to teach concepts.
- A **skill** is the ability to do something.
- Students can develop some skills by reading literature books.

INTRODUCTION

This chapter presents a lesson combining concept teaching and skill teaching; the concept is patterns, and the major skill is classification. It capitalizes on a person's natural curiosity in trying to find out an answer to a mystery or puzzling situation. Although the lesson is designed to be used with a group of early elementary or middle grade students, it would also work well with a class of college methods students.

CONCEPTS

A concept is an idea (or mental image) that is expressed in a word or a phrase. Examples of concepts include

- fractions
- magnetic force
- freedom of speech
- color
- topic sentence
- fair play
- musical tone

When a person hears or sees a word or phrase like one of those listed above, many images flash through the mind, and that is why teaching is so challenging. Teachers need to lead a student to develop proper and accurate meanings of the innumerable concepts they encounter in their lives. Teachers can define a concept for a student (i.e., the expository method of teaching); on the other hand, teachers can use a more inductive approach by having students encounter examples or nonexamples of concepts or by personally discovering a concept.

SKILLS

A skill is the ability to do something and usually involves movement requiring a mind or motor connection. The following are some examples of skills in the early elementary and middle schools:

1. A student will exhibit listening skills by repeating the directions that were given for a playground game.
2. A student will draw a two-dimensional figure.
3. A student will operate a piece of scientific equipment.

Educators sometimes include other statements as skills even though there is no movement exhibited; for example, "A student will compare the size of the two fractional parts." In this case the invisible thought process is considered to be a thinking skill.

COMBINING CONCEPTS WITH SKILLS

The following lesson plan, with its attention to classifying fingerprints, ties in with the concept attainment model (Sunal, 1990, p. 58), which contains the following steps: (1) information is presented, (2) students make observations, (3) additional information is presented, (4) additional observations are made, (5) generalizing inferences are made, and (6) closure is made.

Certain skills overlap many subjects of the curriculum and thereby promote integration. Although his background is scientific, Carin (1993, p. 8) realizes some skills that people consider to be in the realm of science, such as investigation, hypothesizing, and problem solving, are really lifelong learning skills independent of any particular subject area.

The general population thinks of basic skills as the 3 Rs—reading, 'riting, and 'rithmetic—and they are thought to be tied to content areas. However, there are other skill categories, such as study skills, intellectual skills, socialization skills, and motor skills, that span the content areas. It is just as important that a student should possess motor skills for handling a paint brush as for dribbling a basketball.

The following lesson plan on fingerprints requires students to practice some skills that are important in many ways. Sunal and Haas (1993, p. 46) have categorized these broad skills in this way:

(1) Data gathering skills

(2) Data organizing skills

(3) Data processing skills

(4) Communicating skills

(5) Overall thinking skills

As students organize and process data in this lesson, they must act on observations they have made. They order their observations, interpret their observations, classify, find relationships, and find patterns. Lemlech (1994, pp. 138–166) suggests that through these skills we are encouraging students to be researchers.

LESSON PLAN

TITLE: **FINGERPRINTS**

Ages/Grades: Early elementary, later elementary, or middle school

Time: One hour

**Content
Areas:**
 Anthropology, Science

 Reading

 Writing

Materials: Paper

Ink pads (all of the same color)

Wallet

Magnifying lenses

Cleaning rags and dampened towelettes

Objectives:
- Students realize the commonalties and differences of their classmates.

- Students identify, compare, and contrast patterns and use patterns to understand and interpret past and present events and predict future events.

- Students construct meaning from a variety of printed materials.

- Students use research tools to locate sources of information and ideas relevant to a specific need or problem.

• Students communicate ideas and information to a variety of audiences for a variety of purposes in a variety of modes through writing.

Beginning: Ask students to look at their right index fingers and think how they would describe them. Then have them pair up. Each person should explain to the partner how his or her fingers appear to be different from the other person's. Comments may be:

Justin: My finger is longer than yours.

Takisha: Yes, but mine has a longer fingernail.

Justin: Yours has paint on it, too.

Takisha: Oh, Justin, that's fingernail polish.

Justin: I know that! You've got a ring on. Let me see if it fits my finger. (He tries it on, but it won't fit.) There! It works on my little finger.

Takisha: Your fingers are bigger around than mine.

Give each pair a magnifying lens and ask them to look closely at their fingers to find something they didn't notice before. As someone mentions that he/she can see lines and holes (prints and pores), follow up on this point that everyone has finger-prints and that police take impressions of people's fingerprints when they want to find clues in cases they are trying to solve.

Middle: Divide the class into four groups with roughly six or seven students in each group. Distribute two Post-it™ notes to each student. Have each student roll his/her index finger onto a water-based ink pad and then roll the finger on the two Post-it™ notes. Provide rags or dampened towelettes for removal of all the excess ink from the students' fingers. Each student should write his/her name on the front side of one Post-it™ note and on the back side of the other Post-it™ note.

Each of the four groups is given a large sheet of paper that they tape to a wall. They place the Post-it™ notes with the identifying names on this sheet of paper. The entire class places the other Post-it™ note (with the name on the back side) on a large sheet of paper that is kept by the teacher. With a magnifying lens the students—in their groups of six or seven—examine the master sheet of paper for their group to observe the patterns that are shown in the fingerprints of all the other students in their group. They decide if they can see any patterns in the appearance of their group's prints.

They then move to another part of the room to look at another group's poster. Each group should come up with a classification scheme that would accommodate the various kinds of fingerprints that they have seen. For example, one group might believe that they can put all the fingerprints into two groups—lines that are bunched closely together and lines that are further apart.

Next, the teacher should distribute photocopies of the way experts have classified fingerprints: arches, loops, and whorls (see fig. 6.1.) The four groups can decide how this new information alters the way they have organized their classification patterns.

End: Bring the entire class back together and present the following scenario:

> One of the street crossing patrol guards found a wallet lying on the grass next to the street outside the school. She took it to the school principal, but he could not find the name of the owner inside the wallet. There was no other identification either. However, it may be possible to determine if it belongs to anyone in this room if we examine the fingerprints. There was some money in the wallet, so it needs to be returned to the proper person.

> Take one of the Post-it™ notes (with the student's name on the backside) and tape it to the chalkboard so that everyone can come up to get a close look at it with a magnifying lens. They should compare this print with the others around the room to see if they can find a match.

Assessment of Student Learning: When time has been allowed for students to gather, organize, and process data, students should communicate their conclusions by writing their findings. Their write-up might appear as follows:

I think that _____ is the owner because of the following reasons:

1. (It looks like both have a small mark on the left side.)

2. (It looks like both have the same shape at the top of the arch.)

Have a number of books available in the room for the students to read (see fig. 6.2). Explain that all the books in the collection have something to do with mysteries, detectives, or examining something very carefully for clues.

FIGURE 6.1

Types of Fingerprints

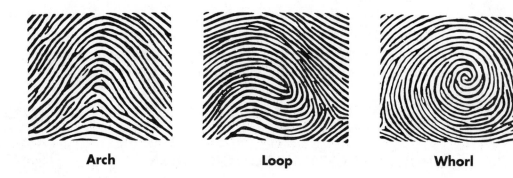

Arch   **Loop**   **Whorl**

FIGURE 6.2

Books Related to the Lesson

Ahlberg, J., & Ahlberg, A. *Each peach pear plum: An I-Spy story.*
Bonsall, C. *The case of the hungry stranger.*
Christian, M. B. *Sebastian (Super Sleuth) and the start-in-his-eyes-mystery.*
Crowther, R. *The most amazing hide-and-seek alphabet book.*
Docekal, E. M. *Nature detective: How to solve outdoor mysteries.*
Dubanevich, A. *Pigs in hiding.*
Geisert, A. *Pigs from 1 to 10.*
Hill, E. *Where's Spot?*
Hoban, T. *Look! Look! Look!*
Micklethwait, L. *I Spy: An alphabet in art.*
Quackenbush, R. M. *Sherlock chick's first case.*
Sharmat, M. W. *Nate the Great and the lost list.*
Sobol, D. J. *Encyclopedia Brown tracks them down.*

REFERENCES

Bridges, B. C. (1963). *Practical fingerprinting.* New York: Funk & Wagnalls.

Carin, A. A. (1993). *Teaching science through discovery* (7th ed.). New York: Macmillan.

Jarolimek, J., & Foster, C. D. (1989). *Teaching and learning in the elementary school* (4th ed.). New York: Macmillan.

Lemlech, J. K. (1994). *Curriculum and instructional methods for the elementary and middle school* (3rd ed.). Englewood Cliffs, NJ: Macmillan.

Saul, W. (1993). *Science workshop: A whole language approach.* Portsmouth, NH: Heinemann.

Sunal, C. (1990). *Early childhood social studies.* Columbus, OH: Merrill Publishing Company.

Sunal, C. S., & Haas, M. E. (1993). *Social studies and the elementary/middle school student.* Orlando, FL: Harcourt Brace Jovanovich College Publishers.

Weiser, M. P. K. (1972). *Fingerprint owls and other fantasies.* Philadelphia: Lippincott.

BOOK SUGGESTIONS FOR CHILDREN

Ahlberg, J., & Ahlberg, A. (1978). *Each peach pear plum: An I-spy story.* New York: Viking Penguin.

Aruego, J., & Dewey, A. (1979). *We hide, you seek*. New York: Greenwillow Books.

Baker, K. (1991). *Hide and snake*. San Diego, CA: Harcourt Brace Jovanovich.

Blake, Q. (1992). *Cockatoos*. Boston: Little, Brown & Co., Inc.

Bonsall, C. (1992). *The case of the hungry stranger*. New York: HarperCollins.

Butler, W. (1994). *The kid detective's handbook*. Boston: Little, Brown.

Caufield, D. E. (1966). *The incredible detectives*. New York: Harper & Row.

Christian, M. B. (1987). *Sebastian (Super Sleuth) and the start-in-his-eyes-mystery*. New York: Macmillan.

Crowther, R. (1978). *The most amazing hide-and-seek alphabet book*. New York: Viking Penguin.

Cushman, D. (1993). *The ABC mystery*. New York: Harper Collins.

Docekal, E. M. (1989). *Nature detective: How to solve outdoor mysteries*. New York: Sterling Publishing Co.

Dubanevich, A. (1983). *Pigs in hiding*. New York: Four Winds Press.

Geisert, A. (1986). *Pigs from A to Z*. Boston: Houghton Mifflin Co.

Geisert, A. (1992). *Pigs from 1 to 10*. Boston: Houghton Mifflin Co.

Hildick, E. W. (1995). *The case of the absent author: A McGurk mystery*. New York: Macmillan.

Hill, E. (1980). *Where's Spot?* New York: Putnam Berkley Group, Inc.

Hoban, T. (1981). *Take another look*. New York: Greenwillow Books.

Hoban, T. (1984). *What is it?* New York: Greenwillow Books.

Hoban, T. (1988). *Look! Look! Look!* New York: Greenwillow Books.

Levy, E. (1995). *Something queer at the scary movie*. Westport, CT: Hyperion.

Micklethwait, L. (1992). *I spy: An alphabet in art*. New York: Greenwillow Books.

Quackenbush, R. M. (1993). *Sherlock and the giant egg mystery*. New York: Parents Magazine Press.

Quackenbush, R. M. (1993). *Sherlock Chick's first case*. New York: Parents Magazine Press.

Sharmat, M. W. (1974). *Nate the Great goes undercover*. New York: Dell.

Sharmat, M. W. (1981). *Nate the Great and the lost list*. New York: Dell.

Sharmat, M. W. (1981). *Nate the Great and the phony clue*. New York: Dell.

Sharmat, M. W. (1981). *Nate the Great and the sticky case*. New York: Dell.

Sobol, D. J. (1972). *Encyclopedia Brown tracks them down*. New York: Pocket Books.

Sobol, D. J. (1994). *Encyclopedia Brown and the case of the two spies*. New York: Delacorte.

Winterfield, H. (1956). *Detectives in togas*. New York: Harcourt, Brace.

BOOTS AND SHOES

KEY IDEAS

■ **Social mathematics** can be used with all ages of students.

■ Venn diagrams show shared and separate content.

■ Common forms of **graphs** include picture, bar, circle, and line.

INTRODUCTION

This chapter combines the areas of mathematics, social studies, and reading. Collecting, analyzing, and recording data are certainly part of mathematics; examining the behavior of people is characteristic of social studies; and enjoying literary experiences is part of reading. The lesson plan in this chapter is designed to be used with students in early elementary, later elementary, or middle school.

SOCIAL MATHEMATICS

A general definition of mathematics is the science of pattern and order. Hartoonian defined social mathematics as "the study and use of **statistics** and probability applied to the social world" (1989, p. 51). Since that time, a wider view of the term has been adopted by educators, namely, that students can use data to help understand their social environment. As Locklege suggests (1993), mathematics can become the language and tool of social studies.

Hollister (1995) states that he has developed hundreds of files of data that could be used in a secondary American or world history class. Some of his files include (1) male/female ratios in the United States from 1790 to 1990, (2) disease patterns in various countries, and (3) winning percentages of twentieth-century baseball teams. He discusses at great length how mathematics, science, and social studies can be integrated to draw conclusions from North American bison population in the nineteenth and twentieth centuries.

Data for younger children often can be obtained by them in response to questions in which they have a personal interest. For example, one girl surveyed her classmates to find the best time of the school day for everyone to eat Valentine cupcakes (Whitin, 1993). Another young child canvassed her classmates to find their favorite *Sesame Street* characters. Hollister (1995, pp. 14–16) presents a question secondary students have investigated, How many students in our school are left- or right-handed? with intriguing follow-up questions:

> How many students in other schools in the community are left- or right-handed?
>
> What percentage of the people in the United States are left- or right-handed?
>
> What ratio can be established between our school and the nation?

Charts and tables are common ways to display data on such questions; however, there are alternatives for students who are not able to work with these forms or who prefer to work with other forms. Freeland and Brewer (1989) discuss how simple picture graphs can be used as a precursor to more complicated graphs. Burton (1993) explains how students can display information by using drawings or graphs.

VENN DIAGRAM

A Venn diagram was discussed in chapter 1, indicating that it organizes information and displays likenesses and differences. Figure 7.1 shows a simple Venn diagram in which the left part of circle A lists unique characteristics of a dog, the right part of circle B lists unique characteristics of a horse, and the overlapping part of the two circles indicates what the two have in common.

GRAPHS

There are four basic types of graphs that students can work with (Freeland & Madden, 1990). All four of these present information in a form that is easy to understand. Ranging from the simplest to the most difficult, they are (1) the picture graph, (2) the bar graph, (3) the circle graph, and (4) the line graph (see fig. 7.2). Graphs illustrate relationships among quantities, thus making them ideal for teaching social mathematics.

FIGURE 7.1

Venn Diagram

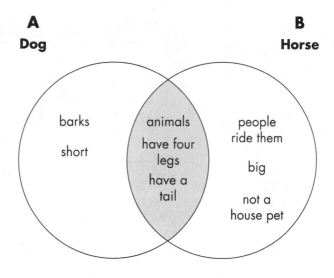

FIGURE 7.2

Graphs

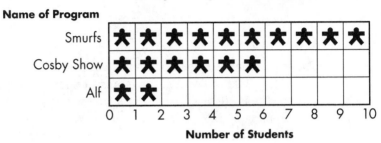

Picture Graph
Popularity of TV Programs

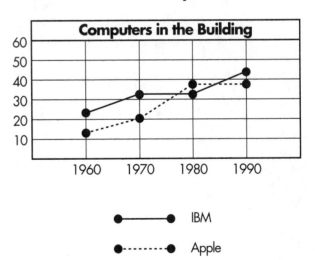

Line Graph

FIGURE 7.2 *Continued*

Bar Graph
Popularity of TV Programs

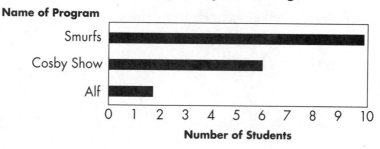

Name of Program

Smurfs	
Cosby Show	
Alf	

0 1 2 3 4 5 6 7 8 9 10

Number of Students

Circle Graph
Lost & Found Articles

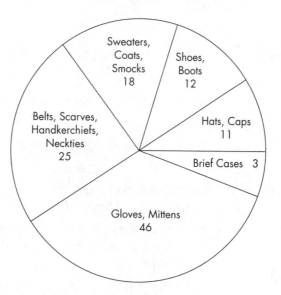

LESSON PLAN

TITLE: **BOOTS AND SHOES**

Ages/Grades: Early elementary, later elementary, middle school

Time: Two hours

Content Areas:

 Mathematics

 Social Studies

 Reading

Materials: A cardboard wheel

Rubber bands

Shoes and boots that children might wear

Clothespins

Materials to make graphs, e.g., rulers, paper, etc.

Objectives:
- Students will manipulate information and communicate ideas using a variety of forms of computation.
- Students will observe, analyze, and interpret human behaviors to acquire a better understanding of self, others, and human relationships.
- Students will enjoy reading materials that relate to the topic of the lesson.

Beginning: Ask students to look around the room and notice what their classmates are wearing on their feet. They probably will find a variety of footwear such as sandals, work boots, hiking shoes, loafers, sneakers, dress shoes, and cowboy boots. Tell the members of the class you would like them to make a list of characteristics for two kinds of footwear—boots and tennis shoes—on a sheet of paper.

Middle: Have students make a Venn diagram, recording the characteristics that are unique to each piece of footwear along with the characteristics the two share. This allows the class to focus on the similarities and differences between the two. The results may appear as shown in figure 7.3.

Next, ask students to think about some brand names of sneakers they may buy and write them on the chalkboard. Narrow this list down to four brand names. Take a large circle of cardboard (which can be obtained from a pizza business) and stretch two rubber bands around it so that they divide the circle into quarter sections. Label the four sections with the four brand names of the sneakers. Ask each student to select one of the four he/she would most want to buy. Give each student a clothespin and ask the students to clamp the clothespins on the edge of the quarter section that represents his/her preference. After the voting is completed, write the results on the chalkboard, indicating how many votes each of the four brands of sneakers received.

End: Ask the class to work in pairs and to use the data from the chalkboard to create a bar graph showing the class's preference results for the four brands of sneakers. Review some of the essential elements of a good bar graph:

- Give the graph a title.
- Label the horizontal and vertical axes.
- Divide one of the axes into units of sneakers.
- Arrange one of the axes to show sneaker brands.

It may be helpful to give the students the following scoring guide (see fig. 7.4) so they can see how their work can be assessed. *Top Notch* shows an exemplary bar graph; *Good* represents one that is adequate; and *Keep Working* indicates that more attention needs to be given to the product.

Assessment of Student Learning:

Have students exchange graphs and have each apply the scoring guide to another classmate's graph. An alternative would be for the teacher to gather the graphs and apply the scoring guide.

At the end of this lesson, encourage students to visit the reading center in the classroom, where the following books could be on display. All of them relate to the word *shoes*.

Angelou, Maya. *All God's Children Need Traveling Shoes.*

Curtiss, Lora Lee. *Who Wants to Wear Boots?*

Farnsworth, Frances J. *Winged Moccasins, the Story of Sacajawea.*

Garst, Shannon. *Silver Spurs for Cowboy Boots.*

Gaulke, Gloria. *Where Is My Shoe?*

Grimm, Jakob. *The Elves and the Shoemaker.*

Hart, Christeen M. *High Button Shoes.*

Hurd, Edith Thacher. *Johnny Lion's Rubber Boots.*

Hurwitz, Johanna. *New Shoes for Sylvia.*

Miller, Margaret. *Whose Shoe?*

Mitchell, Barbara. *Shoes for Everyone: A Story about Jan Matzeliger.*

Patrick, Denise L. *Red Dancing Shoes.*

Turner, Glennette. *Take a Walk in their Shoes.*

FIGURE 7.3

Venn Diagram

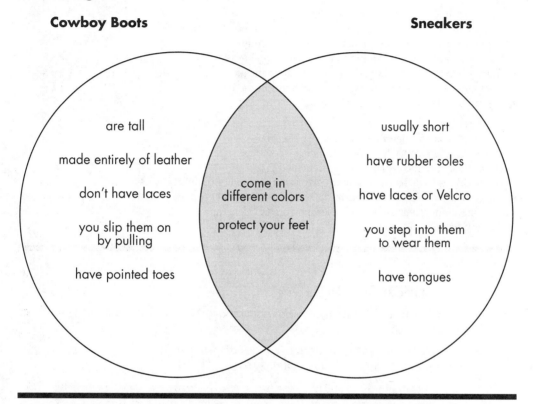

Cowboy Boots   **Sneakers**

are tall

made entirely of leather

don't have laces

you slip them on
by pulling

have pointed toes

come in
different colors

protect your feet

usually short

have rubber soles

have laces or Velcro

you step into them
to wear them

have tongues

FIGURE 7.4

Scoring Guide for Bar Graph

Top Notch
- The graph has an appropriate title with no misspellings.
- The horizontal **axis** has a logical label, spelled correctly.
- The vertical axis has a logical label, spelled correctly.
- The horizontal axis is divided into the proper number of units.
- The vertical axis shows brand names of all four sneakers spelled correctly.
- The number of sneakers is measured exactly by the bars.
- The graph is very easy to read.

Continued

FIGURE 7.4 *Continued*

Good
- The graph has an appropriate title with no misspellings.
- The horizontal axis has a logical label, spelled correctly.
- The vertical axis has a logical label, spelled correctly.
- The horizontal axis is divided into the proper number of units.
- The vertical axis shows brand names of all four sneakers, three spelled correctly.
- The number of sneakers contains a slight error in the bars.
- The graph is fairly easy to read.

Keep Working
- The graph has no title or has some misspellings.
- The horizontal axis has no label or is misspelled.
- The vertical axis has no label or is misspelled.
- The horizontal axis has one or more errors in the number of units.
- The vertical axis shows brand names of less than four sneakers or more than one shoe is misspelled.
- The number of tennis shoes has several errors in the bars.
- The graph is not easy to read.

REFERENCES

Beech, L. W. (1989). *Building visual skills: Charts and graphs*. New York: Sniffen Court Books.

Burton, G. (1993, September/October). Drawing from data. *Social Studies and the Young Learner, 6*(1), 10–16, 27.

Carratello, J. (1990). *Beginning charts, graphs, and diagrams: Skill building activities for the primary child*. Huntington Beach, CA: Teacher Created Materials.

Carratello, J. (1990). *Maps, charts, graphs, and diagrams: Skill building activities for visual literacy*. Huntington Beach, CA: Teacher Created Materials.

Freeland, K., & Brewer, S. (1989, Spring). Graphs for early elementary social studies. *Ohio Council for the Social Studies Review, 25*(1), 32–36.

Freeland, K., & Madden, W. (1990, Fall). Helping young children understand graphs: A demonstration study. *Louisiana Social Studies Journal, 17*(1), 37–39.

Froman, R. (1972). *Venn diagrams*. New York: Crowell.

Hartoonian, H. M. (1989). Social mathematics. In *From information to decision making: New challenges for effective citizenship* (Bulletin No. 83). Washington, DC: National Council for the Social Studies.

Hollister, B. C. (1995, January). Social math in the history classroom. *Social Education, 59*(1), 14–16.

Lockledge, A. (1993, September/October). Math as the Language and Tool of Social Studies. *Social Studies and the Young Learner, 6*(1), 3–6.

National Geographic Society. (1987). *Adventures with charts and graphs computer file: Project Zoo.* Washington, DC: Author.

Porter, P. (1993, September/October). Activities for social math. *Social Studies and the Young Learner, 6*(1), (pullout feature).

Vance, A. (1985). *Math fun graphs computer file.* Santa Barbara, CA: AV Systems, Inc.

Whitin, D. J. (1993, September/October). Dealing with data in democratic classrooms. *Social Studies and the Young Learner, 6*(1), 7–9.

BOOK SUGGESTIONS FOR CHILDREN

Angelou, M. (1986). *All God's children need traveling shoes.* New York: Random House.

Compton's interactive encyclopedia (Ed.). (1996). [CD-ROM]. Chicago: Compton's New Media, Inc.

Curtiss, L. L. (1972). *Who wants to wear boots?* Minneapolis, MN: Denison.

De Angeli, M. (1938). *Copper-toed boots.* New York: Doubleday, Doran.

de La Fontaine, J. (1965). *The rich man and the shoe-maker.* New York: Franklin Watts.

Farnsworth, F. J. (1954). *Winged moccasins: The story of Sacajawea.* New York: J. Messner.

Fox, M. (1989). *Shoes for Grandpa.* New York: Orchard Books.

Garst, S. (1946). *Cowboy boots.* New York: Abingdon-Cokesbury Press.

Garst, S. (1949). *Silver spurs for cowboy boots.* New York: Abingdon-Cokesbury Press.

Gaulke, G. (1965). *Where is my shoe?* New York: Holt, Rinehart and Winston.

Grimm, J. (1981). *The elves and the shoemaker.* Mahwah, NJ: Troll Associates.

Hart, C. M. (1987). *High button shoes.* Bowling Green, KY: C. M. Hart.

Haviland, V. (1961). Boots and the Troll. In *Favorite fairy tales.* Boston: Little, Brown & Co.

Hosford, J. (1972). *You bet your boots I can.* New York: T. Nelson.

Hurd, E. T. (1972). *Johnny Lion's rubber boots.* New York: Harper & Row.

Hurwitz, J. (1993). *New shoes for Sylvia*. New York: Morrow Junior Books.

Kirstein, L. (1992). *Puss in Boots*. Boston: Little, Brown & Co.

Lawrence, M. (1949). *Sand in her shoes*. New York: Harcourt, Brace.

Milhous, K. (1951). *Patrick and the golden slippers*. New York: Scribners.

Miller, M. (1991). *Whose shoe?* New York: Greenwillow Books.

Mitchell, B. (1986). *Shoes for everyone: A story about Jan Matzeliger*. Minneapolis, MN: Carolrhoda.

Nunaroff, L. (1993). *Dogs don't wear sneakers*. New York: Simon & Schuster Books for Young Readers.

Patrick, D. L. (1993). *Red dancing shoes*. New York: Tambourine Books.

Rice, E. (1979). *New blue shoes: Story and pictures*. New York: Puffin Books.

Steiner, C. (1957). *My slippers are red*. New York: Knopf.

Streatfeild, N. (1937). *Ballet shoes*. New York: Random House.

Streatfeild, N. (1939). *Circus shoes*. New York: Random House.

Streatfeild, N. (1945). *Theater shoes, or other people's shoes*. New York: Random House.

Turner, G. (1989). *Take a walk in their shoes*. New York: Cobblehill Books.

Ungerer, T. (1964). *One, two, where's my shoe?* New York: Harper & Row.

MUSEUM

KEY IDEAS

- Museums containing paintings, photographs, antiques, or other objects provide good learning experiences.
- Students need to use maps in real-life situations.

INTRODUCTION

This lesson combines social studies, fine arts, and language arts, which works well if students visit a museum. If this type of field trip activity is not possible, then paintings, statues, or other art pieces can be displayed in several rooms or hallways of the building. In either situation, students will walk about the area with the aid of a **map** that they sketch. They can use walkie-talkies to communicate to a partner and to interpret the maps they are making.

MUSEUMS AND ART

Museums often are thought of as buildings in large cities where a person can go to view paintings. Although this certainly is one purpose of a museum, it is not limited to this description, for it can house any kind of material that provides information about a person, community, group, or segment of society. One can spend weeks in the Smithsonian Institution in Washington, DC, or one can spend a few minutes in a small town's one-room tribute to a local hero. A museum can contain a wide assortment of objects, as does the Chicago Museum of Science and Industry, or it can be very specialized, as is the Quilt Museum, located in Paducah, Kentucky.

To find out about museums on the World Wide Web, a person can look up *museums* using one of the many search engines (see chapter 10 for a more detailed explanation of using technological databases). For example, one of the subtopics on the Web is "World Wide Arts Resources," and this list of museums—arranged by continents—offers information about museums connected to the Internet. Under *North America* is a long list of museums and their specialties. Another option is to go directly into a Web site.

A museum contains a collection of items designed to indicate something about the people who made them or are portrayed in them. It's always a wise procedure for the teacher to prepare the students beforehand for the museum visit (Stopsky & Lee, 1994, p. 407). Perhaps the museum can supply literature the students can read before the day of the trip. Some museums have designed educational packets that students can use as they make their way through the building. Even if there is nothing formally prepared, the teacher should discuss what the students will be seeing when they walk through the museum rooms and look at the displays.

Norton (1995) explores the *visual elements* contained in children's illustrated books. *Lines*, whether curved, jagged, vertical, horizontal, diagonal, thin, or heavy, give suggestions to the viewer. These can be interpreted as motion, danger, or delicacy. The illustrators of *The Girl Who Loved Wild Horses* and *Cinderella* effectively use lines in their illustrations.

Colors such as bright yellow, pastel hues, muted red, and dark blue convey sensations of warmth, energy, and bleakness. Pictures in *Letting Swift River Go* and *In Coal Country* show what colors can do.

Shapes can be round to free-form. Artists in *Arrow to the Sun* and *Mirette on the High Wire* create different effects with their shapes.

Texture invites the reader to touch the illustrations. Illustrations in *Owl Moon* and *Bear* are examples of texture depicted in art.

Artists employ **design**, **media**, and **style** to vary the way that the visual elements appear. The *Night before Christmas* and *Will's Mammoth* supply unique design combinations of *line*, *color*, *shape*, and *texture*. The media of ink, wood, and paint give expression to visual elements in such books as *The Crane Wife* and *The Very Hungry Caterpillar*. Men and women have artistic styles that appeal to students. Illustrators of *Paddle-to-the-Sea* and *Swimmy* are examples.

GEOGRAPHIC ORIENTATION

According to the National Geography Standards (1994), geography is supposed to have a utilitarian value in our lives. More than memorizing names of cities, mountains, and countries found on a map or globe, it applies geographic information in our situations. We need to orient ourselves in our environment by using geographic terms. Following are some important pieces of information that will help students as they try to understand the application of a map.

A Geographic Vocabulary

1. A **map** is a two-dimensional representation of the earth's surface.

2. **Symbols** are pictorial or abstract representations of real objects.

3. *Location* indicates a position on the earth's surface.

4. *Distance* is the length of the path between the points being measured.

5. A person follows a certain *direction* (or bearing) to an intended point. The direction could be cardinal (north, south, east, or west), or it could be intermediate (northeast, northwest, southeast, or southwest).

6. A *key*, or legend, on a map is a collection of **symbols** that have been used.

7. Maps show *scale*, that is, they show a distance on paper that bears some relationship to the actual distance on the ground.

8. Bodies of water and land have unique *shapes*, or outline appearances.

9. The *size* of an object can be different on various maps, but the nature of the object remains the same.

10. A *route* is a selected path a person chooses to travel.

11. A compass rose is a circle found on maps that shows at least the four cardinal directions.

12. Proper *proportion* must be shown on a map so that one object has the appropriate size relative to other objects.

LESSON PLAN

TITLE: **MUSEUM**

Ages/Grades: Early elementary, later elementary, middle school

Time: Two hours

Content Areas:

 Language Arts

 Fine Arts

 Geography

Materials: Walkie-talkies

Exhibits in art gallery

Maps of world and the United States

Writing materials

Compass

Outline maps (floor plans) of art gallery

Objectives:
- Students will engage in informal communication.
- Students will examine and construct meaning from visual art.
- Students will express information and ideas using technology.
- Students will use geographic sources of information and data for a purpose.

- Students will use a variety of means to identify absolute and relative location.

- Students will recognize that everything has a location.

- Students will identify and express arts concepts in visual arts.

- Students will observe and explore a variety of artistic styles and forms in visual arts.

Beginning: Gather students on the floor in one of the areas of an art gallery to review prerequisite skills discussed previously in the section about geographic orientation in this chapter: map, symbol, location, distance, direction, key, scale, shape, size, route, compass, proportion.

Inform the students about proper museum etiquette: speak quietly, walk—don't run—in the building; don't touch paintings, statues, or other exhibit pieces. Next, allow them a short time to browse through the museum to get a quick overview of the facilities. Gather them back as a group and have them reflect on what they noticed as they walked through the museum.

Distribute printed information and/or tell students something about the featured artist or artists. If appropriate, distribute a map of relevant places; for example, the artist's birthplace and in what part of the country or world the scenes are located.

Orient the students with a compass to the cardinal directions (north, south, east, and west) and the intermediate directions (northeast, southeast, northwest, and southwest) in the museum. They should position themselves so that the compass needle and themselves are lined up with north.

Middle: Request that the students walk through the gallery for the purpose of selecting a favorite piece of art. Each student takes a sheet of 8½ by 11 paper showing outlines (which the teacher has drawn) of the gallery areas. The purpose of this part of the assignment is for students to identify their favorite artwork and place it on the map. Students should draw appropriate symbols and directions so that another person would be able to interpret the map and locate the favorite piece.

Pair the students and ask them to exchange maps. Select just one pair and give a walkie-talkie to that pair; the other walkie-talkie will remain with the teacher and the rest of the group. One of the persons in this pair will orient himself or herself to the partner's map and try to follow the correct route. That person should speak into the walkie-talkie, explaining what he or she is doing; for example, "I am starting to walk about 10 feet east toward the stairway"; "Now I am going down the stairs to the lower level"; "At the bottom of the steps I turn left and face the south wall"; "My partner's favorite painting will be the second one on the left as I face the south wall."

The group listens to the comments and will ask for clarifying comments when appropriate. For example, the teacher may say, "When you reached the bottom of the stairs and turned left, did you turn east or west?" People in the large group can attempt to trace the route as they hear the information from the speaker on the walkie-talkie.

As the two people are traveling the route (each with the partner's map), the student who drew the map will give corroborating or correcting information until the favorite piece is correctly identified. Oral communication is thereby used to enable students to give expression to their geographic understanding.

End: The rest of the class will pair up, exchange maps, and proceed to locate the partner's favorite piece in the same way as the first pair did. This time, however, the walkie-talkie will not be used to relay the conversations between the students. It is up to each pair to decide how helpful to be to one another. For example, one pair may stipulate that each will respond only to questions with a yes or no answer. Once the piece is located, the person will explain what he/she liked about it to qualify it as a favorite piece.

**Assessment
of Student
Learning:**   Assessment of the success of the activity can be done in three
ways: (1) By a show of hands find out how many students were
able to locate a partner's favorite piece. This indicates if map
reading can be done. (2) Anecdotal records can be kept by the
teacher to report on the students' oral ability to communicate
with geographical terms. (3) The actual maps can be examined
to decide on the authenticity of the symbols, directions,
locations, proportions, shapes, etc.

A debriefing session should be held at the end to discuss how
communication can occur through spoken words and through
symbols on a map.

REFERENCES

Blizzard, G. S. (1992). *Come look with me: Exploring landscape art with children*. Charlottesville, VA: Thomasson-Grant, Inc.

Cleaver, J. (1988). *Doing children's museums: A guide to 225 hands-on museums*. Charlotte, VT: Williamson Pub.

Geography for life: National Geography Standards 1994. (1994). Washington, DC: National Geographic Research & Exploration.

George, G., & Sherrill-Leo, C. (1986). *Starting right: A basic guide to museum planning*. Nashville: TN: American Association for State and Local History.

Koetsch, P. (1994, September/October). Museum in progress: Student learning environments. *Social Studies and the Young Learner, 7*(1), 15–18.

Lacy, L. E. (1986). *Art and design in children's picture books*. Chicago, IL: American Library Association.

Norton, D. (1995). *Through the eyes of a child* (4th ed.). Englwood Cliffs, NJ: Prentice-Hall, Inc.

Stopsky, F., & Lee, S. (1994). *Social studies in a global society*. Albany, NY: Delmar Publishers Inc.

BOOK SUGGESTIONS FOR CHILDREN

(See also the suggestions for students in chapter 11.)

Arnosky, J. (1982). *Drawing from nature*. New York: Lothrop, Lee & Shepard.

Arnosky, J. (1988). *Sketching outdoors in summer*. New York: Lee & Shepard.

Bang, M. (1991). *Picture this: Perception and composition*. Boston, MA: Little, Brown.

Blizzard, G. S. (1992). *Come look with me: Animals in art*. Charlottesville, VA: Thomasson-Grant, Inc.

Bolognese, D. (1982). *Drawing spaceships and other spacecraft*. New York: Watts.

Brown, L. K., & Brown, M. (1986). *Visiting the art museum*. New York: Dutton.

Carle, E. (1971). *The very hungry caterpillar*. New York: Crowell.

Davidson, R. (1994). *Take a look: An introduction to the experience of art*. New York: Viking.

Goble, P. (1978). *The girl who loved wild horses*. New York: Bradbury.

Greenberg, J., & Jordan, S. (1991). *Painter's eye*. New York: Delacorte.

Greenberg, J., & Jordan, S. (1993). *Sculptor's eye*. New York: Delacorte.

Hendershot, J. (1987). *In coal country*. New York: Knopf.

Holling, H. C. (1941). *Paddle-to-the-sea*. Boston: Houghton Mifflin.

Janson, H. W., & Janson, A. F. (1992). *History of art for young people* (4th ed.). New York: Abrams.

Konisburg, E. L. (1967). *From the mixed-up files of Mrs. Basil Frankweiler*. New York: Atheneum.

Knox, B. (1992). *The great art adventure*. New York: Rizoli.

Lionni, L. (1963). *Swimmy*. New York: Pantheon.

Martin, R. (1989). *Will's mammoth*. New York: Putnam.

McCully, E. A. (1992). *Mirette on the high wire*. New York: Putnam.

McDermott, G. (1974). *Arrow to the sun*. New York: Viking.

McLanathan, R. (1990). *Leonardo da Vinci*. New York: Abrams.

Moore, C. (1980). *The night before Christmas*. New York: Holiday House.

Perrault, C. (1985). *Cinderella*. New York: Dial.

Schoenherr, J. (1991). *Bear*. New York: Philomel.

Sills, L. (1993). *Visions: Stories about women artists*. Morton Grove, IL: Whitman.

Strickland, C. (1992). *The annotated Mona Lisa: A crash course in art history from prehistoric to post-modern*. Kansas City: Andrews and McMeel.

Turner, R. M. (1992). *Portraits of women artists for children: Georgia O'Keeffe*. Boston: Little, Brown.

Yagawa, S. (1981). *The crane wife*. New York: Morrow.

Yolen, J. (1987). *Owl moon*. New York: Philomel.

Yolen, J. (1992). *Letting Swift River go*. Boston: Little, Brown.

SHELTER

KEY IDEAS

- Students enjoy working with inquiries from anthropology.
- The five themes from geography enable students to investigate their world.
- The National Council of Teachers of Mathematics encourages integration of the curriculum.
- Students can relate to the topic of houses.

INTRODUCTION

This chapter combines the areas of **anthropology**, **geography**, reading, writing, mathematics, and practical living skills. Literature provides a focus for these three topics. Because the mathematics in the lesson plan involves **geometry** (specifically determining the area of a geometric shape), the plan works best with middle school students.

ANTHROPOLOGY

Anthropology has been defined as the study of culture, where culture means *way of life*. As such, this area of social studies is very broad, for it includes topics such as art, religion, music, sports, and entertainment; and it includes concepts such as artifacts, technology, tools, rituals, and adaptation. Anthropology is fascinating for students because it requires them to investigate questions that ask why:

Why do people in other countries enjoy fast foods that are different from ours?

Why does a particular piece of fashion apparel appeal to so many of the students in this school?

Why is basketball enjoyed by people around the world?

Lacks (1992) discusses how young children can learn about cultures by studying common objects found in other countries (such as a ball) to find how the objects are alike and different. Bernson and Lindquist (1989) use the first and last names of people around the world to find out about the cultures of a variety of countries.

GEOGRAPHY

There are two aspects to geography: physical and human. The first focuses on the rivers, mountains, and natural features, whereas the second emphasizes how people relate to their natural physical environment. Geography is not only the study of maps and globes; for this reason, it is wise to have students use the five geographic themes to investigate the world around them:

1. Location: position on the earth's surface

2. Place: physical and human characteristics

3. Relationships within places: humans and environments

4. Movement: humans interacting with one another on the earth

5. Regions: how they form and change

In Lacks's reference to the ball (1992), students could locate Japan to find this country whose citizens relish baseball; they could study how people travel from all parts of the earth to attend the World Cup in soccer; or they could see how people change the environment to build arenas or stadiums to enjoy basketball games.

GEOMETRY IN MATHEMATICS

The National Council of Teachers of Mathematics (1989) has encouraged schools to broaden their curriculum by integrating mathematics with other subject areas from preschool to secondary school. Whitin (1994) takes mathematics beyond rules to be memorized to extend them as relevant aspects of children's lives. Everyday events in school offer a tie between mathematics and literature for young children; for example, celebrating birthdays *(Happy Birthday, Sam)* and taking attendance *(Two Ways to Count to Ten)*. Miller and Mitchell (1995) present one-to-three-week outlines of mathematics and science activities that are derived from the business world. Their activities demonstrate how middle school students can do random sampling to investigate quality control of the manufacture of camera film.

Renga (1994) presents many activities related to the topic of the postal system to correlate mathematics with art, social studies, and reading. Strickland and Kuykendoll's activities (1992) very cleverly display connections between mathematics and physical education.

Van de Walle (1990) feels that students should study geometry in mathematics for many reasons, including (1) developing problem-solving skills and (2) because it is used by many people daily in their professions. The lesson plan in this chapter attempts to point out these real-life applications for geometry.

HOUSES

It is said that humans have three basic needs: food, clothing, and shelter. We satisfy our need for shelter by building houses of varying sizes, shapes, and materials. The following lesson plan allows students to ask questions about a variety of buildings that house people. The lesson can be used with middle school students.

LESSON PLAN

TITLE: **HOUSES**

Ages/Grades: Middle school

Time: One hour

**Content
Areas:**
 Geography

 Mathematics

 Anthropology

 Reading

 Writing

 Practical living

Materials: A collection of literature books (see section at end of this chapter)

Large pictures of houses and homes representing those found in countries from around the world

Measuring tools (rulers, calculators, string, graph paper, plastic counters, etc.)

Objectives:
- Students will describe cultural universals, similarities, and differences.
- Students will apply appropriate computational methods (estimation, mental arithmetic, paper and pencil) to solve problems in real-life situations.
- Students will create alternative approaches to a task.
- Students will be able to write some differences in homes occupied by people around the world.
- Students will enjoy making the connections found in literature books on the topic of houses.

Beginning: Ask students to think about the houses they live in and some words they would use to describe them: tall, wet, windows, small, apartment, rats, cold, paint. Show a collection of photographs or pictures depicting houses found in other cultures. Students form pairs to look at a particular illustration and make a list of all the questions they would like to find the answers to when looking at it. Some possibilities may be:

- Why are there no walls?
- What do the decorations above the door represent?
- What is the house made of?
- Is this big enough for the whole family to live in?
- Where do the people go to the bathroom?

Two pairs of students form a group of four and compare their two illustrations to find similarities and differences. As students share their information about the pictures, point out that people around the world don't all live in the same kind of houses. Why is this? Some prefer square houses, some rectangular houses, and some round houses.

Middle: After students have arrived at some opinions about why some cultures design houses of different shapes, ask them if there could be a reason related to efficiency for the differences; in other words, are there some shapes that allow more interior living space for a family?

Have the students form groups to investigate this problem of the various areas of interiors of houses by discussing the procedure a person may use to determine how much space would be contained within a geometric shape. As they come up with the formulas, write them on the board:

Rectangle: $A = l \times w$

Parallelogram: $A = b \times h$

Triangle: $A = \frac{1}{2} b \times h$

Circle: $A = \pi r^2$

Encourage the students to think of ways a person may determine an area without the use of mathematical formulas. Some, for instance, may say that you could draw the shapes on graph paper so that the perimeters are identical for a square house and a rectangular house. Then you could count the small squares inside to see which is greater. What if you had identical perimeters for a circular house and a rectangular house? Which results in a larger area? How about between a triangular house and a square house? Students could use a variety of materials, such as beans, coins, plastic counters, to determine area.

End: After each group has performed the comparisons on several kinds of house perimeters, record their findings on a large chart. The chart may show, for example,

Group A found more area in a rectangle than a parallelogram.

Group B found more area in a square than a triangle.

Group C found more area in a circle than an oval.

**Assessment
of Student
Learning:**   As a large group, have students tell the shape they selected and record the various answers on the chalkboard. As it turns out, a circle results in the greatest interior area. Ask the class the following questions to get them to think about why some cultures choose to build houses of other shapes and designs.

1. Why is it that we see very few round houses?

2. What cultures build houses with a circular base (some North American Indians with tepees, some Eskimos with igloos, some African tribes with huts)?

The students may offer some thoughts to the effect that it's difficult to arrange furniture in a round house, or lumber for sale at a building supply store does not lend itself to circular construction.

Have a supply of books on houses for the students to read. All the books in the following list connect with the topic of houses.

Aardema, Verna. *Who's in Rabbit's House: A Masai Tale.*

Byars, Betsy. *The House of Wings.*

Carle, Eric. *A House for Hermit Crab.*

Cisneros, Sandra. *The House on Mango Street.*

Dragonwagon, Crescent. *Home Place.*

Dugan, William. *All about Houses.*

Felix, Monique. *The House.*

Gibbons, Gail. *How a House Is Built.*

Godden, Rumer. *Mouse House.*

Goodall, John. *The Story of a Castle.*

Grifalconi, Ann. *The Village of Round and Square Houses.*

Hoberman, Mary Ann. *A House Is a House for Me.*

James, Alan. *Homes in Cold Places.*

Lobel, Arnold. *Owl at Home.*

MacDonald, Fiona. *A Medieval Castle.*

Morris, Ann. *Houses and Homes.*

Shapp, Martha. *Let's Find out about Houses.*

Steele, Philip. *House through the Ages.*

REFERENCES

Bernson, M. H., & Lindquist, T. L. (1989, March/April). What's in a name? Galloping toward cultural insights. *Social Studies and the Young Learner, 1*(4), 13–15.

Houses and homes around the world. (1980). Poster study prints teaching aid. London: Macmillan Children's Books.

Joint Committee on Geographic Education. (1984). *Guidelines for geographic education: Elementary and secondary schools*. Washington, DC: Association of American Geographers and the National Council for Geographic Education.

Lacks, C. (1992, January/February). Sharing a world of difference: International education in the early years. *Social Studies and the Young Learner, 4*(3), 6–8, 30.

Miller, L. D., & Mitchell, C. E. (1995, February). Using quality control activities to develop scientific and mathematical literacy. *School Science and Mathematics, 95*(2), 58–60.

National Council of Teachers of Mathematics. (1989). *Curriculum and evaluation standards for school mathematics*. Reston, VA: Author.

Renga, S. (1994, April). Ideas: Moving the mail. *Arithmetic Teacher, 41*(8), 463–472.

Sheffield, S. (1995). *Math and literature (K–3), book two*. Sausalito, CA: Math Solutions Publications.

Strickland, J. F., & Kuykendoll, N. J. (1992, Fall). Mathematics and physical education: Providing opportunities for interactions in the middle school. *Education, 113*(1), 93–95.

Thompson, G. (1991). *Teaching through themes*. New York: Scholastic.

Van de Walle, J. A. (1990). *Elementary school mathematics: Teaching developmentally*. New York: Longman.

Whitin, D. (1994, January). Literature and mathematics in preschool and primary. *Young Children, 49*(2), 4–11.

BOOK SUGGESTIONS FOR CHILDREN

Aardema, V. (1979). *Who's in Rabbit's house: A Masai tale*. New York: Dial Books for Young Readers.

Angelou, M. (1994). *My painted house, my friendly chicken*. New York: Scholastic.

Blal, R. (1994). *Shaker house*. Boston: Houghton Mifflin.

Byars, B. (1972). *The house of wings*. New York: Viking Press.

Caldecott, R. (1989). *This is the house that Jack built*. Danbury, CT: Grolier Educational Corporation.

Carle, E. (1991). *A house for Hermit Crab*. Saxonville, MA: Picture Book Studio, Ltd.

Cisneros, S. (1983). *The house on Mango Street*. Houston, TX: Arte Publico.

Cooper, F. (1994). *Coming home: From the life of Langston Hughes*. New York: Philomel Books.

Curry, N. (1968). *The littlest house*. Glendale, CA: Bowmar Pub. Corp.

dePaola, T. (1973). *Nana upstairs, Nana downstairs*. New York: Putnam Berkley Group, Inc.

Dee, R. (1988). *Two ways to count to ten*. New York: Holt.

Dorros, A. (1992). *This is my house*. New York: Scholastic.

Dragonwagon, C. (1990). *Home place*. New York: MacMillan.

Dugan, W. (1975). *All about houses*. New York: Golden Press.

Falwell, C. (1992). *Shape space*. New York: Clarion.

Felix, M. (1993). *The house*. Columbus, OH: American Education Publishing.

Gibbons, G. (1991). *How a house is built*. New York: Holiday House, Inc.

Godden, R. (1968). *Mouse house*. New York: Viking Press.

Goodall, J. S. (1986). *The story of a castle*. New York: Margaret K. McElderry Books.

Grifalconi, A. (1986). *The village of round and square houses*. Boston: Little, Brown.

Griffith, H. V. (1987). *Grandaddy's place*. New York: Greenwillow Books.

Harris, D. J. (1973). *The house mouse*. New York: F. Warne.

Hamilton, V. (1968). *The house of Dies Drear*. New York: Macmillan.

Hamilton, V. (1987). *Mystery of Drear House*. New York: Greenwillow Books.

Hoban, T. (1974). *Circles, triangles, and squares*. New York: Macmillan.

Hoberman, M. A. (1982). *A house is a house for me*. New York: Puffin Books.

Horwitz, E. L. (1982). *How to wreck a building*. New York: Pantheon Books Inc.

Hutchins, P. (1986). *Happy birthday, Sam*. New York: Mulberry.

Ichikawa, S. (1986). *Nora's castle*. New York: Putnam Berkley Group, Inc.

James, A. (1989). *Homes in cold places*. Minneapolis, MN: Lerner Publications Co.

James, A. (1989). *Homes in hot places*. Minneapolis, MN: Lerner Publications Co.

James, A. (1989). *Homes on water*. Minneapolis, MN: Lerner Publications Co.

Lionni, L. (1968). *The biggest house in the world*. New York: Pantheon.

Lobel, A. (1975). *Owl at home*. New York: Harper & Row.

Macaulay, D. (1973). *Cathedral: The story of its construction*. Boston: Houghton Mifflin.

Macdonald, F. (1990). *A medieval castle*. New York: Peter Bedrick Books.

MacLachlan, P. *Through Grandpa's eyes*. (1983). New York: HarperCollins.

McBratney, S. (1989). *The ghosts of Hungryhouse Lane*. New York: Henry Holt & Co.

Milne, A. A. (1956). *The house at Pooh Corner*. New York: Dutton.

Morris, A. (1992). *Houses and homes*. New York: Lothrop, Lee & Shepard Books.

Pienkowski, J. (1979). *Haunted house*. New York: E. P. Dutton.

Rosen, M. J. (1992). *Home*. New York: HarperCollins.

Rylant, C. (1993). *Everyday house*. New York: Bradbury.

Shapp, M. (1962). *Let's find out about houses*. New York: Watts.

Shemie, B. (1989). *Houses of snow, skin, and bones*. Plattsburgh, NY: Tundra.

Steele, P. (1994). *House through the ages*. Mahwah, NJ: Troll Associates.

Weik, M. H. (1972). *A house on Liberty Street*. New York: Atheneum.

Wilder, L. I. (1932). *Little house in the big woods*. New York: Harper & Row.

Wood, A. (1984). *The napping house*. San Diego, CA: Harcourt Brace & Co.

TECHNOLOGY AND CURRICULUM

KEY IDEAS

- On-line technology is becoming an important learning tool for students.
- News and events become instantaneously available to students through technology.
- All content areas of a curriculum can benefit from electronic learning media.

INTRODUCTION

Technology is becoming an important instrument for educating students, and it also is becoming a significant factor in teachers' professional development. Students and teachers can join bulletin boards to engage in discussions about topics that interest them. If more extensive research is required, they can search, locate, read, and download the files they wish to investigate further.

SCIENCE, TECHNOLOGY, AND SOCIETY

Science, technology, and society (STS) is a topic that is taught in many schools. Craig (1992) presents some questions related to technology that students in the elementary grades can investigate: How does technology help or hinder people as they do their jobs at school? How do people differ in their use of technology? How has technology changed our community?

TELEVISION

Television is one form of technology that has been used in the classroom for many decades. C-Span, public television, the Discovery Channel, and other cable facilities provide opportunities for learning in the areas of mathematics, language, reading, social studies, and science. *Channel One*, a twelve-minute newscast was quite popular in the early 1990s. More than eight million secondary students watched this commercial venture in schools (Tiene & Whitmore, 1995).

In addition, a new instructional technique, called distance learning, where one teacher can work simultaneously with many remote sites, enables hundreds or even thousands of students at a time to learn interactively from television that transmits through fiber optics.

MULTIMEDIA AND COMPUTERS

Teachers have used audiotapes, phonograph records, films, and videotapes for many years to supplement the traditional educational experience. Recently audio compact discs and visual laser discs have been available to bring sounds and sights to their students.

A CD-ROM (compact disc read-only memory) can hold not only text and music, but also photographs and video clips. Illustrations from postcards, maps, magazines, and calendars can be captured with a scanning device and converted to a digital format (Jackson, 1995). Thousands of these images can then be stored on one CD.

Laser discs provide publishers such as National Geographic *(Solar System)*, Smithsonian *(Dinosaurs)*, and the BBC *(Encyclopedia of Animals)* the opportunity to bring technological wizardry into the classrooms. Using a bar code reader, teachers or students can bring into action K–12 topics in a variety of curriculum areas. Children in early elementary grades are developing databases in content areas.

Classroom computers have a number of uses besides running software games. For years, teachers have been using computers for drill and practice, tutorials, and simulations. Recently, educational applications have been extended into a variety of communication possibilities, some of which are described below.

THE INTERNET

There is simply too much information available in the world for students to be able to access it only by reading books. Computers can store vast amounts of data economically and can allow a student to retrieve information quickly. The **Internet** is a worldwide computer hookup delivered through telephone lines. There are commercial providers (such as Prodigy, CompuServe, and America Online), while some states have taken the initiative to link colleges, universities, and K–12 schools. Once a site is **on line**, a number of services are available.

The following lesson plan presents a way for middle school students to carry out an assignment using electronic communication. Students use Gopher to participate in a scavenger hunt, seeking information. **Gopher** is a software tool enabling someone to search for items using a menu on a computer screen.

LESSON PLAN

TITLE: **TECHNOLOGY SCAVENGER HUNT**

Ages/Grades: Middle school

Time: Two hours

**Content
Areas:**   Social Studies

    Language Arts

    Practical Living

    Health

Materials: Computer and printer

Newspaper article

Internet access

Objectives: • Students will analyze economic situations that are of national importance.

• Students will demonstrate knowledge of the function of elected political officials.

• Students will identify health-related facilities in a community.

• Students will perceive technology as a more integral part of their lives.

• Students will gather and manipulate data.

• Students will write to support their ideas.

Beginning: The students in this middle school classroom have been performing a community service project with a nearby nursing home for several months. Each student has "adopted" one of the residents and has made weekly visits to that person. Through conversation, running errands, and doing helpful favors, friendships have developed between the senior citizens and the youngsters. The middle school students have acquired a new insight into the life of senior citizens. In particular, they have realized how much the senior citizens are dependent upon their retirement income. Without paychecks from jobs, most of the men and women in the home have little money to spend. The middle school class has decided they want to study the topic of Social Security benefits for retired citizens.

A newspaper article was selected that describes the potential conflict between a lobby (the American Association of Retired Persons) and the United States Congress over cutbacks in Social Security benefits. Figure 10.1 and the other newspaper clipping in this chapter are from a medium-sized city's newspaper. However, these types of articles can commonly be found in many local, state, and national papers.

Congressional members will apparently need to decide whether to cut benefits to senior citizens in order to save money. For the past week the class has been discussing the pros and cons of both sides of this issue.

The teacher will let students select a state and prepare a letter to mail to one of that state's elected officials in either the United States Senate or the House of Representatives. Ask the students how they would go about finding the mailing address of a United States senator.

Remind them that Congress contains a large number of members (100 senators and 435 representatives) with offices in several buildings in the nation's capital. A zip code also needs to be included. Some students may suggest contacting the post office and asking an official to consult a postal directory to locate the address. Ask the students if they would need to know the name of a specific senator to give to the post office.

Tell the class there is a quick way to locate names and addresses of congressional members by looking them up in a computer database. An additional option is to have the students search for the e-mail address of their congressional representative and send their message electronically.

Middle: Arrange the class so they are working at computers in the school's computer lab. It is important that the computers are networked so that the Internet can be accessed. Gopher is a menu-driven arrangement that allows a person to search for and retrieve information. The information is supplied by a server that supplies resources on the terminal screen.

Once a student types *gopher* on the computer's keyboard, a menu of choices should appear. Once a selection is made, another menu appears. This type of branching (or *burrowing*) eventually will lead to the specific information the student seeks.

End: If the teacher distributes the question regarding the names of congressional representatives along with the steps to follow as outlined in Figure 10.2, a student should be able to find the name and address of any United States senator.

The exact wording of this menu's entry numbers and phrases may vary, so the teacher should run through this procedure to see how it appears on the gopher server used in his or her school. Ask the students to select the name of a senator or congressman who they think would have a very important impact on Social Security legislation.

Assessment of Student Learning: Each student should prepare a written justification for the senator or congressman who was selected. For example, a student might have selected a member from Florida because many retirees live in this state. Another might have selected one from Arizona, because a great number of retired people live there as well. Some students might have chosen a congressional figure because they know that person serves on an important congressional committee that deals with Social Security legislation.

FIGURE 10.1

Newspaper Article

Senior groups to fight Social Security cuts

AARP leading charge in battle with Congress

Associated Press

WASHINGTON—Senior citizens groups are mobilizing to stop a move in Congress to reduce cost-of-living increases for the millions of Americans who collect Social Security.

The country's most powerful senior citizens lobby, the American Association of Retired Persons, weighed in yesterday with a news conference to attack an effort to shave the annual cost-of-living increases by one-third.

Spokesmen for other senior citizens groups said in interviews that they also intend to fight proposed cuts in Social Security benefit increases, and promised to alert millions of elderly Americans through direct mail campaigns and other grass roots tactics to pressure Congress.

"People will see this as a stark cut in their income, money right out of their pockets, and they'll react, even if (the amount) seems little in Washington," said Dan Schulder. He is legislative director of the National Council of Senior Citizens, a liberal-leaning group representing 5 million older Americans.

"We're going to ask them to get on the backs of all members of Congress and the White House," he said. "This is one of the last things Congress will try to sneak through (this year), so we have time."

Max Richtman, executive vice president of the National Committee to Preserve Social Security and Medicare, said his group would take its case against cost-of-living cuts to its 6.5 million members with direct mail.

Later, one of AARP's leading critics, Sen. Alan Simpson, R-Wyo., fired back, saying the organization had come charging out of its $17-million-a-year "cavern . . . rioting like the four horses of the Apocalypse . . . hauling out distortions" and perpetuating untruths about cost-of-living adjustments.

Politicians of both parties promised last year that Social Security benefits would be left untouched as Congress tries to balance the budget.

Congress could save billions of dollars through lower benefit payments and higher taxes with such a plan, and ease the pressure to make deep cuts in Medicare and Medicaid that are now a part of the GOP blueprint to balance the budget by 2002.

Reprinted, with permission, from the Associated Press.

FIGURE 10.2

Using the Gopher Menu

QUESTION: WHAT ARE THE NAMES AND ADDRESSES OF U.S. CONGRESSIONAL REPRESENTATIVES?

1. gopher

2. 6. other gophers & info services

3. 6. gophers by location

4. 2. United States gopher servers

5. 50. Washington, D.C.

6. 82. United States Senate

7. 4. Members of the United States Senate

As a follow-up to this lesson, students could investigate health-related topics and their impact on senior citizens by connecting with a resource on the Internet. One of these resources is the Network Engineering and Resources Development Specialists, which can be accessed if students first go into the **World Wide Web (WWW)**, which is a network of sites on the Internet that can be accessed with hypertext. Once into WWW, the student can go into **Yahoo**, which is a search utility arranged with menus offering choices for the user. Students should execute the following steps when menus appear on the screen:

   1.   Yahoo

   2.   Health

   3.   Geriatrics and aging

   4.   Guide to Retirement Living

The publication "Guide to Retirement Living" features articles related to aging and retirement life, with topics such as home health care, nursing care facilities, continuing care communities, assisted living facilities, etc. A toll-free telephone number (1-800-394-9990) is provided if someone wishes to call and request this free publication. The e-mail address is Steve_D._Gurney@csgi.com.

Alta Vista, a **search engine** begun in 1995, is a large index of the Web. It is used by way of a key word search. For example, the middle school students in this chapter's lesson could access Alta Vista and type the phrases "Social Security and retirement." This supplies about 100,000 items, one of which is the following web site address: http://www.rain.org/~ssa/sbdo/qa.htm. This address supplies many questions and answers on the topic of Social Security.

Webcrawler is another search utility, but it requires a person to seek out information by typing a key word related to the topic to be investigated. Suppose a student needs to contact science museums to request newsletters, brochures, packets, or literature. The student would follow this procedure:

1. Access the WWW
2. Select the Webcrawler Search Form
3. Type "science and children"
4. Select Science Museums (Bill Beaty's Homepage)
5. Select Hands on Science Centers Worldwide

What appears on the screen is a list of museums around the world. A student could then read about the services offered and decide which ones may have information he or she desires. Addresses and telephone numbers are provided. This method of accessing museums also provides information for the physically disabled or handicapped.

In 1995 the Art Institute of Chicago exhibited works by impressionist artist Claude Monet (fig. 10.3).

After students read the newspaper article, they could use World Wide Web to learn more about Monet and impressionism. Once they accessed Webcrawler, they could type the name *Monet* for the subject search. On the next menu, they could select *Impressionists Subject Page* because twenty-two of Monet's masterpieces can be viewed, three of which are *Water Lilies*, *The Road to Giverny*, and *Gare St-Lazare*. Vincent Van Gogh, Georges Seurat, and Camille Pissarro are other artists whose works can be displayed on the screen.

Here is another instance where the World Wide Web and Webcrawler can be used, this time to introduce the curriculum area of music. The newspaper article in figure 10.4 describes the importance of beginning music instruction at an early age.

To learn about the importance of practicing musical instruments, students should type the word *music* as a subject search in Webcrawler and perform these actions:

FIGURE 10.3

Monet Art Exhibit

Monet mania generates frenzy for scarce tickets

Associated Press

CHICAGO—Tom Vickery flew up from Florida to see it. Ted Scott's mother won't come to town unless she gets in. People have been standing in line every day even though tickets have been sold out for weeks.

Chicago—meet Monet mania.

A blockbuster show by impressionist master Claude Monet at The Art Institute of Chicago is drawing art lovers from across the country.

Scalpers and ticket brokers are getting more than six times face value ($10 weekdays, $12.50 weekends) for passes.

The exhibit opened July 22 and runs through Nov. 26, but advance passes sold out in late September.

"Monet panic is what we're into at this point," Art Institute spokeswoman Eileen Harakal said.

The museum offers up to 400 daily passes.

Harakal said the lines with up to 700 people form several hours before the ticket office opens.

Reprinted, with permission, from the Associated Press.

1. Select "Music"

2. Select "Instruments: piano"

3. Select "The piano education page"

4. Select "Just for kids"

Electronic mail (e-mail) is a very convenient way to send messages electronically to or converse with people or organizations around the world. The sender or receiver must be assigned an e-mail address, some of which can be extremely long. There are directories for e-mail addresses, some of which can be located by using Webcrawler on the World Wide Web. For example, if a student accesses Webcrawler, types *e-mail*, then selects the menu item Internet and Related Online Resources for Not-for-Profits, a

---

FIGURE 10.4

Music Article

Study finds music virtuosos must start by age 12

Associated Press

WASHINGTON—To become a violin virtuoso, you have to start practicing by the age of 12. Thirteen is too late, say scientists who have studied the brains of musicians.

Edward Taub of the University of Alabama, Birmingham, said magnetic images of the brains of people who play stringed instruments show that larger and more complex neuron circuits form in violinists who started their training at an early age than among those who began later in life.

"There is an abrupt change at between ages 12 and 13 that appears to be quite dramatic," said Taub.

Violinists who started studies between ages 3 and 12 showed no significant differences in the brain circuitry. But there was a distinctly reduced level of development, said Taub, in the brains of those who didn't start musical studies until after the age of 13.

What causes this dramatic shift at that moment in life, said Taub, "is still unknown, but it is very clear."

Taub is co-author of a study of musical brains, which will be published today in Science, the journal of the American Association for the Advancement of Science.

Taub said the study measures the way in which the brain adapts to dexterity challenges and training.

Reprinted, with permission, from the Associated Press.

---

lengthy list of e-mail addresses appears for academic, educational, governmental, and scientific resources in the United States. The topics of concern related to this list of resources are primarily housing, health, and human services.

There are a number of fascinating opportunities for students to communicate with others in many places. For instance, if they want to send a message to the President of the United States, they send it to: president@whitehouse.gov.

FIGURE 10.5

Fire Safety

Three Calif. homes burned at scene of '91 firestorm

Associated Press

OAKLAND, Calif.—A brush fire broke out yesterday in the Oakland hills, injuring one person and burning three homes near the scene of the 1991 firestorm that killed 25 people and destroyed almost 3,000 dwellings.

The flames were contained about half an hour after the fire began.

Firefighters evacuated residents of the immediate neighborhood as a plume of white smoke spread over the area. They were allowed to return about two hours later.

One person was hospitalized for smoke inhalation.

Temperatures were in the 80s and winds were gusting at up to 25 mph.

It wasn't immediately known what caused the blaze.

Reprinted, with permission, from the Associated Press.

There is a **Listserv** program that facilitates discussion groups. Students can subscribe to this service very easily. If a student wishes to connect with a pen pal, the e-mail address to write to is: listserv@vml.nodak.edu.

The following command must be in the text of the student's message: SUB KIDLINK Your-first-name Your-last-name.

McKinley is another search vehicle that students can use. After reading the article on out-of-control fires (fig. 10.5), students could enter the World Wide Web and select the McKinley option. When asked to type the subject to be searched, enter *fire safety*. If students select the menu item *Firesave Company*, they are connected to a home page set up by a company that sells a portable fire fighting system to homeowners, who can spray a stream of foam on the house, trees, and other property items to diminish the threat of a forest fire.

There is a method to locate sites on the World Wide Web directly, and this is to use **hypertext transfer protocol (http)**. For example, students in one state who are studying the topic Crime and Violence could experience the social studies aspect by logging on the World Wide Web and searching with the words *crime* and *violence*.

This will offer choices of different web sites where crime and violence are discussed with the purpose of encouraging students to look for solutions to the problems of violence in schools.

The following are other hypertext site addresses:

Environmental education (activities, resources, and tips on recycling)
http://penbiz.com/stellar/green

Science (information about solar energy)
http://lesowww.epfl.ch/other_links.html

Food (information about chocolate from Godiva Chocolatier)
http://www.godiva.com

Political science (provides links to states and cities for student research)
http://www.NeoSoft.com/citylink

Writing (provides examples of newspaper headlines)
http://www.newslink.org

Antarctica (information from experts on life and conditions of this continent)
http://quest.arc.nasa.gov/livefrom/livefrom.html

Time (various times around the world using time zones)
http://www.hilink.com.au/

Two capabilities that will allow a student to actually connect with other computers are **Telnet** and **File Transfer Protocol (FTP)**. Telnet is the facility to log on to a computer at a remote site. One way a student can access KIDLINK is by typing the Telnet address: 165.190.8.35.

A student who finds a file at another location can then transfer it back into his or her computer system using FTP. For example, a student could view a Supreme Court ruling by entering: ftp.cwru.edu/hermes.

CONCLUSION

As powerful and helpful as the computer is, there are attendant problems. A major problem for students who have easy access to the Internet is that they might find—intentionally or unintentionally—controversial material. Chat rooms, bulletin boards, and images can contain material that is inappropriate for young people. Teachers need to warn their students about the possibility of encountering information or visual images that may upset them.

Obviously schools have grown in their utilization of technology. It began with a computer in a classroom where a student could go when his or her work was done to play a software game. Later, teachers found a variety of ways to make use of that single computer, including large group instruction to promote discussion, small group instruction to prompt cross-group interactions, as a presentation tool to enliven demonstrations, and as a learning center to track students' progress.

What will the future hold? Results from a survey of publishers and schools that appeared in *Technology and Learning* (January, 1995) revealed new products will be increasingly available in both Macintosh and PC formats. Over eighty percent of the publishers plan to disseminate new products in CD-ROM format. Delivering on-line resources is in the plan for over half of the publishers. It appears that nearly all of the schools that currently do not have multimedia plan to make such purchases within four years.

The big challenge is for teachers to know what is available in the realm of electronic learning. Experts indicate that only about ten percent of teachers can be considered proficient users of technology (Riley, 1995). To this end, it is important that pertinent journals and resources are read regularly. Some of these include:

- *Children's Software* (713)-467-8686

- *Computerworld* (800)-343-6474

- *Electronic Learning* (800)-955-5570

- *Instructor* (800)-544-2917

- *Internet* (415)-525-4300

- *Learning* (800)-753-1843

- *Macworld* (800)-288-6848

- *Media and Methods* (215)-587-9706

- *MultiMedia Schools* (800)-248-8466

- *Multimedia World* (800)-766-3294

- *PC Computing* (415)-578-7059

- *PC Magazine* (303)-665-8930

- *PC World* (415)-978-3212

- *Technology and Learning* (800)-543-4383

- *Windows Magazine* (800)-829-9150

A quick perusal of titles of publications such as the ones above reveals some intriguing topics: How can I assess students using electronic portfolios? What can I do with just one computer in my classroom? How can I create a personal home page? How can I help my students surf the Net? What kind of special software is there for my special students?

REFERENCES

Craig, C. (1992, Fall). Science, technology, and society: Philosophy, rationale, and implications for elementary social studies. *Canadian Social Studies, 27*(1), 11–16.

Feil, C. (1995, October). Your in-class communication center. *Instructor, 104*(3), 60–63.

Jackson, C. (1995, Fall). A note on photo CDs: A valuable resource for the classroom. *Canadian Social Studies, 30*(1), 28–29, 32.

Kennedy, D. A. M., & Spangler, S. (1990). Science and technology in fact and fiction: A guide to children's books. New York: Bowker.

Riedl, J. (1995). *The integrated technology classroom: Building self-reliant learners*. Needham Heights, MA: Allyn & Bacon.

Riley, R. (1995, November/December). An action plan for educational technology. *Teaching PreK–8, 26*(3), 6.

Ross, T. W., Jr., & Bailey, G. D. (1995). *Technology-based learning: A handbook for principals and technology leaders*. New York: Scholastic.

Taking the fast lane on the information superhighway (1995, October). *Teaching PreK–8, 26*(2), 34–39.

Tiene, D., & Whitmore, E. (1995, February). TV or not TV? that is the question: A study of the effects of *Channel One. Social Education, 59*(3), 159–164.

RESOURCE SUGGESTIONS FOR CHILDREN
(Dealing with computers and other forms of technology)

Bender, L. (1991). *Invention*. New York: Alfred A. Knopf.

Bendick, J., & Bendick, R. (1993). *Eureka! It's television*. Brookfield, CT: Millbrook.

Bookshelf '96 [CD-ROM].(1996). Redmond, WA: Microsoft.

Cameron, E. (1954). The wonderful flight to the Mushroom Planet. Boston: Little, Brown.

Christopher, J. (1967). *The White Mountains*. New York: Macmillan.

Complete Reference Library [CD-ROM]. (1996). Novato, CA: Mindscape.

Encarta 96 World Atlas [CD-ROM]. (1996). Redmond, WA: Microsoft.

Farmer, N. (1994). *The ear, the eye, and the arm*. New York: Scholastic, Inc.

Hamilton, V. (1981). *The gathering*. New York: Greenwillow Books.

Hughes, M. (1984). *The keeper of the Isis light*. New York: Atheneum.

Infopedia [CD-ROM]. (1996). Cambridge, MA: Softkey International.

Juster, N. (1961). *The phantom tollbooth*. New York: Random House.

L'Engle, M. (1962). *A wrinkle in time*. New York: Farrar, Straus, & Giroux.

L'Engle, M. (1973). *A wind in the door*. New York: Farrar, Straus, & Giroux.

Lowry, L. (1993). *The giver*. Boston: Houghton Mifflin.

Macaulay, D. (1988). *The way things work: From levers to lasers, cars to computers—a visual guide to the world of machines*. Boston: Houghton Mifflin. Note: This is also available on CD-ROM from Dorling Kindersley, DK Multimedia, 95 Madison Ave., NY 10016; (800)-225-3362.

Marney, D. (1985). *The computer that ate my brother*. New York: Scholastic.

Marzollo, J., & Marzollo, C. (1982). *Jed's junior space patrol: A science fiction easy-to-read*. New York: Dial Books for Young Readers.

Math, I. (1992). *Tomorrow's technology: Experiments with the science of the future*. New York: Scribners.

McCaffrey, A. (1981). *Dragonquest*. New York: Ballantine.

O'Brien, R. (1971). *Mrs. Frisby and the rats of NIMH*. New York: Atheneum.

Platt, R. (1994). *The Smithsonian visual timeline of inventions*. New York: Dorling Kindersley.

Rendal, J. (1995). *A very personal computer*. New York: Harper Collins.

Skurzynski, G. (1994). *Get the message: Telecommunications in your high-tech world*. New York: Bradbury.

Wilkins, M. J. (1991). *Everyday things and how they work*. New York: Warwick.

CHAPTER 11

ART CRITIC

KEY IDEAS

■ Students having limited or no access to art galleries and museums of art can locate visual art masterpieces on CD-ROM databases and in local bookstores and libraries.

■ Students should have opportunities to write in many real-life genres about visual arts, i.e., visual art editorials, museum exhibit brochures, tour guide scripts, and art video documentary scripts.

■ Picture books provide authentic visual art for visual art critiquing and writing.

■ Writers need to know their audience.

■ Language and the arts provide the means for people to create, recreate, revise, and transform "wholly fresh products, systems, and even worlds of meaning" (Gardner, 1982, p. 5).

INTRODUCTION

The lesson in this chapter is designed to give later elementary and middle school writers opportunities to connect the content area of **visual arts** with an "authentic audience" of readers and/or listeners through observing and writing about works of art. Another purpose for this lesson is to "bring to life" one of the most neglected areas of curricular study, the fine arts. According to Bolen, "the arts enjoy barely a toehold in the curriculum of most of the nation's schools" (1989, p. 11).

The founding of Harvard Project Zero by Nelson Goodman in the early 1960s has begun to yield, under the observant eyes of Howard Gardner (1982) and his research colleagues, a body of knowledge about children's spontaneous aesthetic, creative, and artistic development. This research supports teachers providing experiences to help children gain mastery of various techniques and media while introducing young artists to issues and concepts about standards and criticism as children create their own written masterpieces.

Another avenue for broadening visual arts education has grown out of the work of Elliott Eisner and the Getty Center for Education in the Arts. This approach, known as discipline-based art education (**DBAE**), calls for students having experiences in art making, art history, art criticism, and aesthetics (Brandt, 1988).

Pairing the more linear means of expressing ideas in writing with ideas expressed in a more nonlinear mode in the arts involves the learner mentally, physically, and emotionally. Further, combining observation and investigation of works of fine art with students' writing in many forms and for a variety of audiences about art pieces allows for individualization of learning. Also, integrated writing and fine arts lessons allow for exploration and a combination of divergent and convergent thinking.

VISUAL ARTS

The neglect of fine arts education, in general, and visual arts education, in particular, often results from schools having little or no access to museums of art and art galleries. With the advent of computer technology, several CD-ROM art libraries can be accessed by students in the school computer laboratory or classroom (fig. 11.1).

In addition to viewing works of art by way of CD-ROM art galleries, students can visit local community bookstores and public and school libraries to view reproductions of masterpieces. Finally, students can critique art by analyzing Caldecott Medal picture books, which are widely available. The books contain award-winning art, which should be tapped as a visual resource for young writers (fig. 11.2). These picture books also include examples of well-written text.

FIGURE 11.1

CD-ROM and Internet Libraries

American Art from The National Gallery [Laserdisc]. Full views and details of over 2,600 works representing three centuries of American paintings, sculptures. More than 1,000 drawings, watercolors, and prints from the Index of American Design and a complete index of the works.

Art Gallery: The Collection of the National Gallery, London [Microsoft, Macintosh and MPC CD-ROM]. Contains an alphabetic list of artists with visual descriptions of their works. A convenient cross-indexing is present for artist names and title of work (all ages).

Great Artists. Attica Cybernetics, 9234 Deering Avenue, Chatsworth, CA 91311 (1-800-721-2475). Looks at the lives and works of Botticelli, Cezanne, Rembrandt, and thirty-seven western European masters, framing each study within the context of the artists' times. Students can analyze details of one artist's work; listen to commentary; and read short articles on perspective, scale, and other technical aspects of a piece (grades 7 and up).

High Museum of Art. The Atlanta Art Museum offers a World Wide Web tour of its exhibits. The museum tour includes images of contemporary art; nineteenth- and twentieth-century furniture; American and European paintings; African art; folk art; and photography. Access it by e-mail: comp.infosystems.www.mise or http://isotropic.com/highmuse/highhome.html.

The Louvre: Volumes I–III [CD-ROM, Macintosh and Windows]. About 4,500 of the world's greatest works of art on laserdiscs. Thirty thousand full-color images with detailed, close-up views. On-screen information precedes each work. Fragile and rarely exhibited works are included and documented in guidebook. Distributed through Davis Publications, Inc., Worchester, MA.

The National Gallery of Art [Laserdisc w/software]. Over 1,600 images from the United States National Museum. Full and close-up views. On-screen identifying captions. A guided tour is presented by a museum director. Guidebooks included.

Web Museum. Allows viewing of many wonderful paintings. Access it through the Internet at http://sunsite.unc.edul.

With Open Eyes: Images from the Art Institute of Chicago: Great Art for Kids (and Their Grown Ups) [Voyager, Macintosh and Windows hybrid CD-ROM]. Contains over 200 art pieces. A unique feature is the capability of zooming in on the art (all ages); call 1-800-446-2001 for publication date.

FIGURE 11.2

Caldecott Awards 1938–1996

1938
Animals of the Bible by Dorothy P. Lathrop (Helen Dean Fish), New York: HarperCollins.
Honor Books: ***Seven Simeons*** by Boris Artzybasheff, New York: Viking; ***Four and Twenty Blackbirds*** by Robert Lawson (Helen Dean Fish), New York: HarperCollins.

1939
Mei Li by Thomas Handforth, Garden City, NY: Doubleday.
Honor Books: ***The Forest Pool*** by Laura Adams Armer, White Plains, NY: Longmans; ***Wee Gillis*** by Robert Lawson (Munro Leaf), New York: Viking; ***Snow White and the Seven Dwarfs*** by Wanda Gag, New York: Coward; ***Barkis*** by Clare Newberry, New York: HarperCollins; ***Andy and the Lion*** by James Daugherty, New York: Viking.

1940
Abraham Lincoln by Ingri and Edgar Parin d'Aulaire, Garden City, NY: Doubleday.
Honor Books: ***Cock-a-Doodle Doo . . .*** by Berta and Elmer Hader, New York: Macmillan; ***Madeline*** by Ludwig Bemelmans, New York: Viking; ***The Ageless Story***, by Lauren Ford, Long Beach, CA: Dodd, Mead.

1941
They Were Strong and Good by Robert Lawson, New York: Viking.
Honor Books: ***April's Kittens*** by Clare Newberry, New York: HarperCollins.

1942
Make Way for Ducklings by Robert McCloskey, New York: Viking.
Honor Books: ***An American ABC*** by Maud and Miska Petersham, New York: Macmillan; ***In My Mother's House*** by Velino Herrera (Ann Nolan Clark), New York: Viking; ***Paddle-to-the-Sea*** by Holling C. Holling, Burlington, MA: Houghton Mifflin; ***Nothing at All*** by Wanda Gag, New York: Coward-McCann.

1943
The Little House by Virginia Lee Burton, Burlington, MA: Houghton Mifflin.
Honor Books: ***Dash and Dart*** by Mary and Conrad Buff, New York: Viking; ***Marshmallow*** by Clare Newberry, New York: HarperCollins.

1944
Many Moons by Louis Slobodkin (James Thurber), New York: Harcourt Brace.
Honor Books: ***Small Rain: Verses from the Bible*** by Elizabeth Orton Jones (selected by Jessie Orton Jones), New York: Viking; ***Pierre Pigeon*** by Arnold E. Bare (Lee Kingman), Burlington, MA: Houghton Mifflin; ***The Mighty Hunter*** by Berta and Elmer Hader, New York: Macmillan; ***A Child's Good Night Book*** by Jean Charlot (Margaret Wise Brown), Glenview, IL: Scott, Foresman; ***Good Luck Horse*** ill. by Plato Chan (Chih-Yi Chan), Eau Claire, WI: E. M. Hale.

1945
Prayer for a Child by Elizabeth Orton Jones (Rachel Field), New York: Macmillan.
Honor Books: ***Mother Goose*** by Tasha Tudor, New York: Walck; ***In the Forest*** by Marie Hall Ets, New York: Viking; ***Yonie Wondernose*** by Marguerite de Angeli, Garden City, NY: Doubleday; ***The Christmas Anna Angel*** by Kate Seredy (Ruth Sawyer), New York: Viking.

1946
The Rooster Crows . . . (traditional Mother Goose) by Maud and Miska Petersham, New York: Macmillan.
Honor Books: ***Little Lost Lamb*** by Leonard Weisgard (Golden MacDonald), Garden City, NY: Doubleday; ***Sing Mother Goose*** by Marjorie Torrey (Opal Wheeler), New York: Dutton; ***My Mother Is the Most Beautiful Woman in the World*** by Ruth Gannett (Becky Reyher), New York: Lothrop, Lee & Shepard; ***You Can Write Chinese*** by Kurt Wiese, New York: Viking.

1947
The Little Island by Leonard Weisgard (Golden MacDonald), Garden City, NY: Doubleday.
Honor Books: ***Rain Drop Splash*** by Leonard Weisgard (Alvin Tresselt), New York: Lothrop, Lee & Shepard; ***Boats on the River*** by Jay Hyde Barnum (Marjorie Flack), New York: Viking; ***Timothy Turtle*** by Tony Palazzo (Al Graham), New York: Viking; ***Pedro, the Angel of Olvera Street*** by Leo Politi, New York: Scribner's; ***Sing in Praise: A Collection of the Best Loved Hymns*** by Marjorie Torrey (Opal Wheeler), New York: Dutton.

Continued

FIGURE 11.2 *Continued*

1948
White Snow, Bright Snow by Roger Duvoisin (Alvin Tresselt), New York: Lothrop, Lee & Shepard.
Honor Books: ***Stone Soup*** by Marcia Brown, New York: Scribner's; ***McElligot's Pool*** by Dr. Seuss, New York: Random House; ***Bambino the Clown*** by George Schreiber, New York: Viking; ***Roger and the Fox*** by Hildegard Woodward (Lavinia Davis), Garden City, NY: Doubleday; ***Song of Robin Hood*** by Virginia Lee Burton (edited by Anne Malcolmson), Burlington, MA: Houghton Mifflin.

1949
The Big Snow by Berta and Elmer Hader, New York: Macmillan.
Honor Books: ***Blueberries for Sal*** by Robert McCloskey, New York: Viking; ***All Around the Town*** by Helen Stone (Phyllis McGinley), New York: HarperCollins: ***Juanita*** by Leo Politi, New York: Scribner's; ***Fish in the Air*** by Kurt Wiese, New York: Viking.

1950
Song of the Swallows by Leo Politi, New York: Scribner's.
Honor Books: ***America's Ethan Allen*** by Lynd Ward (Stewart Holbrook), Burlington, MA: Houghton Mifflin; ***The Wild Birthday Cake*** by Hildegard Woodward (Lavinia Davis), Garden City, NY: Doubleday; ***The Happy Day*** by Marc Simont (Ruth Krauss), New York: HarperCollins; ***Bartholomew and the Oobleck*** by Dr. Seuss, New York: Random House; ***Henry Fisherman*** by Marcia Brown, New York: Scribner's.

1951
The Egg Tree by Katherine Milhous, New York: Scribner's.
Honor Books: ***Dick Whittington and His Cat*** by Marcia Brown, NY: Scribner's; ***The Two Reds*** by Nicholas Mordvinoff (William Lipkind), New York: Harcourt Brace; ***If I Ran the Zoo*** by Dr. Seuss, New York: Random House; ***The Most Wonderful Doll in the World*** by Helen Stone (Phyllis McGinley), New York: HarperCollins; ***T-Bone, the Baby Sitter*** by Clare Newberry, New York: HarperCollins.

1952
Finders Keepers by Nicholas Mordvinoff (William Lipkind), New York: Harcourt Brace.
Honor Books: ***Mr. T. W. Anthony Woo*** by Marie Hall Ets, New York: Viking; ***Skipper John's Cook*** by Marcia Brown, New York: Scribner's; ***All Falling Down*** by Margaret Bloy Graham (Gene Zion), New York: HarperCollins; ***Bear Party*** by William Pene du Bois, New York: Viking; ***Feather Mountain*** by Elizabeth Olds, Burlington, MA: Houghton Mifflin.

1953
The Biggest Bear by Lynd Ward, Burlington, MA: Houghton Mifflin.
Honor Books: ***Puss in Boots*** retold and illustrated by Marcia Brown (Charles Perrault), New York: Scribner's; ***One Morning in Maine*** by Robert McCloskey, New York: Viking; ***Ape in a Cape*** by Fritz Eichenberg, New York: Harcourt Brace; ***The Storm Book*** by Margaret Bloy Graham (Charlotte Zolotow), New York: HarperCollins; ***Five Little Monkeys*** by Juliet Kepes, Burlington, MA: Houghton Mifflin.

1954
Madeline's Rescue by Ludwig Bemelmans, New York: Viking.
Honor Books: ***Journey Cake, Ho!*** by Robert McCloskey (Ruth Sawyer), New York: Viking; ***When Will the World Be Mine?*** by Jean Charlot (Miriam Schlein), Glenview, IL: Scott, Foresman; ***The Steadfast Tin Soldier*** by Marcia Brown (Hans Christian Andersen), New York: Scribner's; ***A Very Special House*** by Maurice Sendak (Ruth Krauss), New York: HarperCollins; ***Green Eyes*** by A. Birnbaum, Irvington, NY: Capitol.

1955
Cinderella, or the Little Glass Slipper retold and illustrated by Marcia Brown (Charles Perrault), New York: Scribner's.
Honor Books: ***Book of Nursery and Mother Goose Rhymes*** by Marguerite de Angeli, Garden City, NY: Doubleday; ***Wheel on the Chimney*** by Tibor Gergely (Margaret Wise Brown), New York: HarperCollins; ***The Thanksgiving Story*** by Helen Sewell (Alice Dalgliesh), New York: Scribner's.

1956
Frog Went A-Courtin' by Feodor Rojankovsky (John Langstaff), New York: Harcourt Brace.
Honor Books: ***Play with Me*** by Marie Hall Ets, New York: Viking; ***Crow Boy*** by Taro Yashima, New York: Viking.

Continued

FIGURE 11.2 *Continued*

1957
A Tree Is Nice by Marc Simont (Janice May Udry), New York: HarperCollins.
Honor Books: *Mr. Penny's Race Horse* by Marie Hall Ets, New York: Viking; *1 Is One* by Tasha Tudor, New York: Walck; *Anatole* by Paul Galdone (Eve Titus), Blacklick, OH: McGraw-Hill; *Gillespie and the Guards* by James Daugherty (Benjamin Elkin), New York: Viking; *Lion* by William Pene du Bois, New York: Viking.

1958
Time of Wonder by Robert McCloskey, New York: Viking.
Honor Books: *Fly High, Fly Low* by Don Freeman, New York: Viking; *Anatole and the Cat* by Paul Galdone (Eve Titus), Blacklick, OH: McGraw-Hill.

1959
Chanticleer and the Fox adapted and illustrated by Barbara Cooney, New York: HarperCollins.
Honor Books: *The House That Jack Build* by Antonio Frasconi, New York: Harcourt Brace; *What Do You Say, Dear?* by Maurice Sendak (Sesyle Joslin), Glenview, IL: Scott, Foresman; *Umbrella* by Taro Yashima, New York: Viking.

1960
Nine Days to Christmas by Marie Hall Ets (Aurora Labastida, Marie Hall Ets), New York: Viking.
Honor Books: *Houses from the Sea* by Adrienne Adams (Alice E. Goudey), New York: Scribner's; *The Moon Jumpers* by Maurice Sendak (Janice May Udry), New York: HarperCollins.

1961
Baboushka and the Three Kings by Nicholas Sidjakov (Ruth Robbins), East Orleans, MA: Parnassus.
Honor Books: *Inch by Inch* by Leo Lionni, New York: Obolensky.

1962
Once a Mouse . . . by Marcia Brown, New York: Scribner's.
Honor Books: *Fox Went Out on a Chilly Night* by Peter Spier, Garden City, NY: Doubleday; *Little Bear's Visit* by Maurice Sendak (Else Holmelund Minarik), New York: HarperCollins; *The Day We Saw the Sun Come Up* by Adrienne Adams (Alice E. Goudey), New York: Scribner's.

1963
The Snowy Day by Ezra Jack Keats, New York: Viking.
Honor Books: *The Sun Is a Golden Earring* by Bernarda Bryson (Natalia M. Belting), New York: Holt; *Mr. Rabbit and the Lovely Present* by Maurice Sendak (Charlotte Zolotow), New York: HarperCollins.

1964
Where the Wild Things Are by Maurice Sendak, New York: HarperCollins.
Honor Books: *Swimmy* by Leo Lionni, New York: Pantheon; *All in the Morning Early* by Evaline Ness (Sorche Nic Leodhas), New York: Holt; *Mother Goose and Nursery Rhymes* by Philip Reed, New York: Atheneum.

1965
May I Bring a Friend? by Beni Montresor (Beatrice Schenk De Regniers), New York: Atheneum.
Honor Books: *Rain Makes Applesauce* by Marvin Bileck (Julian Scheer), New York: Holiday House; *The Wave* by Blair Lent (Margaret Hodges), Burlington, MA: Houghton Mifflin; *A Pocketful of Cricket* by Evaline Ness (Rebecca Caudill), New York: Holt.

1966
Always Room for One More by Nonny Hogrogian (Sorche Nic Leodhas), New York: Holt.
Honor Books: *Hide and Seek Fog* by Roger Duvoisin (Alvin Tresselt), New York: Lothrop, Lee & Shepard; *Just Me* by Marie Hall Ets, New York: Viking; *Tom Tit Tot* by Evaline Ness, New York: Scribner's.

1967
Sam, Bangs and Moonshine by Evaline Ness, New York: Holt.
Honor Books: *One Wide River to Cross* by Ed Emberley (Barbara Emberley), Englewood Cliffs, NJ: Prentice-Hall.

1968
Drummer Hoff by Ed Emberley (Barbara Emberley), Englewood Cliffs, NJ: Prentice-Hall.
Honor Books: *Frederick* by Leo Lionni, New York: Pantheon; *Seashore Story* by Taro Yashima, New York: Viking; *The Emperor and the Kite* by Ed Young (Jane Yolen), Cleveland, OH: World.

Continued

FIGURE 11.2 *Continued*

1969
The Fool of the World and the Flying Ship by Uri Shulevitz (Arthur Ransome), New York: Farrar, Straus & Giroux.
Honor Books: ***Why the Sun and the Moon Live in the Sky*** by Blair Lent (Elphinstone Dayrell), Burlington, MA: Houghton Mifflin.

1970
Sylvester and the Magic Pebble by William Steig, New York: Windmill.
Honor Books: ***Goggles!*** by Ezra Jack Keats, New York: Macmillan; ***Alexander and the Wind-up Mouse*** by Leo Lionni, New York: Pantheon; ***Pop Corn and Ma Goodness*** by Robert Andrew Parker (Edna Mitchell Preston), New York: Viking; ***Thy Friend, Obadiah*** by Brinton Turkle, New York: Viking; ***The Judge*** by Margot Zemach (Harve Szemach), New York: Farrar, Straus & Giroux.

1971
A Story—A Story by Gail E. Haley, New York: Atheneum.
Honor Books: ***The Angry Moon*** ill. by Blair Lent (retold by William Sleator), Boston: Little, Brown; ***Frog and Toad Are Friends*** by Arnold Lobel, New York: HarperCollins; ***In the Night Kitchen*** by Maurice Sendak, New York: HarperCollins.

1972
One Fine Day by Nonny Hogrogian, New York: Macmillan.
Honor Books: ***If All the Seas Were One Sea*** by Janina Domanska, New York: Macmillan; ***Moja Means One: Swahili Counting Book*** by Tom Feelings, (Muriel Feelings), New York: Dial; ***Hildilid's Night*** by Arnold Lobel (Cheli Duran Ryan), New York: Macmillan.

1973
The Funny Little Woman by Blair Lent (retold by Arlene Mosel), New York: Dutton.
Honor Books: ***Anansi the Spider*** adapted and ill. by Gerald McDermott, New York: Holt; ***Hosie's Alphabet*** by Leonard Baskin (Hosea, Tobias, and Lisa Baskin), New York: Viking; ***Snow White and the Seven Dwarfs*** by Nancy Ekholm Burkert (translated by Randal Jarrell), New York: Farrar, Straus & Giroux; ***When Clay Sings*** by Tom Bahti (Byrd Baylor), New York: Scribner's.

1974
Duffy and the Devil by Harve Zemach, ill. by Margot Zemach, New York: Farrar.
Honor Books: ***Three Jovial Huntsmen*** by Susan Jeffers, Scarsdale, NY: Bradbury; ***Cathedral: The Story of Its Construction*** by David Macaulay, New York: Houghton Mifflin.

1975
Arrow to the Sun retold and ill. by Gerald McDermott, New York: Viking.
Honor Books: ***Jambo Means Hello*** by Tom Feelings (Muriel Feelings), New York: Dial.

1976
Why Mosquitoes Buzz in People's Ears by Leo and Dian Dillon (retold by Verna Aardema), New York: Dial.
Honor Books: ***The Desert Is Theirs*** by Peter Parnall (Byrd Baylor), New York: Scribner's; ***Strega Nona*** retold and ill. by Tomie de Paola, Englewood Cliffs, NJ: Prentice-Hall.

1977
Ashanti to Zulu: African Traditions by Margaret Musgrove, New York: Dial Press.
Honor Books: ***The Amazing Bone*** by William Steig, New York: Farrar, Straus & Giroux; ***The Contest*** retold and ill. by Nonny Hogrogian, New York: Greenwillow; ***Fish for Supper*** by M. B. Goffstein, New York: Dial; ***The Golem*** by Beverly Brodsky McDermott, New York: HarperCollins; ***Hawk, I'm Your Brother*** by Peter Parnall (Byrd Baylor), New York: Scribner's.

1978
Noah's Ark by Peter Spier, New York: Doubleday.
Honor Books: ***Castle*** by David Macaulay, Burlington, MA: Houghton Mifflin; ***It Could Always Be Worse*** by Margot Zemach, New York: Farrar, Straus & Giroux.

1979
The Girl Who Loved Wild Horses by Paul Goble, Scarsdale, NY: Bradbury.
Honor Books: ***Freight Train*** by Donald Crews, New York: Greenwillow; ***The Way to Start a Day*** by Peter Parnall (Byrd Baylor), New York: Scribner's.

Continued

FIGURE 11.2 *Continued*

1980
Ox-Cart Man by Barbara Cooney (Donald Hall), New York: Viking.
Honor Books: *Ben's Trumpet* by Rachel Isadora, New York: Greenwillow; *The Treasure* by Uri Shulevitz, New York: Farrar, Straus & Giroux; *The Garden of Abdul Gasazi* by Chris Van Allsburg, Burlington, MA: Houghton Mifflin.

1981
Fables by Arnold Lobel, New York: HarperCollins.
Honor Books: *The Bremen-Town Musicians* by Ilse Plume, Garden City, NY: Doubleday; *The Grey Lady and the Strawberry Snatcher* by Molly Bang, New York: Four Winds; *Mice Twice* by Joseph Low, New York: Atheneum; *Truck* by Donald Crews, New York: Greenwillow.

1982
Jumanji by Chris Van Alsburg, Burlington, MA: Houghton Mifflin.
Honor Books: *On Market Street* by Anita Lobel (Arnold Lobel), New York: Greenwillow; *Outside Over There* by Maurice Sendak, New York: HarperCollins; *A Visit to William Blake's Inn: Poems for Innocent and Experienced Travelers* by Alice and Martin Provensen (Nancy Willard), New York: Harcourt Brace; *Where the Buffaloes Begin* by Stephen Gammell (Olaf Baker), New York: Warner.

1983
Shadow by Marcia Brown (Blaise Cendrars), New York: Scribner's.
Honor Books: *Chair for My Mother* by Vera B. Williams, New York: Greenwillow; *When I Was Young in the Mountains* by Diane Goode (Cynthia Rylant), New York: Dutton.

1984
The Glorious Flight: Across the Channel with Louis Bleriot by Alice and Martin Provensen, New York: Viking.
Honor Books: *Little Red Riding Hood* retold and ill. by Trina Schart Hyman, New York: Holiday House; *Ten, Nine, Eight* by Molly Bang, New York: Greenwillow.

1985
St. George and the Dragon by Trina Schart Hyman (retold by Margaret Hodges), Boston: Little, Brown.
Honor Books: *Hansel and Gretel* by Paul O. Zelinsky (retold by Rika Lesser), Long Beach, CA: Dodd, Mead; *Have You Seen My Duckling?* by Nancy Tafuri, New York: Greenwillow; *The Story of Jumping Mouse* retold and ill. by John Steptoe, New York: Lothrop, Lee & Shepard.

1986
The Polar Express by Chris Van Alsburg, Burlington, MA: Houghton Mifflin.
Honor Books: *The Relatives Came* by Stephen Gammell (Cynthia Rylant), Scarsdale, NY: Bradbury; *King Bidgood's in the Bathtub* by Don Wood (Audrey Wood), New York: Harcourt Brace.

1987
Hey, Al by Richard Egielski (Arthur Yorinks), New York: Farrar, Straus & Giroux.
Honor Books: *The Village of Round and Square Houses* by Ann Grifalconi, Boston: Little, Brown; *Alphabatics* by Suse MacDonald, Scarsdale, NY: Bradbury; *Rumpelstiltskin* by Paul O. Zelinsky, New York: Dutton.

1988
Owl Moon by Johen Schoenherr (Jane Yolen), New York: Philomel.
Honor Books: *Mufaro's Beautiful Daughters* by John Steptoe, New York: Lothrop, Lee & Shepard.

1989
Song and Dance Man by Stephen Gammell (Karen Ackerman), New York: Knopf.
Honor Books: *The Boy of the Three-Year Nap* by Allen Say (Dianne Snyder), Burlington, MA: Houghton Mifflin; *Free Fall* by David Wiesner, New York: Lothrop, Lee & Shepard; *Goldilocks* by James Marshall, New York: Dial; *Mirandy and Brother Wind* by Jerry Pinkney (Patricia C. McKissack), New York: Knopf.

1990
Lon Po Po: A Red-Riding Hood Story from China by Ed Young, New York: Philomel.
Honor Books: *Bill Peet: An Autobiography* by Bill Peet, Burlington, MA: Houghton Mifflin; *Color Zoo* by Lois Ehlert, New York: HarperCollins; *Hershel and the Hanukkah Goblins* by Trina Schart Hyman (Eric Kimmel), New York: Holiday House; *The Talking Eggs* by Jerry Pinkney (Robert D. SanSouci), New York: Dial.

Continued

FIGURE 11.2 *Continued*

1991
Black and White by David Macaulay, Burlington, MA: Houghton Mifflin.
Honor Books: *"More, More, More" Said the Baby: 3 Love Stories* by Vera Williams, New York: Greenwillow; *Puss in Boots* by Fred Marcellino (Charles Perrault, translated by Malcolm Arthur), New York: Farrar, Straus & Giroux.

1992
Tuesday by David Wiesner, New York: Clarion.
Honor Books: *Tar Beach* by Faith Ringgold, New York: Crown.

1993
Mirette on the High Wire by Emily Arnold McCully, Chicago: Putnam.
Honor Books: *Stinky Cheese Man* by Lane Smith (Jon Scieszka), New York: Viking; *Working Cotton* by Carole Byard (Sherely Anne Williams), New York: Harcourt Brace; *Seven Blind Mice* by Ed Young, New York: Philomel.

1994
Grandfather's Journey by Allen Say, Burlington, MA: Houghton Mifflin.
Honor Books: *Owen* by Kevin Henkes, New York: Greenwillow; *Peppe, the Lamplighter* by Elisa Bartone, New York: Lothrop, Lee & Shepard; *Raven* by Gerald McDermott, New York: Harcourt Brace; *In the Small, Small Pond* by Denise Fleming, New York: Holt; *Yo! Yes?* by Chris Raschka, Santa Cruz, CA: Orchard.

1995
Smoky Nights by Eve Bunting, ill. by David Diaz, New York: Harcourt Brace.
Honor Books: *Swamp Angel* by Anne Issacs, ill. by Paul Zelinksy, New York: Viking Penguin; *John Henry* by Julius Lester, ill. by Jerry Pinkney, New York: Dial; *Time Flies* by Eric Rohman, New York: Crown Books.

1996
Officer Buckle and Gloria by Peggy Rathmann, Chicago: Putnam.
Honor Books: *Alphabet City* by Stephen T. Johnson, New York: Viking; *Zin! Zin! Zin! A Violin* (Text: Lloyd Moss) by Marjorie Priceman, New York: Simon & Schuster; *The Faithful Friend* (Text: Robert D. San Souci) by Brian Pinkney, New York: Simon & Schuster; *Tops & Bottoms* by Janet Stevens, New York: Harcourt Brace.

The learner must have resources "to feed himself with the accumulated heritage from the [geniuses of art]" (Bolen, 1989). Access to artists, original works of art, books of art reproductions, museums, models of well-written critiques about art, and ideas must be made available to learners. Award-winning picture books, one of the most accessible and authentic artifacts for investigating, observing, and critiquing art, should be borrowed from the library (Pappas, Levstik, & Kiefer, 1995). Other resources for viewing selected masterpieces, such as computer-based encyclopedias and art galleries, should be provided if funding and availability permit. Oversized texts (fig. 11.3), kits and large reproductions (fig. 11.4), and videos of original masterpieces in school and public libraries (fig. 11.5) also should be investigated. Resources needed to provide support for writing about art include discussions with artists and art critics, opportunities to read art commentaries, a CD-ROM art library and other reference materials, peer-editing and revising sessions, and access to a file of exemplars of well-written genre for art audiences (fig. 11.6).

FIGURE 11.3

Selected Library Materials
Examples of Oversized Art Books

Cubism
Green, C. (1987). *Cubism and its enemies.* New Haven, CT: Yale University Press.
I Fabre, J. P. (1990). *Picasso cubism.* New York: Rizzoli.

Impressionism
Boyle, R. J. (1974). *American impressionism.* Boston: New York Graphic Society.
Gerdts, W. H. (1984). *American impressionism.* New York: Abbeville Press.
Renior, A. (1989). *Renoire: A retrospective.* New York: Park Lane: Distributed by
    Nicholas Wadley.

Realism
Neuhaus, R. (1987). *Unsuspected genius: The art and life of Frank Duveneck.*
    San Francisco: Bedford Press.

Surrealism
Gaunt, W. (1972). *The surrealists.* New York: Putnam.
Gaunt, W. (1974). *Painters of fantasy: From Hieronymus to Salvador Dali.*
    London: Phaidon.
Meuris, J. (1990). *Reni Magritte.* Woodstock, NY: Overlook Press.
Schneede, U. M. (1974). *Surrealism.* New York: H. N. Abrams.

FIGURE 11.4

Kits and Reproductions
Brommer, G. F. *Discovering art history.* Worchester, MA: Davis Publications,
    Inc.
Chapman, L. H. *Adventures in art 1–6.* Worchester, MA: Davis Publications,
    Inc.
Chapman, L. H. *Art: Images and ideas.* Worchester, MA: Davis Publications,
    Inc.
Chapman, L. H. *A world of images.* Worchester, MA: Davis Publications, Inc.
Colbert, C., & Tauton, M. *Discover art kindergarten.* Worchester, MA: Davis
    Publications, Inc.
Schell, K. D. (Ed.). *Teacher's guide to art history.* Peterborough, NH: Cobblestone
    Publishing, Inc.

Continued

FIGURE 11.4 *Continued*

Large Reproductions

Distributed by Davis Publications
(For address, see Appendix B.)

- Black Artists in America
- Discovering Art History
- Folk Art Prints
- Haiku
- Mask Prints
- Modern Art Styles
- Multicultural I
- Multicultural Print Sets
- Native American Prints
- Native American Reproductions
- Sculptue Art Prints
- The Visual Experience
- Three Dimensional Art Prints
- Women Artists

FIGURE 11.5

Videotapes about Art

African American art: Past and present. Worchester, MA: Davis Publications, Inc.

African-American artists: Affirmation today. Worchester, MA: Davis Publications, Inc.

Art and music in America. Worchester, MA: Davis Publications, Inc.

Beyond tradition: American Indian art. Worchester, MA: Davis Publications, Inc.

Footloose in history. Worchester, MA: Davis Publications, Inc.

Gente del Sol. Worchester, MA: Davis Publications, Inc.

Latino art and culture in the United States. Worchester, MA: Davis Publications, Inc.

Masks from many cultures. Worchester, MA: Davis Publications, Inc.

Monsieur Reni Magritte. Chicago, IL: Home Vision.

Multicultural artist series. Worchester, MA: Davis Publications, Inc.

Oriental art. Worchester, MA: Davis Publications, Inc.

Picasso: Joie de vivre. Northbrook, IL: Roland Collection.

Picasso, war, peace, love. Indianapolis, IN: Kartes Video Communications.

The cubist epoch. Indianapolis, IN: Kartes Video Communications.

The impressionists. Worchester, MA: Davis Publications, Inc.

The impressionists: Rebels in art. Washington, DC: Museum One, Inc.

The life and art of William H. Johnson. Worchester, MA: Davis Publications, Inc.

Tribal design. Worchester, MA: Davis Publications, Inc.

FIGURE 11.6

Writing Exemplars for Art Audiences

Brochures describing holdings of art galleries

Newspaper clippings critiquing visual art shows

Magazine features about artists and their work

Audiotapes of tours through art galleries

Videotapes of guided tours through art galleries and museums

Maps showing layouts of art galleries and museums

Interviews with artists, videographers, photographers, writers

Textbooks and software describing art

Slide shows with scripts of art work

WRITING ACROSS THE CURRICULUM

In addition to having works of art about which to write, writers about art must demonstrate *reader awareness* in the products they produce.

> Providing the context allows the reader to enter into the writing in a way that allows him/her to understand why the topic is important and why he/she may be interested in reading about it. These writers also provide enough detail for the reader to see the point and an organization that allows a reader to follow the author's thinking throughout the piece. Writers also demonstrate reader awareness by the word choice they employ, the attention they give to sentence structure and by providing conventions that allow the reader to understand the writers' text (Lewis, 1995, p. 7).

One of the most typical writing assignments given in school to help writers with audience identification is letter writing. Though letter writing helps the writer and reader more easily identify the audience who will read the piece, young writers need to become aware of the audience for all products they write. The writing coach asks, "How else may reader awareness be developed in the young writer?"

According to Pappas, Levstik, and Kiefer, "Language and arts are our human vehicles for constructing and conveying meaning" (1990, p. 190). These two communication tools can and should be integrated to give writers opportunities to write to a specific audience about real-life content.

The following lesson plan is designed to provide writers with a wide scope of writing opportunities directed at different types of audiences who are all learning about art. The writers will address the readers and listeners who want to learn about the pieces in an art show by writing and producing an audiotape to highlight artworks for the "art tourist." They may choose to write editorials and critiques for readers who want to know the quality of artists' work; they may decide to write video scripts for documentaries shown to students of art, art educators, and historians; and they could design maps and brochures to guide artists through a gallery of art.

LESSON PLAN

TITLE: **ART CRITIC**

Ages/Grades: Later elementary and middle school

Time: Two hours

Content Areas:

 Language Arts

 Visual Arts

Materials: Hardware: Computers and printers

Software: Word-processing program, graphics program, and CD-ROM libraries and encyclopedias

Library: art and picture books

Bookstore: art and picture books

Art museum and/or gallery

Artists

Writers

Museum directors

Paper and pencils

Filmstrips, slides, and video libraries of artworks

Copy machine

Recorders and audiotapes

Portfolios

File of exemplars (e.g., brochures, audiotapes, newspaper and magazine editorials, and reviews of art exhibits)

Objectives:
- Students will locate sources, using appropriate technology, to view visual artworks.

- Students will read art critiques written about artworks by professional writers.

- Students will observe a variety of artworks.

- Students will interview real artists, writers, and museum directors.

- Students will analyze, organize, interpret, and evaluate pieces of art and information about art gathered from reading, writing, interviewing, and observing.

- Students will write a critique of an art piece using appropriate art terminology and applying effective writing techniques and skills.

Beginning:
Provide students with many examples of visual arts to observe; for example, authentic art at a museum or a gallery, and picture books and vicarious connections to visual art via CD-ROM libraries, books, and/or slide or videotape presentations. The search engine of Netscape has web site addresses for many of the major museums in the world. Also provide an opportunity for students to speak with people involved in the world of art, like artists, museum curators, art consumers, art historians, art critics, photographers, and videographers. Ask the students to take notes of their discoveries about the visual arts pieces they investigate and observe by writing their descriptions and discoveries in a notebook and/or by tape-recording their observations.

Give students an opportunity to explore well-written exemplars of newspaper articles or magazine critiques related to visual arts; for example, tour guide booklets, newspaper editorials, maps of museums, and video and audio scripts. After students have looked at art pieces and the file of genre exemplars, ask them individually to review the notes they have gathered about them.

Middle: Have the students choose partners. The partners listen to each other describe their visual arts investigations and then make suggestions to each other about narrowing the genre, audience, and topic for the writing assignment. The writers decide, with support from their peers and the teacher, who will be the audience for their production (e.g., a reader of an art brochure or art museum map; someone who views a video or listens to a recorded tour guide; a consumer, buyer, viewer of art shows or artwork; or an interviewer of an artist for a television or radio program.

End: The students write a first draft about the art piece(s) they have selected as their focus. Teachers and peers conduct regular daily or weekly conferences using the Content Writing Response Sheet for Teacher and Peer Conferences (fig. 11.7) and editing symbols (fig. 11.8) to edit and revise the piece of writing.

Assessment of Student Learning: Criteria on the scoring guide shown in figure 11.9 may be used to assess the degree of proficiency demonstrated in a piece of writing. Conferencing, editing, and revision sessions throughout the process provide continuous opportunities for authentic and qualitative assessment.

FIGURE 11.7

Content Writing Response Sheet for Teacher and Peer Conferences

1. Summarize in one or two sentences what you think the writer is trying to say or write in this piece of writing.

PURPOSE_____

_____

2. Describe who the author's intended audience may be for this piece of writing.

AUDIENCE _____

_____

3. Which words, phrases, and/or sentences work especially well to provide insight into the author's topic? Write some here; point out others.

WORDS_____

PHRASES_____

SENTENCES _____

_____

4. What else would you like to know? Write at least three questions that may help the author acquire information that is lacking, or take a new direction.

QUESTIONS _____

_____

5. Name some forms of writing—other than that which the writer has chosen for the first draft, e.g., news story, brochure, advertisement, interview, script for video- or audiotapes.

GENRE_____

_____

FIGURE 11.8

Selected Editing Symbols

PURPOSE	SYMBOL
move together	⌣
spread apart	#
move	↻→
reverse order	∼
check spelling	(sp)
indent for paragraph	¶
omit	~~word~~
insert word	∧
capitalize	≡
change to lowercase	⊄
insert period	⊙
insert comma	⤳
insert apostrophe	⤵
insert quotation mark	⋎ ... ⋎

FIGURE 11.9

Kentucky Writing Assessment
Holistic Scoring Guide

NOVICE
- Limited awareness of audience and/or purpose
- Minimal idea development; limited and/or unrelated details
- Random and/or weak organization
- Incorrect and/or ineffective sentence structure
- Incorrect and/or ineffective language
- Errors in spelling, punctuation, and capitalization are disproportionate to length and complexity

APPRENTICE
- Some evidence of communicating with an audience for a specific purpose; some lapses in focus
- Unelaborated idea development; unelaborated and/or repetitious details
- Lapses in organization and/or coherence
- Simplistic and/or awkward sentence structure
- Simplistic and/or imprecise language
- Some errors in spelling, punctuation, and capitalization that do not interfere with communication

PROFICIENT
- Focused on a purpose; communicates with an audience; evidence of voice and/or suitable tone
- Depth of idea development supported by elaborated, relevant details
- Logical, coherent organization
- Controlled and varied sentence structure
- Acceptable, effective language
- Few errors in spelling, punctuation, and capitalization relative to length and complexity

DISTINGUISHED
- Establishes a purpose and maintains clear focus; strong awareness of audience; evidence of distinctive voice and/or appropriate tone
- Depth and complexity of ideas supported by rich, engaging, and/or pertinent details; evidence of analysis, reflection, insight
- Careful and/or subtle organization
- Variety in sentence structure and length enhances effect
- Precise and/or rich language
- Control of spelling, punctuation, and capitalization

Continued

FIGURE 11.9 *Continued*

SCORING CRITERIA

Criteria	Overview
Purpose/Audience	The degree to which the writer • establishes and maintains a purpose • communicates with the audience • employs a suitable voice and/or tone
Idea Development/Support	The degree to which the writer provides thoughtful, detailed support to develop main idea(s)
Organization	The degree to which the writer demonstrates • logical order • coherence • transitions/organizational signals
Sentences	The degree to which the writer includes sentences that are • varied in structure and length • constructed effectively • complete and correct
Language	The degree to which the writer exhibits correct and effective • word choice • usage
Correctness	The degree to which the writer demonstrates correct • spelling • punctuation • capitalization

INSTRUCTIONAL ANALYSIS

Examining instructional strengths can assist in improving writing and learning in your school. Student portfolios can provide evidence of instructional practices. This section of the Holistic Scoring Guide is provided to assist teachers in identifying sustained evidence of instructional practices through examination of student products. When scoring a student portfolio, scorers may identify *any number* of the instructional strengths listed on the following page.

Continued

FIGURE 11.9 *Continued*

The sustained performance in this portfolio demonstrates that the student has applied instruction in the following areas:

- Establishing focused, authentic **purposes**
- Writing for authentic **audiences**, situations
- Employing a suitable **voice and/or tone**
- **Developing ideas** relevant to the purpose
- **Supporting ideas** with elaborated, relevant details
- **Organizing ideas** logically
- Using effective **transitions**
- Constructing effective and/or correct **sentences**
- Using **language** effectively and/or correctly
- **Editing** for correctness

COMPLETE/INCOMPLETE PORTFOLIOS

A portfolio is *incomplete* if any of the following apply:

- Table of Contents does not contain required information
- Table of Contents does not note study area information (including the Letter to the Reviewer)
- There are fewer than 7 different entries, including Table of Contents and the Letter to the Reviewer
- One or more entries are plagiarized (must be proven)
- One or more entries are different than those listed in the Table of Contents
- One or more entries are written in a language other than English
- One or more entries demonstrate only computational skills, or consist of only diagrams or drawings
- Portfolio contains a group entry
- Entries are out of order without clear descriptors on the Table of Contents

A portfolio is *complete* and *will be scored* according to how well it fulfills the criteria of the Holistic Scoring Guide if one or more entries are:

- out of order with clear descriptors on the Table of Contents
- questionable concerning fulfillment of the purpose for which it is intended
- questionable concerning plagiarism, but the plagiarism cannot be proven

Courtesy of the Kentucky Department of Education. To order, contact the Kentucky Department of Education Publications Center, 500 Mero Street, Frankfort, KY 40601.

REFERENCES

Bolen, L. (1989). The importance of the arts in the early childhood curriculum. *Dimensions, 18*(1), 11–13.

Brandt, R. (1988). On discipline-based art education: A conversation with Elliott Eisner. *Educational Leadership, 45*(4), 6–9.

Cole, E., & Schaefer, C. (1990). Can young children be art critics? *Young Children, 45*(2), 33–38.

De Porter, D., & Kavanaugh, R. (1978). Parameters of children's sensitivity to painting styles. *Studies in Art Education, 20*(1), 43–48.

Dewey, J. (1934). *Art as experience.* New York: Minton, Balch & Company.

Dixon, G. T., & Chalmers, F. G. (1990). The expressive arts in education. *Childhood Education, 67*, 12–17.

Dixon-Krauss, L. (1996). *Vygotsky in the classroom: Mediated literacy instruction and assessment.* White Plains, NY: Longman Publishers USA.

Dyson, A. H. (1990). Symbol makers, symbol weavers: How children link play, pictures and print. *Young Children, 46*(2), 50–57.

Eisner, E. W. (1977). *Reading, the arts, and the creation of meaning.* Reston, VA: National Art Education Association.

Ernst, K. (1995, November/December). Seeing meaning: Connecting writing and art. *Teaching K–8, 28*(1), 33–34.

Feeney, S., & Moravcik, E. (1989). A thing of beauty: Aesthetic development in young children. *Young Children, 42*(6), 7–15.

Gardner, H. (1980). Artful scribbles: *The significance of children's drawings.* New York: Basic Books.

Gardner, H. (1982). *Art, mind and brain: A cognitive approach to creativity.* New York: Basic Books.

Gardner, H. (1988). Toward more effective arts education. *Journal of Aesthetic Education, 22*, 157–167.

Gee, K., & Dewitt, J. (1994). *Different ways of knowing: Institute discovery journal—creating your classroom community.* Los Angeles, CA: The Galef Institute.

Hall, B. A. (1979, January). *The arts and reading: Coming to our senses—why the visual and performing arts are fundamental to reading and language development.* Paper presented at the annual meeting of the Claremont California Reading Conference, Claremont, CA.

Hoffman, S., Kantner, L., Colbert, C., & Sims, W. (1991). Nurturing the expressive arts. *Childhood Education, 19*, 23–26.

Isaacs, N. (1974). *Children's ways of knowing*. New York: Teachers College Press, Columbia University.

Jacobs, H. H. (Ed.). (1989). *Interdisciplinary curriculum: Design and implementation*. Alexandria, VA: Association for Supervision and Curriculum Development.

Kentucky Department of Education. (1995). *Kentucky Early Learning Profile* (2nd ed.). Frankfort, KY: Author.

Kentucky Department of Education. (1995). *Transformations: Kentucky's curriculum framework, volumes I and II*. Frankfort, KY: Author.

LaDuke, B. *Africa through the eyes of women artists*. Worchester, MA: Davis Publications, Inc.

LaDuke, B. *Contemporary American women artists*. Worchester, MA: Davis Publications, Inc.

Lasky L., & Mukerji, R. (1980). *ART: Basic for young children*. Washington, DC: National Association for the Education of Young Children.

Lewis, S. (1995, Summer). Just what is "audience awareness," anyway? *Kentucky Writing Teacher*, *1*(2), 1–8.

Mecca, J. T. (1992). *Plays that teach: Plays, activities, and songs with a message*. Nashville, TN: Incentive Pub., Inc.

Norton, D. (1995). *Through the eyes of a child: An introduction to children's literature* (4th ed.). Englewood Cliffs, NJ: Prentice Hall.

Pappas, C., Kiefer, B. Z., & Levstik, L. S. (1990). *An integrated language perspective in the elementary school: Theory into action*. White Plains, NY: Longman Publications USA.

Pappas, C., Kiefer, B. Z., & Levstik, L. S. (1995). *An integrated language perspective in the elementary school: Theory into action* (2nd ed.). White Plains, NY: Longman Publications USA.

Piaget, J. (1955). *The language and thought of the child*. New York: Meridian.

Randhawa, B. S., & Coffman, W. E. (Eds.). (1978). *Visual learning, thinking, and communication*. New York: Academic Press.

Schirrmacher, R. (1986). Talking with children about their art. *Young Children*, *41*(5), 3–7.

Wassermann, S. (1990). *Serious players in the primary classroom*. New York: Teachers College Press.

Watson, D., Burke, C., & Harste, J. (1989). *Whole language: Inquiring voices*. New York: Scholastic.

BOOK SUGGESTIONS FOR CHILDREN
Artists

Agee, J. (1988). *The incredible paintings of Felix Clousseau*. New York: Farrar, Straus & Giroux.

Blegvad, E. (1979). *Self-portrait: Erik Blegvad*. New York: Addison-Wesley.

Bonafoux, P. (1992). *A weekend with Rembrandt*. Boston: Rizzoli International.

Goffstein, M. B. (1983). *Lives of the artists*. New York: HarperCollins.

Greenfield, H. (1990). *Leonardo da Vinci*. New York: Abrams.

Harris, N. (1987). *Leonardo and the Renaissance*. Chicago: Franklin Watts/Bookwright.

Heselwood, J. (1993). *Introducing Picasso*. Boston: Little, Brown.

Hyman, T. (1981). *Self-portrait: Trina Schart Hyman*. New York: Addison-Wesley.

Kastner, J. (1992). *John James Audubon*. New York: Abrams.

Lasky, K. (1992). *Think like an eagle: At work with a wildlife photographer*. Boston: Little, Brown.

McLanthan, R. (1990). *Leonardo da Vinci*. New York: Abrams.

Meltzer, M. (1985). *Dorthea Lange: Life through the camera*. New York: Viking.

Meryman, R. (1991). *Andrew Wyeth*. New York: Abrams.

Metropolitan Museum of Arts Series: What makes a Breugel? (1995). Placerville, CA: Bluestocking Press.

Metropolitan Museum of Arts Series: What makes a Degas? (1995). Placerville, CA: Bluestocking Press.

Metropolitan Museum of Arts Series: What makes a Monet? (1995). Placerville, CA: Bluestocking Press.

Metropolitan Museum of Arts Series: What makes a Raphael? (1995). Placerville, CA: Bluestocking Press.

Metropolitan Museum of Arts Series: What makes a Rembrandt? (1995). Placerville, CA: Bluestocking Press.

Metropolitan Museum of Arts Series: What makes a Van Gogh? (1995). Placerville, CA: Bluestocking Press.

Meyer, S. E. (1990). *Mary Cassatt*. New York: Abrams.

Monet, C. (1996). *Monet: The artist speaks*. San Francisco, CA: Collins Publishers.

Moore, R. (1993). *Native artists of North America*. Sante Fe, NM: John Muir Publications.

Munthe, N. (1983). *Meet Matisse*. Boston: Little, Brown.

Niemark, A. E. (1992). *Diego Rivera: Artist of the people*. New York: HarperCollins.

Provensen, A., & Provensen, M. (1984). *Leonardo da Vinci*. New York: Viking.

Raboff, E. (1988). *Henri Matisse*. New York: Lippincott.

Richmond, R. *Introducing Michelangelo*. Boston: Little, Brown.

Rodari, F. (1991). *A weekend with Picasso*. New York: Rizzoli International.

Skira-Ventrui, R. (1991). *A weekend with Renoir*. New York: Rizzoli International.

Skira-Ventrui, R. (1992). *A weekend with Degas*. New York: Rizzoli International.

Turner, R. M. (1991). *Portraits of women artists for children: Georgia O'Keeffe*. Boston: Little, Brown.

Turner, R. M. (1991). *Rosa Bonheur*. Boston: Little, Brown.

Turner, R. M. (1992). *Mary Cassatt*. Boston: Little, Brown.

Turner, R. M. (1993). *Frida Kahlo*. Boston: Little, Brown.

Turner, R. M. (1993). *Portraits of women artists for children*. Boston: Little, Brown.

Ventura, P. (1984). *Great painters*. New York: Putnam.

Waldron, A. (1991). *Claude Monet*. New York: Abrams.

Waldron, A. (1992). *Francisco Goya*. New York: Abrams.

Welton, J. (1992). *Monet*. New York: Houghton Mifflin.

Zhensun, Z., & Low, A. (1991). *A young painter: The life and paintings of Wang Yani, China's extraordinary young artist*. New York: Scholastic.

Art History

Arenas, J. F. (1990). *The key to Renaissance art*. Minneapolis, MN: Lerner.

Brown, L. K., & Brown, M. (1990). *Visiting the art museum*. New York: Dutton.

Caserani, G. P. (1983). *Grand constructions*. New York: Putnam.

Conner, P. (1982). *Looking at art: People at home*. New York: Atheneum.

De Trevino, E. B. (1965). *I, Juan de Pareje*. New York: Farrar, Strayss, & Giroux.

Evertt, G. (1993). *John Brown: One man against slavery*. New York: Rizzoli International.

Ford, A. (1988). *John James Audubon*. New York: Abbeville Press.

Gates, F. (1982). *North American Indian masks: Craft and legend*. New York: Walker.

Glubok, S. (1972). *The art of the new American nation*. New York: Macmillan.

Greenburg, J., & Jordan, S. (1991). *The painter's eye: Learning to look at contemporary American art*. New York: Delacorte.

Highwater, J. (1978). *Many smokes, many moons: A chronology of American Indian history through Indian art*. New York: Lippincott.

Janson, H. W., & Janson, A. F. (1987). *History of art for young people*. New York: Abrams.

National Gallery of Art. (1991). *An illustrated treasury of songs*. Boston: Rizzoli International.

Strikland, C. (1992). *The annotated Mona Lisa: A crash course in art history from prehistoric to post-modern*. New York: Andrews and McMeel.

Sullivan C. (Ed.). (1991). *Children of promise: African-American literature and art for young people*. New York: Abrams.

Waterfield, G. (1982). *Looking at art: Faces*. New York: Atheneum.

Stories, Poetry, and Stylized Art Examples

Bagay, S. (1996). *Navajo: Visions and voices across the mesa*. New York: Scholastic.

Baker, J. (1991). *Window*. New York: Greenwillow.

Bjork, C. (1985) *Linnae in Monet's garden*. Illustrated by L. Anderson. New York: R & S.

Blizzard, G. S. (1993). *Come look with me: World of play*. New York: Thomasson-Grant.

Brandenburg, J. (1993). *To the top of the world: Adventures with arctic wolves*. New York: Walker.

Bruchac, J. (1996). *A boy called Slow*. New York: Philomel.

Clark, A. N. (1991). *In my mother's house*. New York: Viking.

de Paola, T. (1985). *Tomie de Paola's Mother Goose*. New York: Putnam.

Everett, G. (1992). *Li'l Sis and Uncle Willie: A story based on the life and paintings of William H. Johnson*. Boston: Rizzoli International.

Freedman, R. (1992). *An Indian winter*. Paintings and photographs by K. Bodmer. New York: Holiday House.

Han, S. C. (1996). *The rabbit's escape*. New York: Holt.

Jones, H. (Ed.). (1971). *Trees stand shining*. New York: Dial.

Knox, B. (1992). *The great art adventure*. New York: Rizzoli International.

Konigsburg, E. L. (1967). *From the mixed-up files of Mrs. Basil Frankweiler*. New York: Antheneum.

Lessac, F. (1987). *Caribbean canvas*. New York: Lippincott.

Lewis, J. P. (1996). *Black Swan White Crow*. New York: Atheneum.

Marcum, P. M. (1993). *The little painter of Saba Grande*. New York: Bradbury.

Panzer, N. (Ed.). (1995). *Celebrate America in poetry and art*. New York: Hyperion.

Rosen, M. J. (1996). *A school for Pompey Walker*. New York: Harcourt Brace.

Scherttle, A. (1996). *Advice for a frog*. New York: Lothrop Lee.

Sky-Peck, K. (Ed.). (1991). *Who has seen the wind? An illustrated collection of poetry for young people*. Boston: Rizzoli.

Smith-Baranzini, M., & Egger-Bovet, H. (1994). *Book of American Indians*. Boston: Little, Brown.

Soto, G. (1996). *Chato's kitchen*. New York: Putnam.

Sullivan, C. (Ed.). (1989). *Imaginary gardens: American poetry and art for young people*. New York: Abrams.

Art Elements and Techniques

Baylor, B. (1972). *When Clay sings*. New York: Scribner's.

Baylor, B. (1992). *One small blue bead*. New York: Scribner's.

Christina, D. (1990). *Drawer in a drawer*. New York: Farrar Straus & Giroux.

Cummings, P. (1992). *Talking with artists* (Vol. 1). New York: Bradbury.

Cummings, P. (1996). *Talking with artists* (Vol. 2). New York: Simon & Schuster.

Davidson, R. (1995). *Take a look: An introduction to the experience of art*. New York: Viking.

de Paula, T. (1989). *The art lesson*. New York: Putnam.

Fisher, L. E. (1986). *Look around: A book about shape*. New York: Viking.

Hoban, T. (1978). *Is it red? Is it yellow? Is it blue?* New York: Greenwillow.

Hoban, T. (1984). *Is it rough? Is it smooth? Is it shiny?* New York: Greenwillow.

Hoban, T. (1986). *Shapes, shapes, shapes*. New York: Greenwillow.

Hoban, T. (1987). *Dots, spots, speckles, and stripes*. New York: Greenwillow.

Jenkins, J. (1992). *Thinking about color*. New York: Dutton.

Jonas, A. (1989). *Color dance*. New York: Greenwillow.

Lionni, L. (1959). *Little Blue and Little Yellow: A story for Pippo and Ann and other children*. New York: Astor.

Macaulay, D. (1973). *Cathedral: The story of its construction*. Boston: Houghton Mifflin.

Pekarik, A. (1992). *Behind the scenes: Painting*. New York: Hyperion.

Pekarik, A. (1992). *Behind the scenes: Sculpture*. New York: Hyperion.

Roalf, P. (1992). *Looking at paintings* (Vols. 1–6). New York: Hyperion.

Roalf, P. (1993). *Looking at paintings* (Vols. 1–6). New York: Hyperion.

Rosetti, C. (1992). *Color*. New York: HarperCollins.

Walsh, E. S. (1988). *Mouse paint*. New York: Delacorte.

Woolf, F. (1990). *Picture this: A first introduction to paintings*. New York: Doubleday.

Yenawine, P. (1991). *Colors*. New York: Delacorte.

Yenawine, P. (1991). *Lines*. New York: Delacorte.

Yenawine, P. (1991). *Shapes*. New York: Delacorte.

Yenawine, P. (1991). *Stories*. New York: Delacorte.

MUSICALLY SPEAKING

KEY IDEAS

■ Music is a valuable way to link people together.

■ Real-life situations often require speaking expertise; therefore, students should have opportunities to develop and master public speaking skills (i.e., persuasive genre).

■ Real-life situations often require writing expertise; therefore, students should have opportunities to develop and master persuasive writing.

■ Appreciating musical variety is part of learning music and learning to enjoy music more widely.

■ Music listeners should explore technical elements of music communication.

■ Music listeners should be music readers, too.

■ Speaking about music involves all areas of language arts (e.g., writing, speaking, listening, and reading, as well as knowledge of musical terms, forms, instruments, and other music-related information).

INTRODUCTION

The objective of the lesson in this chapter is to involve students in writing and delivering an effective speech. The speech must be genuinely persuasive and move carefully toward the objective of motivating fellow students to listen to types of music they would not usually choose. This is a project that develops not only the knowledge, skills, and dispositions found in the traditional content area of language arts, it is also one that develops music knowledge, skills, and dispositions. The students' minds are engaged in an integrated curriculum activity concerned with mastery of skills and understanding of concepts in a challenging and creative learning situation. Simply stated, the lesson in this chapter provides interactions for students to learn to write by writing, to read by reading, to speak by speaking, and to listen by listening (Mayher, Lester, & Pradl, 1983).

MUSIC

Music is one of the oldest, most organized, and important areas of artistic communication. It is everywhere: on the radio and television; as part of operas and ballets; in shopping malls, offices, and corporate headquarters; at special events, like the Olympics and parades; as well as an ingredient of celebrations of all types around the world.

One way for music listeners to appreciate and enjoy music is to select a piece and listen to it repeatedly to become familiar with the way the composers and performers use music to communicate to the listener. "Repetition is the key to making a succession of tones magically become a melody in the mind" (Newman, 1995, p. 203). An additional advantage of repeated listening is that the listener can begin to anticipate what comes next.

Repeated listening brings the same joy as re-reading a favorite poem or book. To understand a piece of music in depth, one must listen to it actively. It must be loud enough for the listener to follow the patterns being played or sung, and a variety of styles should be available. Matching the listening time to listeners' attention spans is important, and guiding listening is an essential requisite for music listening activities (Newman, 1995).

Many styles of music should be listened to in order to develop a full appreciation for musical language. Listeners certainly want to hear musical pieces they are familiar with and prefer; however, they should not limit themselves to one type of vocal or instrumental music. There is, however, a great variety of vocal and instrumental music pieces (see fig. 12.1).

FIGURE 12.1

CD/Audiotape/Phonograph Listings

BALLADS
Caroline Mosley (lecturer). (1979). *The Ballad in Folklore.* New York: Everett/Edwards.
Gunfighter ballads and trail songs. (1959). Columbia.

BIG BAND
Buzzard Rock String Band. (1988). I've got the Blues for my Kentucky Band. Whitesburg, KY: June Appal Records.
Elgart, Larry and the Manhattan Swing Orchestra. (1982). *Hooked on Swing Sound.* New York: RCA Records.

BLUEGRASS
Buzzard Rock String Band. (1988). *I've Got the Blues for My Kentucky Home.* Whitesburg, KY: June Appal Records.
Nashville Bluegrass Band. (1993). *Waitin' for the Hard Times to Go.* Durham, NC: Sugar Hill Records.

BLUES
Patton, Charley. (1991). *King of Delta Blues.* Newton, NY: Yazoo.
Williams, Joe. (1984). *Nothin' But the Blues.* Santa Monica, CA: Delos Records.

CHAMBER MUSIC
Hindemith, Paul. (1992). *Kammermusik, nos. 1–7.* London.
Mozart, Wolfgang Amadeus. (1989). *Chamber Music Selections: Clarinet Quintet in A, K. 581; Horn Quintet in E Flat, K. 407; Oboe Quartet in F, K. 370.* Netherlands: Philips.

CHORAL
Purcell, Henry. (1989). *Choral Music Selections: Te Deum & Jubilate Deo: 4 Anthems.* Hamburg: Archiv Produktion.

CLASSICAL
Beethoven, Ludwig van. (1988). *Symphonies, No. 1, Op. 21 in C Major & No. 6 in F Major, Op. 68: Pastorale.* Hayes, Middlesex, England: EMI Records.
Brahms, Johannes. (1990). *Three Violin Sonatas.* Netherlands: Sony Classical.

COUNTRY/WESTERN
Parton, Dolly. (1994). *Dolly: My Life and Other Unfinished Business.* New York: Harper Audio.
Pride, Charley. (1994). *Charley Pride with Jim Henderson.* Los Angeles, CA: Publishing Mills.

Continued

FIGURE 12.1 *Continued*

FOLK

Anthology of American Folk Music. (1997). Washington, DC: Folkway Records.
Seeger, Mike. (1991). *American Folk Songs for Children.* Cambridge, MA: Rounder Records.

GOSPEL/HYMNS

Ronstadt, Linda. (1989). *Cry Like a Rainstorm, Howl Like the Wind.* New York: Elektra Entertainment.
Watson, Doc. (1990). *On Praying Ground.* Durham, NC: Sugar Hill.

JAZZ

Ellington, Duke. (1991). *The Essence of Duke Ellington.* New York: Columbia/Legacy.
Horn, Shirley. (1992). *Here's to Life.* New York: Verve.

MARCHES

United States Marine Band. (1992). *Sound Off!* Washington, DC: U.S. Marine Band.
Williams, John (conductor) and the Boston Pops. (1991). *I Love a Parade.* New York: Sony Classical.

OPERA

Mussorgsky, Modest Petrovitch. (1987). *Introduction to the Opera "Khovantchina Vstuplenie."* New York & London.
Puccini, Giacomo. (1986). *Arias.* New York: CBS Records.

ORATORIOS

Pachelbel, Johann. (1991). *Pachelbel Cannon and Other Baroque Hits.* New York: RCA Victor/Manufactured and distributed by BMG Music.

POP/ROCK 'N ROLL

Domino, Fats. (1973). *Fats Domino Sound Recordings.* Los Angeles, CA: Everest Records.
Presley, Elvis. (1958). *Elvis' Gold Records.* New York: BGM Entertainment.

RAGTIME

The Greatest Ragtime of the Century. (1989). Ocean, NJ: Musical Heritage Society.
Tony Orlando & Dawn. (1973). *Dawn's New Ragtime Follies.* New York: Bell Records.

RAP

Jones, Quincy. (1989). *Back on the Block.* Burbank, CA: Qwest.
Living Colour. (1990). *Time's Up.* New York: Epic.

WALTZES & POLKAS

Stravinsky, Igor. (1988). *Petrushka, Circus Polka, Fireworks, Op. 4.* Ocean, NJ: Musical Heritage Society.
Wiener Johann-Strauss Kammerorchester. (1996). *Johann and Josef Strauss.* Switzerland: Noralis.

Another quality of music is related to different emotions engendered by music. Music libraries offer selections evoking feelings of humor, pride, silliness, sadness, or scariness. Many listeners recall *Peer Gynt*, composed by Edvard Grieg for fellow Norseman and playwright Henrik Ibsen. A scarey selection from *Peer Gynt*, "Night on Bald Mountain," is a well-known piece of music from this play. *Fantasia*, used by Bach and American jazz and swing musicians, is a free musical form written according to a composer's emotional impulse. This type of musical form does not follow a prescribed pattern and is often described as improvisational. *Fantasia* was also the name of an animated, feature-length motion picture produced by Walt Disney, featuring classical theme music.

Musical selections representing different cultures are included in dance libraries beginning with primitive dances and accompanimental music of numerous continental and island civilizations, and continuing with the dances of the Egyptian, Greek, Roman, medieval, and Renaissance periods. From 1600 to the present day, many types of dance and accompanying dance music have continued to develop worldwide, for example, ballet, tap dancing, modern dance, acrobatic and adagio dances of the Orient and Spain, and folk dances of the Norwegians and many countries. Other dances associated with music include the Arab sword dance of the bride described in the Hebrew "Song of Songs," the Russian Cossak dance, the polka of the Czech culture, the mazurka of the Polish people, group dances of the North American Creole and African Americans, the muscle dances of Ancient Persia, the Hawaiian hula and the Spanish flamenco, gesture dances of the Far East, ceremonial dances of the Chinese and Japanese Kabuki dance-drama. A category that represents American culture is square dance music, e.g., "The Virginia Reel" and "Turkey in the Straw." From Europe, waltzes provide an additional musical selection such as "The Vienna Waltz."

The World Wide Web on the Internet can be explored for information about many topics, including music from other cultures (fig. 12.2). To find information about music from many cultures, a learner can search sequentially under Entertainment: Music: Countries and Cultures. Under each country information such as names of performing artists, festivals, magazines, lyrics of songs, reviews of recordings, instruments, and music news can be located.

In addition to listening to various types of vocal and instrumental music, attention can be given to significant musical details such as rhythm and melody (fig. 12.3). For example, children can imagine the beating of the heart with a steady thump-thump as a way to understand what rhythm

FIGURE 12.2

Internet and World Wide Web Access to Information about Music in Other Countries and Cultures

To access the information, use the following guide words:
World Wide Web: Yahoo, Entertainment, Music, Countries and Cultures

- African
- Arabic
- Argentina
- Asian
- Australia
- Austria
- Belgium
- Bolivia
- Brazil
- Canada
- Celtic
- Chile
- China
- Colombia
- Croatia
- Cuba
- Denmark
- Dominican Republic
- Estonia
- Finland
- France
- Germany
- Greece
- Hong Kong
- Iceland

- India
- Indonesia
- Ireland
- Isle of Man
- Italy
- Japan
- Jewish
- Madagascar
- Mexico
- Morocco
- Netherlands
- New Zealand
- Norway
- Peru
- Russia
- Slovenia
- Somalia
- South Korea
- Spain
- Sweden
- Switzerland
- Turkey
- United Kingdom
- Vietnam

FIGURE 12.3

Musical Details to Guide Active Listening

Tone color	Instruments, voices, solo, small group, large group
Rhythm	Beat: strong, weak, none
	Meter: groups of twos, threes, or combinations of twos and threes
	Rhythm patterns: even, uneven, syncopated
Melody	Contour: smooth, jagged
	Direction: higher, lower, repeated tones
	Movement: steps, skips, combination of steps and skips
	Register: low, middle, high
	Pitch range: wide, narrow
	Scale type: major, minor, pentatonic, nontonal, etc.
Harmony	Relation of melody and chords (accompaniment)
	Number of chord changes, types of chords
	Consonance—dissonance
Texture	Melody alone (monophonic)
	Combined melodic lines—rounds, canons (polyphonic)
	Melody with accompaniment (homophonic)
Form	Structure: motive, phrase, AB, ABA, ABACA, etc.
	Repetition: exact, varied, sequences, contrast
	Introduction, interlude, coda
Expression	Tempo: slow, medium, fast, getting faster or slower
	Dynamics: soft, medium, loud, getting louder or softer
	Articulation: separated sounds, connected sounds
	Text: subject matters, relation to the music
Style	Music of different times and places
	Type: folk, popular, classical, etc.

From Newman, G. (1995). Teaching children music (4th ed.). Madison, WI: Brown & Benchmark, p. 204.

means; tone color (timbre) of voice or instrument may be likened to the qualities of objects; a voice might have a gravely sound just like moving a rock across rough cement.

Another focus for listening may include pieces of music featuring many kinds of instruments and various types of instrumental and vocal ensembles (Baines, 1992; Remnant, 1989; Young, 1980; Diagram Group, 1976) (fig. 12.4).

To further broaden and deepen their understanding of the world of music, students are encouraged to read books with musical themes (see Book Suggestions for Children, p. 169). More recently, CD-ROM software has been providing a rapidly expanding music library for listeners and composers (fig. 12.5).

Listeners naturally judge musical compositions according to their importance in their lives; for example, a piece of music is worth listening to if it communicates something that is individually satisfying and meaningful. Although listening to one's favorite pieces of music is a good beginning point for music appreciation and understanding, listeners need to broaden and deepen their experiences with many types of music. One of the chief reasons for arts education is to help people to recognize and to share the gifts others possess. People who judge music only from a personal perspective fail to broaden and deepen their understanding of the ideas, emotions, and cultural understanding conveyed through music.

WRITING AND DELIVERING A PERSUASIVE SPEECH

Throughout life, people speak with others about their preferences for particular types of food, restaurants, makes of cars, vacation spots, books, and forms of music. In some instances, people actively try to persuade others to adopt their own preference. The ability to persuade others to change their viewpoint or switch to a different product is an essential skill for people living in the economic world of the free enterprise system, and because persuasion is a pervasive element of American life, students should be formally introduced to the genres of persuasive writing/reading and speaking/listening. Several principles are recommended to guide the **persuasive speech** writer to induce others to change their minds (fig. 12.6).

The following lesson for later primary and middle grade students provides an opportunity for them to identify musical pieces and convince classmates about the merit of the pieces they have chosen.

FIGURE 12.4

Types of Instruments and Vocal Ensembles for Listening

Instrumental Ensembles
Symphony, orchestra, big band, duet, trio, quartet, quintet

Vocal Ensembles
A cappella motet chorus, opera, operetta, authentic chants, e.g., Gregorian chants, Native American chants, Hindu mantras, Confusian chants, Zen chants, Christian spiritual and gospel singing, duets, trios, barbershop quartet, Bulu songs from the Cameroons

Brass Family
Serpentine, French horn, trombone, trumpet, tuba, euphonium, cornet, bugle, hunting horn, post horn

String Family
Piano, electronic keyboard, organ, clavicord harpsichord, viola, bass, cello, violin, one-stringed fiddle of Indonesia, guitar of Mexico, violino piccolo, lute, Gypsy or Bluegrass mandolin, lute, banjo, Appalachian dulcimer, Gaelic harp, concert harp, double-action harp, Greek lyre, treble viol

Woodwind Family
Fife, flute, recorder, panpipes of Peru, bassoon, oboe, English horn, saxophone, bass clarinet, clarinet, piccolo

Percussion Parade
Drums
Kettledrums, African bongo drum, tambourine, bass drum, Congo drum, tympani drum

Bells and Chimes
Tam-Tam, sleigh bells, chimes, cymbals, marimba, East African xylophone and other xylophones, vibraphone, triangle, cow bells, crash cymbals, Glockenspiel

Sound Effects
Slapstick, cloves, wood blocks, siren, gourd and scraper, temple blocks, maracas, castanets, ratchet, thunder sheet, wind machine

FIGURE 12.5

Sample List of CD-ROM Music Software

The Art of Music Listening (Clearvue) develops active listening skills interactively. It presents numerous types of music and sound, emphasizing depth of emotion and explanations of terms such as melody, harmony, timbre, and rhythm in numerous forms. It also contains a twenty-four volume student encyclopedia and a glossary of important terms and many multiple choice questions linked to either audiovisual examples or the encyclopedia.

Composer Collection (Microsoft) offers a multimedia journey with three very different, uniquely gifted composers, e.g., Mozart, Beethoven, and Schubert.

Encarta (Microsoft) is a multimedia encyclopedia with thousands of up-to-date articles and high-resolution graphics, enlightening animations, stunning video clips, and resonant digital sounds to explore the world's rich multicultural heritage. Includes musical samples from jazz to popular foreign languages, literature readings, and famous speeches. Also includes Funk & Wagnalls' twenty-nine volume encyclopedia.

Morton Subotnick's Making Music (Voyager, Macintosh, and Windows, ages five to adult) is subtitled "the first real (and totally cool) composing space for kids." A collection of inviting and creative musical play areas requiring no reading that will appeal to most musically challenged individuals.

Multimedia Beethoven: The Ninth Symphony (Microsoft) allows the listener to explore the structure of the *Ninth Symphony*.

Multimedia Mozart: The Dissonant Quartet (Microsoft) contains a CD-ROM that includes a digital recording of W. A. Mozart's *String Quartet in C Major, K 465, The 'Dissonant'* performed by the Angeles Quartet, supplemental musical excerpts, and a six-part HyperCard program.

Multimedia Schubert: The Trout Quintet (Microsoft) presents the spirit and sparkling beauty of Schubert's *Trout Quintet in A Major*. This software allows the user to examine the work along with world events that surrounded Schubert during this time period. Game and narration are also included.

Multimedia Stravinski: The Rite of Spring (Microsoft) focuses on the original 1913 Paris production of this powerful, innovative ballet. The user learns about how the combination of Sergi Diaghilev's choreography and Stravinski's music gave the world a jolt. Also included in this package is the *Rite Game*, for one to four players, which tests players on various topics at varied skill levels.

Music and Culture (Clearvue) introduces students to the relationships between music and traditions of Polynesian, African, and North American Indian peoples. Discusses instruments, vocal music, and dance; enhanced by authentic recorded examples of the music and visuals.

Musical Instruments (Microsoft) includes recordings of more than 200 instruments from around the world.

Continued

FIGURE 12.5   *Continued*

The Orchestra: The Instruments Revealed (Warner) includes the complete digital London recording of *The Young Persons Guide to the Orchestra* by the London Symphony Orchestra conducted by Benjamin Britten. Features full-length annotation in sync with the music, an instrument of the orchestra, more than 500 audio examples from sea gulls to Stravinski, and full-color graphics.

FIGURE 12.6

Effective Persuasive Speech Writing and Delivery: Key Admonitions to Induce Others to Change Their Minds

DO

- Spar cautiously and respectfully.
- Work systematically to develop a persuasive speech.
- Recognize and acknowledge there are different points of view.
- Point out areas of agreement among points of view.
- Try to discover what would be a favorable emotional connection.
- Curb your rebuttal instinct.
- Be patient. Lead.
- Establish rapport by showing you are open-minded and that you understand your listeners' points of view.
- Try to make your idea attractive to your listener.
- Try to make him/her want to agree rather than disagree.
- Know how/if humor can help you.
- Consider telling a "good," short, fresh story that fits the situation.
- Practice your speech before you deliver it.

DO NOT

- Verbally bulldoze, engage in head-on collisions, or come out slugging.
- Bludgen listeners into submission with facts and figures.
- Resort to sarcasm.
- Present in a pushy way.
- Step on intellectual or emotional corns.
- Tell off-color stories.

LESSON PLAN

TITLE: SALES TALK: PERSUADING MUSIC LISTENERS TO TRY SOMETHING NEW

Ages/Grades: Later elementary and middle grades

Time: Two hours

Content Areas:

 Music

 Anthropology

 Language Arts

Materials: Music library

General library

Computer hardware with speakers and software

Audio player (phonograph, CD player, tape recorder)

Paper

Writing instruments

Note cards

Audio recorder or video camera (optional, but valuable for self-assessment)

Objectives:
- Students will gather, analyze, compile, evaluate, and use relevant information from a wide variety of musical forms and styles of instruments from a variety of cultures.

- Students will exhibit effective listening strategies for a specific purpose, for example, to write an informative, persuasive, and imaginative speech.

- Students will write a persuasive speech to be delivered to music listeners.

- Students will demonstrate an openness and sensitivity to a variety of musical works.

- Students will compare elements within and among musical works.

- Students will formulate and justify personal preferences based on the perception and reaction to the expressive qualities of music.

- Students will assess the contributions of various cultures to the expression of musical forms.

- Students will listen to others express their views.

- Students will express ideas in a nonconfrontational manner.

- Students will analyze the creative expression and technical quality of their writing and speaking performance using appropriate terminology and concepts.

Beginning: Assisted by their teacher, students locate a wide variety of vocal and instrumental musical selections from many cultures (see figs. 12.1, 12.3, 12.4, and 12.5). After locating the musical selections, allow students a block of time to listen to their choices independently or with classmates at a listening center or in a computer/multimedia laboratory. During and after these listening sessions, students should take notes about what they heard and how they feel about the musical selections.

To organize ideas for their speeches, students should devise a way to classify the information they gather during their listening research sessions.

Middle: After completing their research, students should be given an opportunity to talk with each other about their research findings. Then they should draft, edit, and revise a persuasive speech about their favorite musical selections. Throughout the writing process, teachers and students conduct thirty-second miniconferences and longer small-group or paired-peer conferences. These conferences provide a cooperative learning structure for editing and revising the persuasive speech (see chap. 11). An opportunity to practice their speeches should be provided with the teacher and peer partners serving as coaches throughout the practice session. The guidelines, "Effective Persuasive Speech Writing and Delivery," (fig. 12.6) may be used as a checklist by both the teacher and students to provide constructive feedback to students about their speaking performances.

End: Following the practice session, students deliver their speeches to classmates or other audiences. For example, some students could broadcast their speeches over local radio or community television stations or over their school's closed circuit television network. Also, students may deliver their persuasive speeches to students in other classes. The speeches should be audio- or videotaped for performance assessment purposes.

Assessment of Student Learning: Students and teachers may use a variety of forms to guide assessment of the speaking performance of students. The guidelines in "Effective Persuasive Speech Writing and Delivery" (fig. 12.6) can serve as a guide during the writing process as well as during the speech practice sessions.

The "Self-Assessment Form for Public Speaking Performance" (fig. 12.7) may be used to guide evaluation of specific speaking behaviors after students watch their videotape or listen to their audiotape.

This form requires the students to decide which speaking behaviors were good and which ones need improvement. The final task on this form calls for students to list ideas on improving their speaking performance.

A form for "Self-Assessment of Persuasive Speaking Performance" is a guide for students' reflections related to this lesson (fig. 12.8).

Using this form, students describe in narrative form what they learned throughout the writing process, what they learned from listening to persuasive speeches given by others, and what they learned about other elements related to the lesson.

These documents can be completed and filed in the students' assessment portfolios to provide a record for monitoring writing and speaking progress. Additionally, students' ability to self-assess and reflect on their own learning is demonstrated and recorded.

FIGURE 12.7

Self-Assessment Form for Public Speaking Performance

Directions:

1. Watch the videotape of your speech performance.

2. Complete the self-assessment form by checking performance behaviors as *Good Performance* or *Improvement Needed.*

3. List ideas for improving your speaking performance.

Speaking Performance Behavior	My performance was *good* here	My performance *needs improvement* here
A. Eye contact	_____	_____
B. Facial expressions	_____	_____
C. Posture/Stance	_____	_____
D. Choice of topic for audience	_____	_____
E. Voice variation/modulation	_____	_____
F. Rate of speaking	_____	_____
G. Projection of voice	_____	_____
H. Use of props	_____	_____
I. Use of gestures	_____	_____
J. Use of standard English	_____	_____
K. Articulation	_____	_____
L. Pronunciation of words	_____	_____
M. Persuasive	_____	_____
N. Use of musical elements	_____	_____

O. Ideas for improving my speaking performance:

FIGURE 12.8

Form for Self-Assessment of Persuasive Speaking Performance

1. What did I most like about writing a persuasive speech?

2. What did I learn most from writing the persuasive speech?

3. What did I learn most from delivering the persuasive speech?

4. What did I learn most from listening to persuasive speeches?

5. Musical ideas included in my speech were:

6. Persuasive strategies included in my speech were:

7. I know my speech persuaded listeners to try different music because

8. I know my speech did not persuade listeners to try different music because

9. I found out

10. What I did well:

11. What I will do better next time:

REFERENCES

Baines, A. (Ed.). (1992). *The Oxford companion to musical instruments*. New York: Oxford University Press.

Blake, G., & Bly, R. (1993). *The elements of technical writing*. New York: Macmillan.

Brent, R., & Anderson, P. (1993). Developing children's classroom listening strategies. *The Reading Teacher, 47*(2), 122–126.

Brown, S. L. (1991). *Improving listening skills in young children*. (ERIC Document Reproduction Services No. ED 339 058).

Burley, A. M. (1982). *Listening: The forgotten skill*. New York: Miley.

Burnaford, G. (1993). The challenge of integrated curricula. *Music Educator Journal, 79*(9), 44–47.

Campbell, M. R. (1995). Interdisciplinary projects in music. *Music Education Journal, 82*(2), 37–44.

Cooper, F. (1995). *African-American songs for children*. New York: Scholastic.

Delacre, L. (1989). *Arroz con leche: Popular songs and rhymes from Latin America*. New York: Scholastic.

Diagram Group, Corporation. (1976). *Musical instruments of the world: An illustrated encyclopedia*. New York: Paddington Press.

Ehninger, D., Gronbeck, R., McKerrow, R. E., & Monroe, A. H. (1985). *Principles and types of speech communication* (11th ed.). New York: Scott Foresman & Co.

Fearing, B., & Sparrow, W. K. (Eds.). (1989). *Technical writing: Theory and practice*. New York: The Modern Language Association of America.

Gardner, H. (1991). *The unschooled mind: How children think and how schools should teach*. New York: Basic Books.

Garman, C. G., & Garman, J. F. (1992). *Teaching young children listening skills*. York, PA: William Gladden Foundation.

Goodman, K. S., Bird, L. B., & Goodman, Y. M. *The whole language catalog*. Santa Rosa, CA: American Schools Publications.

Herbert, E. H. (1990). Research direction: Starting with oral language. *Language Arts, 67*, 502–506.

Hunsaker, R. A. (1990). *Understanding and developing the skills of oral communication: Speaking and listening* (2nd ed.). Englewood, CO: Morton.

Jalongo, M. R. (1995, Fall). Promoting active listening in the classroom. *Childhood Education, 72*(1), 13–18.

Johnson, J. W. (1993). *Lift every voice and sing*. New York: Walker.

Lucas, S. (1994). *The art of public speaking* (5th ed.). New York: Random House.

Mayher, J., Lester, N., & Pradl. G. (1983). *Learning to write, writing to learn*. Upper Montclair, NJ: Boynton, Cook.

Newman, G. (1995). *Teaching children music* (4th ed.). Madison, WI: Brown & Benchmark.

Pfeiffer, W. S. (1994). *Technical writing: A practical approach* (2nd ed.). New York: Merrill.

Remnant, M. (1989). *Musical instruments: An illustrated history from antiquity to the present.* Portland, OR: Amadeus Press.

Ross, J. E. (Arr.). (1987). *Spirituals.* New York: Margaret McElderry.

Stewart, C., Smith, C., & Denton, Jr., R. E. (1994). *Persuasion and social movements* (3rd ed.). Prospect Heights, IL: Waveland.

Swanson, C. H. (1989). *Speak out for listening.* (ERIC Document Reproduction Service No. ED 306 606).

Wolf, J. (1992). Let's sing it again: Creating music with young children. *Young Children, 47*(2), 56–61.

Woodward, G. C., & Denton, Jr., R. E. (1996). *Persuasion and influence in American life* (3rd ed.). Prospect Heights, IL: Waveland.

Young, P. T. (1980). *The look of music: Rare musical instruments, 1500–1900.* Seattle, WA: University of Washington Press.

BOOK SUGGESTIONS FOR CHILDREN

Musical Theme Books for Early Elementary Students

Aardema, V. (1975). *The riddle of the drum: A tale from Tizapan, Mexico.* New York: Four Winds.

Ackerman, K. (1988). *Song and dance man.* New York: Knopf.

Adoff, A. (1995). *Street music: City poems.* New York: HarperCollins.

Aliki. (1968). *Hush little baby: A folk lullaby.* New York: Simon & Schuster.

Aliki. (1986). *Go tell Aunt Rhody.* New York: Macmillan.

Angelou, M. (1987). *Now Sheba sings the song.* New York: Dutton/Dial.

Axelrod, A. (1991). *Songs of the wild West.* New York: Simon & Schuster.

Baer, G. (1989). *Thump, thump, rat-a-tat-tat.* New York: HarperCollins.

Balet, J. B. (1951). *What makes an orchestra?* New York: Oxford Press.

Baylor, B. (1982). *Moon song.* New York: Scribner's.

Bodecker, N. M. (1981). *The lost string quartet.* New York: Atheneum.

Brett, J. (1991). *Berlioz the bear.* New York: Putnam.

Britten, B., & Holst, I. (1958). *The wonderful world of music.* New York: Doubleday.

Brott, A. (1990). *Jeremy's decision*. New York: Kane/Miller.

Bruchac-Banai, J. (1995). *The Mishomis book: The voice of the Ojibway*. Hayward, WI: Indian Country Communications.

Bryan, A. (1981). *Beat the story-drum, pum-pum*. New York: Atheneum.

Bryan, A. (1992). *Sing to the sun*. New York: McElderry.

Bulla, C. R. (1959). *Stories of favorite operas*. New York: Crowell.

Carlson, N. (1983). *Loudmouth George and the cornet*. Minneapolis: Caroirhoda.

Doniach, S. (1961). *Every child's book of music and musicians*. New York: Ambassador.

Eversole, R. (1995). *The flute player/la flautista*. New York: Orchard.

Fisher, A. (1969, o. p.). *Sing little mouse*. New York: HarperCollins.

Fleischman, P. (1988). *Rondo in C*. New York: Harper & Row.

Goble, P. (1991). *Sing for the animals*. New York: Bradbury.

Goldstein, M. B. (1972). *A little Schubert*. New York: Harper & Row.

Griffith, H. (1986). *Georgia music*. New York: Greenwillow.

Halsey, D. (1983). *The old banjo*. New York: Macmillan.

Hamanaka, S. (1990). *Bebop-a do-walk!* New York: Simon & Schuster.

Hirlihy, D. (1988). *Ludie's song*. New York: Dial.

Hoffman, M. (1991). *Amazing grace*. New York: Dial.

Hoyt-Goldsmith, D., & Migdale, L. (1991). *Pueblo, storyteller*. New York: Holiday.

Hughes, L. (1954). *The first book of jazz*. New York: Watts.

Isadora, R. (1979). *Ben's trumpet*. New York: Greenwillow.

Jetter, J. (1968). *The cat and the fiddler*. New York: Parent's Magazine Press.

Kaufmann, H. L. (1957). *History's 100 greatest composers*. New York: Grossett.

Kherdian, D. (1990). *The cat's midsummer jamboree*. New York: Philomel.

Komaiko, L. (1987). *I like the music*. New York: Harper & Row.

Kraus, R. (1990). *Musical Max*. New York: Simon & Schuster.

Krementz, J. (1991). *A very young musician*. New York: Simon & Schuster.

Kuskin, K. (1982). *The philharmonic gets dressed*. New York: Harper & Row.

Larrick, N. (Comp.). (1988). *Songs from Mother Goose*. New York: HarperCollins.

Lewis, R. (1991). *All of you was singing*. New York: Atheneum.

Lionni, L. (1979). *Geraldine the music mouse*. New York: Random House.

Martin, B., & Achhambault, J. (1986). *Barn dance*. New York: Henry Holt.

Maxner, J. (1989). *Nicholas Cricket*. New York: Harper & Row.

Medearis, A. S. (1994). *The singing man*. New York: Holiday House.

Melmed, L. K. (1993). *The first song ever sung*. New York: Lothrop.

Monjo, F. N. (1970). *The drinking gourd*. New York: Harper & Row.

Montgomery, E. R. (1953). *The story behind the musical instruments*. New York: Dodd.

Moss, L. (1996). *Zin! Zin! Zin!: A violin*. New York: Simon & Schuster.

Norman, G. (1954). *The first book of music*. New York: Watts.

Palmer, H. (1990). *Homemade band: Songs to sing, instruments to make*. New York: Crown.

Plume, I. (1980). *The Bremen-Town musicians*. New York: Doubleday.

Schick, E. (1984). *The piano for Julie*. New York: Greenwillow.

Schroeder, A. (1989). *Ragtime tumpie*. Boston: Joy Street Books.

Seeger, P. (1986). *Abiyoyo: Based on a South African lullaby and folk story*. New York: Orchard.

Van Laan, N. (1995). *In a circle long ago: A treasury of native lore from North America*. Knopf/Apple Soup.

Velthuijs, M. (1990). *Elephant and Crocodile*. New York: Farrar, Straus, & Giroux.

Williams, V. B. (1984). *Music, music for everyone*. New York: Greenwillow.

Winter, J. (1988). *Follow the drinking gourd*. New York: Knopf.

Yolen, J. (1995). *Granddad Bill's song*. New York: Philomel.

Yorinks, A. (1988). *Bravo Minsky!* New York: Farrar, Straus, & Giroux.

Musical Theme Books for Later and Middle School Students

Angell, J. *Buffalo nickel blues band.* New York: Bradbury.

Bernstein, L. (1959). *The joy of music.* New York: Simon and Schuster.

Best of college marching bands. (1995). Palatine, IL: 800 Video Express.

Caseley, J. (1990). *Kisses.* New York: Knopf.

Commins, D. (1961). *All about the symphony orchestra and what it plays.* New York: Random House.

Copland, A. (1957). *What to listen for in music.* New York: McGraw.

Duder, T. (1986). *Jellybean.* New York: Viking.

Ewen, D. (1994). *The home book of musical knowledge.* New York: Prentice-Hall.

Ewen, D. (1995). *Encyclopedia of opera.* New York: Columbia.

Fenner, C. (1995). *Yolanda's genius.* New York: Simon & Schuster.

Gilson, J. (1979). *Dial Lerio Rupert DJ.* New York: Lothrop.

Grout, D. J. (1960). *The history of Western music.* New York: Norton.

Hilgartner, B. (1986). *A murder for Her Majasty.* Boston: Houghton Mifflin.

Howard, J. T., & Bellows, G. K. (1957). *Short history of music in America.* New York: Crowell.

Lisle, J. T. (1986). *Sirens and spies.* New York: Bradbury.

MacLachian, P. (1988). *The facts and fictions of Minna Pratt.* New York: HarperCollins.

McCaffrey, A. (1995). *Dragonsong.* Lexington, MA: Heath

Monjo, F. N. (1975). *Letters to Horseface: Young Mozart's travels in Italy.* New York: Puffin.

Newton, S. (1983). *I will call it Georgie's Blues.* New York: Viking.

Paterson, K. (1985). *Come sing Jimmy Jo.* New York: Dutton.

Paulson, G. (1985). *Dogsong.* New York: Bradbury.

Plotz, H. (Comp.). (1976). *As I walked out one evening: A book of ballads.* New York: Greenwillow.

Schroeder, A. (1996). *Caroline shout!* New York: Dial.

Sharmatt, M. S., & Sharmatt, C. (1990). *Nate the Great and the musical note*. New York: Putnam.

Springer, N. (1992). *The friendship song*. New York: Atheneum.

Stoddard, H. (1952). *From these comes music: Instruments of the band and orchestra*. New York: Crowell.

Taubman, H. (1958). *How to bring up your child to enjoy music*. New York: Ballantine.

Van Laan, N. (1996). *In a circle long ago: A treasury of native lore from North America*. New York: Knopf/Apple Soup.

Voigt, C. (1983). *Dicey's song*. New York: Atheneum.

Voigt, C. (1992). *Orfe*. New York: Atheneum.

Weller, F. W. (1987). *Boat song*. New York: Macmillan.

Wolfe, V. E. (1991). *The Mozart season*. New York: Henry Holt.

13

MOVEMENT

KEY IDEAS

- Physical education can be the basis for an inter-disciplinary lesson.
- The school curriculum needs to have a global and multicultural orientation.
- Playing games is a way to incorporate physical education with cultural awareness.
- The ability to balance oneself or objects is a skill.

INTRODUCTION

A student who has been instructed with a proper **physical education** program (1) is able to perform skills in a variety of physical activities, (2) participates regularly in physical activity, (3) is cognizant of the value of involvement in physical activities, and (4) appreciates physical activity and how it leads to a healthy life-style (NASPE, 1990).

The curriculum in United States schools needs to be internationalized (Becker, 1990). In a recent article, Butt and Pahnos (1995, p. 48) wrote that teachers should "create a learning environment for their students that provides equity and reflects and embraces the diversity of the world in which we live."

Employing **games** as an instructional technique can be an important avenue to teaching physical education. They should be included in the thematic unit to reflect the unit's goals. Games drawn from around the world can provide a vehicle for exposing students to cultures in other countries; "recreation professionals, thus, have an ideal opportunity to facilitate the development of cultural awareness through the planning and implementation of play-based activities" (Monroe, 1995, p. 24).

Nickell and Kennedy (1987), as an example of this a number of years ago, compiled a wonderful collection of games for children from around the world. They divided the games into these categories: (1) people and nature, (2) competition versus cooperation, (3) war and peace, (4) roles, (5) traditions, (6) worldview, and (7) creating culture games.

The area of games is part of a more basic premise of education; namely, the need for children to play. Vygotsky (1978) believes in the connection between the emotional and intellectual development of the child, and **play** is one avenue where the two can interrelate. Then, of course, play involving games brings in the physical development aspect of education, too.

The lesson in this chapter attempts to make students aware of other world cultures by presenting games that contain elements of physical education. The topic of balancing from the curriculum area of science is also brought into use. The game is intended for a range of interests—early elementary through middle school.

LESSON PLAN

TITLE: **BOTTLE RELAY**

Ages/Grades: Early elementary, later elementary, middle school

Time: 30 minutes

Content Areas:

 Physical education

 Geography

 Science, Anthropology

Materials: Small plastic bottles or cups

Sticks

Four-by-four-inch piece of lumber

World map

Reference books on countries of the world

Objectives:
- Students will develop psychomotor skills, such as creating movement, walking, and running.
- Students will demonstrate fundamental movement concepts (e.g., body and space awareness).

- Students will develop scientific skills, such as identifying variables that cause or influence an outcome.

- Students will explore the similarities and differences among cultures.

- Students will use sources of geographic information for a purpose.

Beginning: Tell the class that this game originated in Uganda, which is a country in the eastern part of Africa. Point out this country on a world map, indicating that its neighbors are Kenya, Sudan, Zaire, Rwanda, and Tanzania. Uganda is a little smaller than the state of Oregon (fig. 13.1). It contains a large lake (Lake Victoria), which is a source of the Nile River.

This is an active playground bottle-relay game that can involve the entire class. Its origin is tied to the practice of Ugandan women where they often carry heavy items on their heads using a coiled cloth (called a kanga cloth) to cushion the load.

Middle: Form the class into three, four, or five teams. Establish a starting line and a turning line as shown in figure 13.2. The two lines should be about ten to twenty feet apart.

Give each player a plastic bottle or cup to balance on his or her head. At a given signal, the first player on each team runs to the turning line while balancing the cup on his or her head. The player touches the turning line, turns around, and runs back to tag the next player in line. After the runner has tagged the next player, he or she goes to the end of the line. If the cup falls off the runner's head, the player must stop and replace it before moving forward. The team that finishes first wins. Play this game for three minutes.

See how many students each group can rotate through during this amount of time. Try it again to see if each team does better or worse. This adds the incentive for each group to improve on its previous performance.

End: Ask the class to think of the physical skills that enabled the classmates on the winning team to be so successful. Was it necessarily speed that was critical to winning the relay event? They should realize that merely being able to run fast is not enough; balance, surefootedness, posture, and agility are necessary characteristics.

Assessment of Student Learning: Discuss the following questions with the class:

1. What similarities can you think of between this game and the life of Ugandan women?

2. Why is this relay game a logical outgrowth of the way that the Ugandan women carry their loads?

3. Do you think that Uganda is the only country in the world where this game is played? Why or why not?

4. Why do you think that this game may be played by Ugandan men, too?

5. How did you try to keep the cup on your head so it wouldn't fall off? Did you try to walk slower? Faster? Did you try to hold your arms out to your side to give yourself better balance?

6. How do you think that high-wire walkers are able to walk on such a thin wire? What techniques do they use?

Invite the class to do some research on the country of Uganda to find out the kind of land that women must travel with their heavy loads; for example, is Uganda extremely flat? Hilly? Mountainous?

Invite the class to conduct a scientific experiment to determine the best length for a stick that might help them balance themselves. They could try to walk on a long wooden four-by-four-inch beam suspended a few inches above the ground.

They could try holding their stick to see how this improves their balancing ability.

Challenge the class to create a game that reflects something about their own culture in the United States.

Have a supply of books available for students to read. These books can be about East Africa, about games or sports that people play in different parts of the world, or about the act of balancing. Some suggestions are listed in Book Suggestions for Children (fig. 13.3).

The women of Uganda cushion heavy loads on their head by using a kanga cloth. Ask students to get a piece of cloth and try to find different ways to use it.

FIGURE 13. 1

Maps

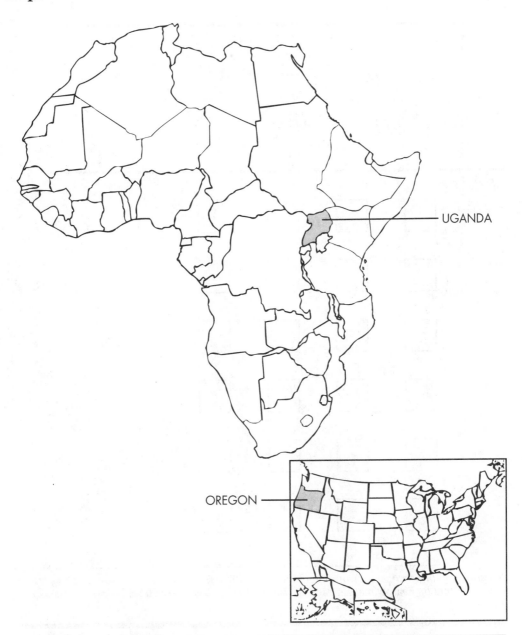

FIGURE 13. 2

Game Formation

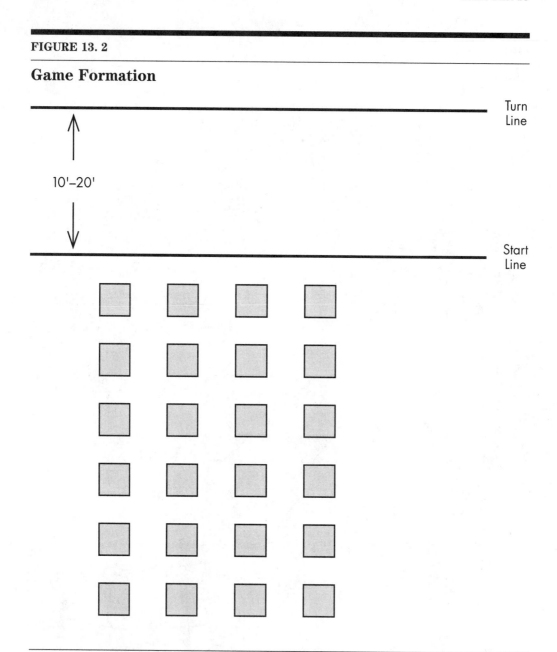

FIGURE 13.3

Book Suggestions for Students

Aardema, Verna. *Bringing the Rain to Kapiti Plain.*

Aardema, Verna. *What Is So Funny, Ketu?*

Adoff, Arnold. *Sports Pages.*

Crutcher, Chris. *Athletic Shorts.*

Ellis, Veronica Freeman. *Afro-Bets First Book about Africa.*

Fairman, Tony. *Bury My Bones But Keep My Words: African Tales for Retelling.*

Feelings, Muriel L. *Moja Means One: Swahili Counting Book.*

Golenbock, Peter. *Teammates.*

Hailey, Gail E. *A Story, A Story.*

Hallet, Jean Pierre. *Congo Kitabu.*

Hamilton, Virginia. *The Magical Adventures of Pretty Pearl.*

Harman, Humphrey. *Men of Masaba.*

Heady, Eleanor B. *When the Stones Were Soft: East African Fireside Tales.*

Knutson, Barbara. *Why the Crab Has No Head.*

Kroll, Virginia. *Masai and I.*

Lester, Julius. *How Many Spots Does a Leopard Have? and Other Tales.*

Maren, Michael. *The Land and People of Kenya.*

McCully, Emily Arnold. *Mirette on the High Wire.*

McDermott, Gerald. *The Magic Tree: A Tale from the Congo.*

Morrison, Lillian. *The Sidewalk Racer and Other Poems of Sports and Motion.*

Musgrove, Margaret. *Ashanti to Zulu: African Traditions.*

Nagenda, John. *Mukasa.*

Rabe, Berniece. *The Balancing Girl.*

Van Stockum, Hilda. *Mogo's Flute.*

Additional games, representing continents besides Africa, can be found in the publications by Nickell and Kennedy (1990) and Nelson and Glass (1992):

Game: Scorpion's Sting

Country: India (Asia)

Curriculum Area: PE: tag game; science: insects; geography: location of India and its description. [The person who is it—the scorpion—scuttles around, trying to touch another player with his leg.]

Game: Bola
Country: Argentina (South America)
Curriculum Area: PE: jumping ability, agility; geography: location of Argentina and its description; science: centrifugal force. [A tennis ball is placed inside a sock, which is tied with a rope. A player stands in the center of a circle and swings this "bola." The players in the circle must jump over the bola as it comes around.]

Game: Muk
Country: Canada/U.S. (Eskimos of North America)
Curriculum Area: PE: movement of body; geography: location of Arctic area and its description; science: length of daylight and darkness hours. [Players sit in a circle and one person goes to the middle. The person in the center uses comical expressions and body gestures in an effort to make the others laugh.]

Game: Sarvisilla
Country: Finland (Europe)
Curriculum Area: PE: movement of body; geography: location of Finland and its description; language arts: A leader of the group says several words in a certain order, which indicates that the rest of the group must perform certain actions. When the leader changes the words he/she gives, the group members must change their responses.

REFERENCES

Ayo, Y. (1995). *Africa*. New York: Alfred A. Knopf.

Becker, J. (1990). Curriculum considerations in global studies. In *Global Education: From Thought to Action* (Chapter 4). The 1991 ASCD Yearbook. Alexandria, VA: Association for Supervision and Curriculum Development.

Butt, K. L., & Pahnos, M. L. (1995, January). Why we need a multicultural focus in our schools. *Journal of Physical Education, Recreation, and Dance, 66*(1), 48–53.

Carpenter, G. (1993, June). The web: Creating an interdisciplinary unit. *Strategies, 6*(2), 26–28.

Culin, S. (1992). *Games of the North American Indians*. Lincoln, NE: University of Nebraska Press.

Elementary Science Study. (1987). *The balance book: A guide for teachers of primary balancing*. Nashua, NH: Delta Education.

Hafkin, J., & Bay, E. G. (Eds.). (1976). *Women in Africa: Studies in social and economic change*. Stanford, CA: Stanford University Press.

Harbin, E. O. (1954). *Games of many nations*. Nashville, TN: Abingdon Press.

Hunt, S. E. (1964). *Games and sports the world around*. New York: Ronald Press Co.

I.C.H.P.E.R. Book of worldwide games and dances. (1967). Washington, DC: International Council on Health, Physical Education, and Recreation.

Jacobs, H. (1989). *Interdisciplinary curriculum: Design and implementation*. Alexandria, VA: Association for Supervision and Curriculum Development.

Jernigan, S., & Vendien, C. L. (1972). *Playtime: A world recreation handbook: games, dances, and songs*. New York: McGraw Hill.

Kane, K. (1994, May). Stories help students understand movement. *Strategies, 7*(7), 13–17.

Kirchner, G. (1992). *Physical education for elementary school children*. Dubuque, IA: Wm. C. Brown Publishers.

Lichtman, B. (1993). *Innovative games*. Champaign, IL: Human Kinetics Publishers.

Monroe, J. E. (1995, October). Developing cultural awareness through play. *Journal of Physical Education, Recreation, and Dance, 66*(8), 24–27.

Morrison, G. S. (1993). *Contemporary curriculum K–8*. Needham Heights, MA: Allyn and Bacon.

National Association for Sport and Physical Education. (1990). *Definition of the physically educated person: Outcomes of quality physical education programs*. Reston, VA: Author.

Nelson, W. E., & Glass, H. "B." (1992). *International playtime: Classroom games and dances from around the world*. Carthage, IL: Fearon Teacher Aids.

Nickell, P., & Kennedy, M. (1990, November/December). Global perspectives through children's games. How to Do It Series 5, Number 3. Pullout section in *The Social Studies*, 1–8.

Orlando, L. (1993). *The multicultural game book: More than 70 traditional games from 30 countries*. New York: Scholastic Professional Books.

Tiedt, P. L., & Tiedt, I. M. (1986). *Multicultural teaching: A handbook of activities, information, and resources*. Boston: Allyn & Bacon.

Vinton, I. (1970). *The Folkways omnibus of children's games*. New York: Hawthorn Books, Inc.

Vogler, C. (1987). *Teaching about Africa: Tradition and change*. Denver, CO: University of Denver Center for Teaching International Relations.

Vygotsky, L. (1978). *Mind in society: The development of higher mental processes*. Cambridge, MA: Harvard University Press.

Wassermann, S., & Ivany, J. W. G. (1988). *Teaching elementary science: Who's afraid of spiders?* New York: Harper & Row, Publishers, Inc.

BOOK SUGGESTIONS FOR CHILDREN

Aardema, V. (1981). *Bringing the rain to Kapiti Plain*. New York: Dial Press.

Aardema, V. (1982). *What is so funny, Ketu?* New York: Dial Books for Young Readers.

Adoff, A. (1986). *Sports pages*. Philadelphia: J. B. Lippincott Co.

Allen, W. D. (1986). *Africa*. Grand Rapids, MI: Fideler Co.

Baker, R. S. B. (1958). *Kamiti: A forester's dream*. Eau Claire, WI: Hale.

Carpenter, F. (1967). *The story of East Africa*. Wichita, KS: McCormick-Mathers Pub. Co.

Crutcher, C. (1991). *Athletic shorts*. New York: Greenwillow Books.

Ellis, V. F. (1990). *Afro-Bets first book about Africa*. East Orange, NJ: Just Us Books.

Fairman, T. (1993). *Bury my bones but keep my words: African tales for retelling*. San Diego, CA: Holt, Rinehart and Winston, Inc.

Feelings, M. L. (1971). *Moja means one: Swahili counting book*. New York: Dial Press.

Golenbock, P. (1990). *Teammates*. San Diego, CA: Harcourt Brace Jovanovich, Inc.

Griffin, M. (1988). *A family in Kenya*. Minneapolis, MN: Lerner Publications.

Hailey, G. E. (1970). *A story, a story*. New York: Atheneum.

Hallet, J. P. (1965). *Congo Kitabu*. New York: Random House.

Hamilton, V. (1983). *The magical adventures of Pretty Pearl*. New York: Harper & Row.

Harman, H. (1965). *African Samson*. New York: Viking.

Harman, H. (1971). *Men of Masaba*. New York: Viking Press.

Harthorn, S. (1972). *Listen to the wild*. New York: Taplinger Pub. Co.

Heady, E. B. (1968). *When the stones were soft: East African fireside tales*. New York: Funk & Wagnalls.

Huxley, E. J. G. (1964). *With forks and hope*. New York: W. Morrow.

Isenberg, B., & Jaffe, M. (1984). *Albert the running bear's exercise book*. Boston: Houghton Mifflin.

Kaula, E. M. (1968). *The land and people of Kenya*. Philadelphia: J. B. Lippincott.

Knutson, B. (1987). *Why the crab has no head*. Minneapolis, MN: Carolrhoda.

Kroll, V. (1992). *Masai and I*. New York: Four Winds Press.

Lester, J. (1989). *How many spots does a leopard have? and other tales*. New York: Scholastic.

Lowery, L. (1995). *Twist with a burger, jitter with a bug*. Boston: Houghton Mifflin.

MacDonald, S.. *Nanta's lion*. New York: Morrow.

Maren, M. (1989). *The land and people of Kenya*. New York: HarperCollins.

Margolies, B. (1990). *Rehema's journey*. New York: Scholastic.

Marson, R. (1993). *Balancing*. Canby, OR: TOPS Learning Systems.

McCully, E. A. (1992). *Mirette on the high wire*. New York: Putnam Berkley Group, Inc.

McDermott, G. (1973). *The magic tree: A tale from the Congo*. New York: Holt, Rinehart and Winston.

Morrison, L. (1977). *The sidewalk racer and other poems of sports and motion*. New York: Lothrop, Lee and Shepard.

Musgrove, M. (1976). *Ashanti to Zulu: African traditions*. New York: Dial Press.

Nagenda, J. (1973). *Mukasa*. New York: Macmillan.

Rabe, B. (1981). *The balancing girl*. New York: E. P. Dutton.

Savory, P. (1971). *Lion outwitted by hare, and other African tales*. Chicago: A. Whitman.

Steig, W. (1992). *Dr. De Soto goes to Africa*. New York: HarperCollins.

Stevenson, W. (1965). *The bushbabies*. Boston: Houghton Mifflin.

Van Stockum, H. (1966). *Mogo's flute*. New York: Viking Press.

CHAPTER

14

ARCHITECTURE

KEY IDEAS

■ Appearance of buildings have changed over time.

■ Architectural styles tell us about a culture.

■ When students construct buildings, they are engaged in problem solving.

■ Students must think about technology as they think of how the structures could be built.

INTRODUCTION

People have been builders ever since they began fashioning crude caves into homes. Most people have not been satisfied to live in caves or log cabins; instead they have aspired to customize the appearance of their houses to achieve beauty and uniqueness. Today, we have trained professionals—called architects—whose job it is to create functional, yet attractive, places for people to live, work, worship, and socialize.

ARCHITECTURE

As students look at books with photographs that depict creations of cultures throughout history—the solid sphinx (Egypt), elegant pagodas (Japan), streamlined Doric columns (Greece), or massive pyramids (Mexico)—they understand that civilizations have different ways of expressing themselves through their art and **architecture**.

Teachers can involve their students in experimenting with the architecture immediately around them—their *built environment*. For instance, students in one elementary school used foam board to make three-dimensional models of buildings in early American architectural styles.

Architecture also can be used to address global studies. Examples of this may be teaching the concepts of technological change, continuity, cultural diffusion, and cultural synthesis; or teaching the skills of visual literacy, chronological sequence, identification of human values, historical analysis, and thinking abilities (Mounkhall, 1994). Daniel (1989) had her elementary students construct a replica of the Ponte Vecchio. This helped them study the importance of this bridge to the city of Florence in Italy.

Logging on to the Internet enables a user to access the topic of *architecture* to find information. A number of hosts, such as the University of Michigan, with its Archigopher, supply images of buildings, bridges, and other structures. To access Archigopher, use a Web browser such as Netscape or Omniweb. The address is: http://libra.caup.umich.edu/Archigopher/.

The following lesson plan—suitable for later elementary students or middle school students—provides an interesting way to investigate architecture. Technical terms come to life as students see examples in the present and past world.

LESSON PLAN

TITLE: **BUILD IT**

Ages/Grades: Later elementary, middle school

Time: Two hours

Content Areas:

 History

 Geography

 Science

 Industrial Technology

 Arts and Architecture

Materials: Wooden Popsicle sticks

Basketball

Pictures, photographs, and videotapes

Objectives:
- Students will recognize continuity and change from historical material.
- Students will examine the interaction between people and their environment.
- Students will create products that convey art concepts.
- Students will discuss artworks using appropriate terminology.

- Students will explore the elements and principles of art forms.
- Students will analyze a situation from different perspectives.
- Students will use models to depict the function of an object.

Beginning: The teacher should show pictures of various kinds of buildings taken from different times in history: log cabins, castles, tepees, igloos, huts, etc. Have students look at the buildings and describe them to a partner; then have them share their descriptions with the entire class. Examples of observations may be as follows if a student were commenting on a picture of an igloo.

1. The igloo is white and rounded.

2. It seems to have some lines showing where the snow blocks were fitted together.

3. It was easy for Eskimos to get materials, because they just had to use the ice that was all around them.

4. If the weather gets too warm, the igloo may melt.

5. It seems like anyone could build an igloo; in our society it takes a trained carpenter or one who knows what he is doing to build a house.

Another good idea is to play a videotape showing the kind of buildings that are in the immediate community. The teacher or student could have recorded this video previously while taking a walk around the area.

The teacher should make a list of all the categories that were mentioned (materials, size, color, difficulty to construct, benefits, disadvantages, shape, texture, permanence, uniqueness, etc.).

Middle: The teacher should pose the following question to the class: Why do you think the rounded igloo stays up and doesn't collapse? Guide the discussion toward the fact that the igloo is rounded in shape. Would this form of dome construction have an effect on the strength of the structure? Inform students that many early buildings were made by placing a flat roof on upright walls (see fig. 14.1). The vertical lines are *posts* and the horizontal lines are *lintels*. Divide students into groups of three and give each group a supply of wooden Popsicle sticks. With these, they can build four walls and place a flat roof on top to represent the post-and-lintel (sometimes called post-and-beam) technique. Show pictures or a videotape of some of our contemporary business or industrial buildings that still retain the post-and-lintel design that has been used for millennia.

Later, the arch was introduced as a design aspect to gain support. The arch somewhat resembles the geometric form of a triangle, which achieves a great deal of support strength (see fig. 14.2). Buildings with an arch could then offer an option in appearance to the boxlike post-and-lintel structures.

As builders wanted to construct taller and more ambitious buildings—such as churches, castles, and cathedrals—they needed more sophisticated construction techniques and materials. One example is the flying buttress, which lent additional support to the walls of a very tall building (see fig. 14.3).

The igloo's design is that of a dome, which must find extra support, because it does not have four upright walls to support a roof.

End: Have students act out the arrangements shown in figures 14.4 through 14.7.

By arranging themselves, students can duplicate the architectural design of (1) post-and-lintel or post-and-beam construction, (2) an arch, (3) a flying buttress, and (4) a dome. Teachers need to use caution when the students form the flying buttress in figure 14.6; if students are not careful, there is a danger of falling down.

Assessment of Student Learning: Ask students to explain the basis for a dome's strength. They should see that it has certain elements of the arch and the flying buttress inasmuch as it has a curved appearance. Moreover, there is an upward and inward push all around the walls toward the top, which keeps it from toppling.

As a homework assignment, ask the class to walk around their community and make a list of buildings that demonstrate each of the four **architectural elements**. Encourage them to make drawings or take photographs of these buildings and bring them to class.

FIGURE 14.1

Post-and-Lintel Structure

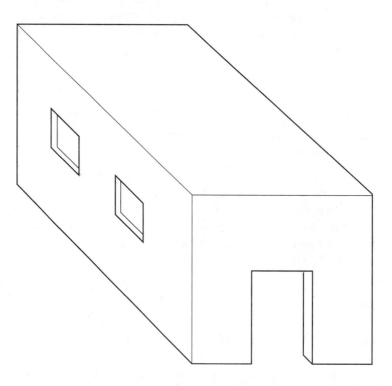

FIGURE 14.2

An Arch

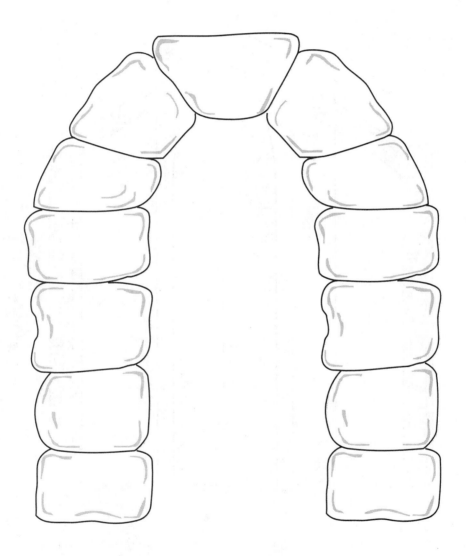

FIGURE 14.3

Flying Buttress

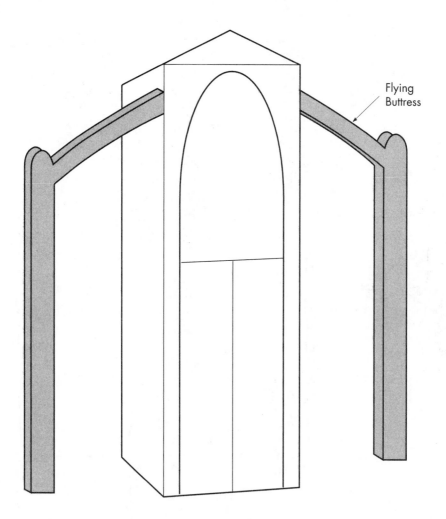

Flying
Buttress

FIGURE 14.4

Post and Beam

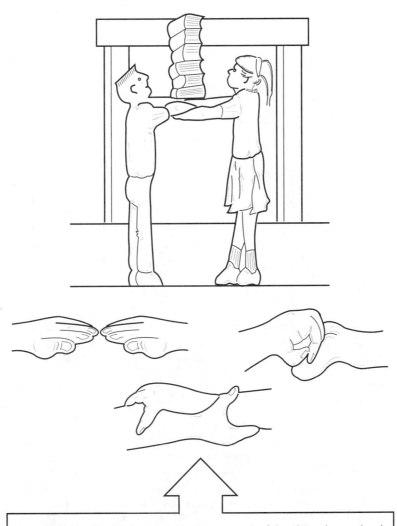

POST AND BEAM To determine the strength of the "best" beam, load books on three different types of "beams" with hands touching, with hands interlocking with hands, and with arms interlockin. Which one works best? Why?

FIGURE 14.5

Arch

ARCH Two students interlock their hands while facing each other. Move feet away as far as you can. Feel the compression in the hands and the tension in the feet.

Reprinted, with permission, from School Zone Institute, American Institute of Architects.

FIGURE 14.6

Flying Buttress

Flying
Buttress

FLYING BUTTRESS Eight students form an arch with two flying buttresses and footings as shown in sketch. Two students form footings and two students stand by to give needed support, if necessary.

Reprinted, with permission, from School Zone Institute, American Institute of Architects.

FIGURE 14.7

Dome

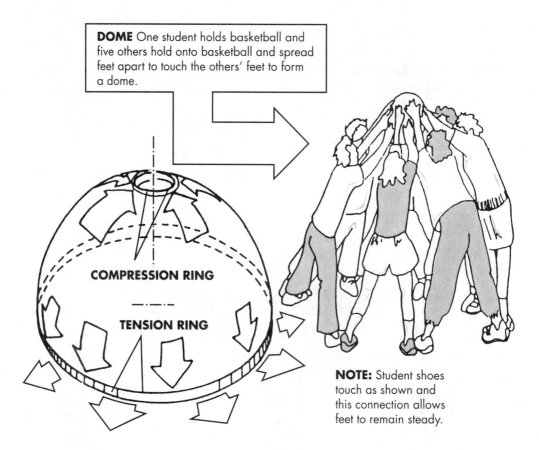

DOME One student holds basketball and five others hold onto basketball and spread feet apart to touch the others' feet to form a dome.

COMPRESSION RING

TENSION RING

NOTE: Student shoes touch as shown and this connection allows feet to remain steady.

Reprinted, with permission, from School Zone Institute, American Institute of Architects.

REFERENCES

America preserved: A checklist of historic buildings, structures, and sites. (1995). Washington, DC: U.S. Government Printing Office.

American Art and Architecture. (No Date). [Videocassettes]. Boulder, CO: Alarion Press.

Brahier, D. (Ed.). (1993, February). Ideas. *Arithmetic Teacher, 40*(6), 325–332.

Butterfield, L., Lange, R. C., Kappel, C., Miller, G., Miller, R., Sinko, K., & Stiadle, K. (1994, October). A fourth grade's architectural journey. *Teaching PreK–8, 25*(2), 46, 47.

Chinese Art and Architecture. (No Date). [CD-ROM]. Boulder, CO: Alarion Press.

D'Alelio, J. (1989). *Discovering architecture with activities and games: I know that building!* Washington, DC: The Preservation Press.

Daniel, L. W. (1989, January/February). Integrating social studies with art and architecture. *Social Studies and the Young Learner, 1*(3), 3–7.

Education Development Agency. (1994). *From the ground up: Modeling, measuring, and constructing houses. Seeing and thinking mathematically in the middle grades.* Portsmouth, NH: Heinemann.

Edwards, K. (1992). *Monument Avenue: History and architecture.* Washington, DC: U.S. Department of the Interior, National Parks Service, Cultural Resources.

Egyptian Art and Architecture. (No Date). [Audiocassettes and Filmstrip]. Boulder, CO: Alarion Press.

Evans, S., Evans, M., & Baker, B. (1993, March/April). This town is your town, this town is my town. *Social Studies and the Young Learner, 5*(4), 6–10.

Greek Art and Architecture. (No Date). [Audiocassettes and Filmstrip]. Boulder, CO: Alarion Press.

Hollingsworth, P. (1993, September/October). Making connections with architecture. *Gifted Child Today, 16*(5), 6–8.

Jorgensen, L. (1992, May). The ABCs of architecture. *School Arts, 91*(9), 34–37.

Kenner, H. (1973). *A guided tour of Buckminster Fuller.* New York: Morrow.

Kropa, S. (1993, October). From shoe box to main street. *Arts & Activities, 114*(2), 24, 25.

Leclerc, D. C. (1978). *Architecture as a primary source for social studies*, Series 2, No. 5, How to Do It Series. Washington, DC: National Council for the Social Studies.

Look and do the Middle Ages. (No Date). [Videocassettes]. Boulder, CO: Alarion Press.

Mounkhall, T. (1994, Fall). Teaching global studies through architecture. *Social Science Record, 31*(2), 37–40.

Purkis, S. (1993). *A teacher's guide to using school buildings.* London: English Heritage.

Raskin, E. (1974). *Architecture and people.* Englewood Cliffs, NJ: Prentice-Hall.

Roman art and architecture. (No Date). [Audiocassettes and Filmstrip]. Boulder, CO: Alarion Press.

Salvadori, M. G. (1990). *The art of construction projects and principles for beginning engineers and architects.* Chicago: Chicago Review Press.

The Sourcebook II. (1988). New York: American Institute of Architects.

Spence, W. P. (1988). *Architecture: Design, engineering, drawing* (5th ed.). Mission Hills, CA: Glencoe Publishing Co.

Todd, R., McCrery, D., & Todd, K. (1985). *Understanding and using technology.* Worcester, MA: Davis Publications, Inc.

Walker, M. E. (1993, March). Architecture is elementary. *School Arts, 92*(7), 35, 36.

Wilson, N. (1988). *What it feels like to be a building.* Washington, DC: The Preservation Press.

BOOK SUGGESTIONS FOR CHILDREN

Buildings and Other Structures

Adkins, J. (1972). *How a house happens.* New York: Walker & Company.

Brown, D. J. (1992). *The Random House book of how things are built.* New York: Random House.

Brown, D. J. (1992). *The Random House book of how things were built.* New York: Random House.

Compton's New Media Encyclopedia. (1996). Chicago: Compton's.

Donati, P. (No Date). *Amazing buildings.* Prairie Village, KS: ArchiSources.

Douglas, G. H. (1995). *Skyscrapers: A social history of the very tall building in America.* Jefferson, MO: McFarland & Company, Inc.

Dupasquier, P. (1995). *A busy day at the building site*. New York: Henry Holt & Co.

Encarta Encyclopedia. (1996). Redmond, WA: Microsoft.

Good, M. (1995). *An Amish barnraising*. Intercourse, PA: Good Books.

Grolier's Multimedia Encyclopedia. (1996). Danbury, CT: Grolier.

Grossman, B. (1995). *The banging book*. New York: HarperCollins Children's Books.

Isaacson, P. M. (1995). *Round buildings, square buildings and buildings that wiggle like a fish*. New York: Knopf.

Jacobs, D. (1969). *Master builders of the Middle Ages*. New York: Harper and Row.

Johnson, S. (1996). *Alphabet city*. New York: Viking.

Klein, M. W. (1986). *Clues to American architecture*. Washington, DC: Elliott & Clark Pub.

Lambert, D., & Osmond, T. (1985). *Great discoveries and inventions*. New York: Facts on File Publications.

Macaulay, D. (1987). *Great moments in architecture*. Boston: Houghton Mifflin Co.

Macaulay, D. (1988). *The way things work*. New York: Houghton Mifflin and Co.

Messenger, N. (1989). *Annabel's house*. New York: Orchard Books.

Parker, S. (1995). *I wonder why tunnels are round: And other questions about building*. New York: Larousse Kingfisher Chambers, Inc.

Seltzer, I. (1992). *The house I live in: At home in America*. New York: Macmillan.

Sloan, E. (1984). *Diary of an early American boy*. New York: Ballantine.

Steltzer, U. (1995). *Building an igloo*. New York: Henry Holt & Co.

Trachtenber, M., & Hyman, I. (1986). *Architecture: From pre-history to post-modernism*. Englewood Cliffs, NJ: Prentice Hall.

Wadsworth, G. (No Date). *Julia Morgan: Architect of dreams*. Prairie Village, KS: ArchiSources.

Wilkinson, P. (1995). *Building*. New York: Random House.

CHAPTER 15

FOOD CHOICES

KEY IDEAS

■ Keeping and analyzing food consumption records provides evidence for analysis of basic food consumption.

■ Comparing individual food consumption data to food consumption recommendations gives eaters an opportunity to objectively compare their basic food consumption to recommended basic food consumption.

■ A written plan for future food choices is a way to guide eaters to maintain well-balanced basic food choices.

■ Graphically representing food choices provides a way for eaters to calculate, analyze, and maintain or modify a plan for making food choices.

■ Graphing gives learners opportunities to compare, count, add, subtract, multiply, divide, calculate percentages and averages, and perform other mathematical operations.

■ Being able to use mathematics (i.e., graphing) in purposeful ways helps learners construct mathematical relationships and understandings related to the real-life issues of making healthy food choices.

INTRODUCTION

In this chapter students are given an opportunity to use mathematics in a meaningful activity within the context of a daily life activity: monitoring and choosing healthy food to eat. "Students should have the opportunity to gather data about their own eating habits and compare that information with the new dietary guidelines published in the food guide pyramid" (Lamphere, 1994, p. 164). Students will gather food intake data, organize their information, analyze their data, and develop a strategy for future food consumption to conform with recommendations of the American Heart Association. A personal food diary (Lamphere, 1994, p. 165) or a data form designed by students on a spreadsheet may be used to record daily food consumption information.

HEALTH/NUTRITION

Nutrition education is "any set of learning experiences designed to facilitate voluntary adoption of eating and other nutrition-related behaviors conducive to **health** and well-being" (Contento, 1995, p. 279). These experiences require opportunities for individuals to make intelligent food choices within the context of their personal lives, for example, in grocery stores, fast-food restaurants, using vending machines, and at home. In other words, a fundamental feature of nutrition education is its emphasis on dietary behavioral change as a result of appropriate educational intervention.

The fourth edition (1995) of "Nutrition and Your Health: Dietary Guidelines for Americans," released in January 1996 by the Agriculture Department and Health and Human Services (HHS), gives the government's advice on a healthy diet recommending "plenty of grain products, vegetables and fruits." A copy of these guidelines may be obtained through home page addresses and other nutrition connections on the Internet (fig. 15.1).

An examination of recently published statistics shows the need for improving eating habits among Americans. According to a comparative study conducted by the Agriculture Department in 1994, Americans' diets contain less fat, but one-third of American adults are overweight (fig. 15.2).

"Instead of eating large quantities of fat, meat and dairy products, Americans should be eating more of the new basics, i.e., fruits, vegetables, and

---

FIGURE 15.1

Nutrition Connections

"Healthy Herb" is a program designed to educate children about fitness and nutrition. The program has videos and a children's club. In addition, it has a downloadable coloring book. Tossed Salad Productions, 1-(407) 855-5457. **Website address: http://www.herb@tossed-salad.com.**

"Team Nutrition In-School Program" is designed to help children make food choices for a healthy diet. The objectives are to add more fruits, grains, and vegetables to their diets and to reduce the amount of fat consumed. There are three objectives: (1) nutrition is the link between agriculture and health, (2) we are all empowered to make food choices for a healthy diet, and (3) food appeals to all of our senses and to our creativity. The program has lesson plans, classroom activities, student worksheets, stories, and articles.

"'Kids Cafe' is a community service project that involves food for the mind and the body. These connections will provide students with "food for thought." Thirty-six fruit and vegetable characters liven up this colorful, extensive site on fruits and vegetables and their importance in the food guide pyramid. Students can e-mail characters, who will write back. A free CD-ROM version of many of the interactive pages of this site is available to schools by calling 1(800)-472-8777, ext. 555. Additional links to resources such as USDA and Team Nutrition can be reached through the <School> button. Wealth of information about children's nutrition. <Information for Parents> is rich with information ranging from a graphically colorful "10 Tips to Healthy Eating for Kids" to well-written articles about nutrition. The <Information for Educators> link has lesson plans and reprints of articles and interactive brochures" (Lindroth, 1995, p. 74).

---

grains" (Bianchi, 1992, p. 77). Figure 15.3 illustrates graphically the "new" **Food Guide Pyramid** recommended by the American Heart Association.

Further evidence for the need to urge people to show more discipline in their eating habits is revealed in the Health and Human Services statistic

FIGURE 15.2

Agriculture Department's Survey of America's Diet

1994 Compared with 1977–78

- Percentage of calories from fat: 33.4, down from 40.1
- Milk, children 5 and younger: 315 grams, down from 380
- Deep yellow vegetables: 8 grams, down from 9 grams

- Daily calories: 1,949, up from 1,854
- Daily snacks: 12 grams, up from 4 grams
- Noncitrus fruit juices and nectars, children 5 and younger: 104 grams, up from 25 grams

- Carbonated soft drinks, children 5 and younger: 74 grams, up from 61
- Dark green vegetables: 10 grams, up from 8 grams
- Percentage of overweight Americans: 30.1, up from 22.2

– There are 28 grams to an ounce.

of 400,000 American deaths resulting "from diet-related illnesses like heart disease, diabetes, hypertension, and stroke." This statistic "details the extent of America's unfitness" (*Lexington-Herald Leader*, 1996, p. A3).

Making improved food choices should be an American priority. To develop autonomous, healthy food-selection behavior, students should be provided opportunities for reflective inquiry to develop personal responsibility for food choices (Contento, 1995). In order to accomplish this goal, there must be a shift from a transmittal-of-information, direct-teaching/telling method of instructional support to an approach involving students in processing information to achieve positive dietary behavioral changes (Sims, 1987). Several programs and kits have been developed specifically to provide intensive, multicomponent activities to improve food choices among America's youth (fig. 15.4).

FIGURE 15.3

The "New" Basic Food Guide Pyramid
A Guide to Daily Food Choices

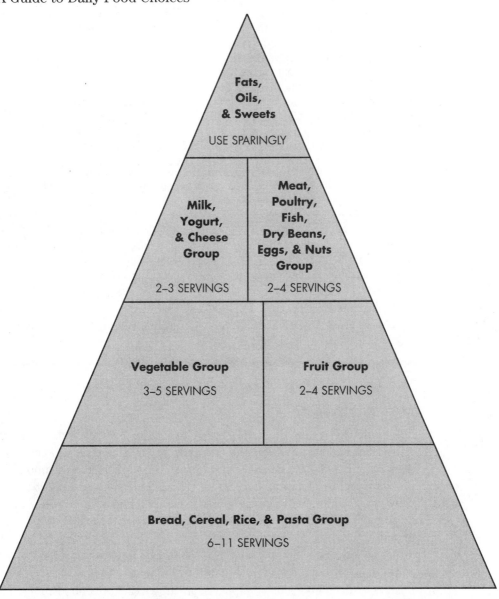

FIGURE 15.4

Nutrition Programs and Kits

Early Childhood Nutrition Program, developed by Jill Randell and Christine Olson, and *Nutrition Comes Alive,* Levels K–3, written by Susan Nelson and Martha C. Mapes, encourage the use of thinking skills to help children

- Develop good habits for nutritional wellbeing
- Know how to select from an array of foods
- Know how to discriminate about dietary advice
- Learn self-restraint when making food choices
- Develop attitudes toward food selection conducive to lifelong health
- Search out and decipher key nutritional information
- Differentiate between fact and opinion when viewing advertisements
- Think about how to make modifications in food choices and ingredients

In Contento, I. R. (1980, Summer). Thinking about nutrition education: What to teach, how to teach it, and what to measure. Teachers College Record, 81, *422–423.*

Nutrition, Food and Culture, 1985 Winner of the Gold Leaf Award for Excellence in Nutrition Education and published by the Education Department National Livestock and Meat Board, includes activities, study prints, and information to help students understand components of a well-balanced daily diet for people around the world, e.g., Finnish, Kenyan, Laps, the Masai, Napalese, Algerian, Mexican, Korean, Japanese, American.

Nutrition, Food and Culture (1982). Education Department of the National Livestock and Meat Board, Chicago, IL.

MATHEMATICS

A good **mathematics** program must cultivate the development of lifelong skills and a positive disposition toward mathematics. Math activities designed for children must spark interest in mathematical solutions to problems and be grounded in children's life experiences. In support of this view of teaching and learning mathematics, *The Curriculum and Evaluation Standards for School Mathematics* (NCTM, 1988) has urgently called for reform in the mathematics education of America's children. According to Price (1989), the "math gap" appears in preschoolers and widens progressively. This deficit leads educators to ask why this is so. Has there been too much emphasis on drill with little opportunity for children to use mathematics in purposeful ways? What will remedy the mathematics performance of America's children?

Although there is no single way to remedy American children's poor mathematical performance, the National Council of Teachers of Mathematics (NCTM) "envisions a curriculum in which children develop an understanding and critical awareness of how and when to use mathematical techniques as well as why they work and how they are developed" (NCTM, 1983). The current view of mathematics education, a movement from pure performance of techniques to include more reflective ways of knowing related to life, is evident in NCTM's key goals for mathematics education (fig. 15.5).

In the context of everyday life situations, effective mathematics teachers provide mathematical tools to aid children in making decisions and solving problems (Tharp, 1988) and promote a *spirit of inquiry* (Pappas, Kiefer, & Levstik, 1995, p. 182). In the context of a problem, teachers conduct a minilesson on different ways to use the computer to represent or calculate results of data collected by demonstrating multiple ways to express their thinking or by conferencing with them to help them solve problems. The most critical factor resulting in children's coming to understand mathematical concepts is to provide authentic learning situations requiring invented or culturally standard mathematical solutions.

In addition to using mathematical tools transmitted by their culture, children naturally communicate mathematical concepts in a variety of ways, for example, by drawing representations of mathematical ideas, by describing situations requiring logico-mathematical intelligence (Gardner, 1993), and by inventing mathematical procedures to represent ideas requiring mathematical explanations (Kamii, 1989). Steffe and Cobb (1988) and Kamii (1989) remind us that children learn more if they have an opportunity to construct an understanding than if they are locked into daily drill and practice sessions and workbooks.

FIGURE 15.5

National Council of Teachers of Mathematics: Key Goals for Students

- To learn to value mathematics
- To become confident in their ability to do mathematics
- To become mathematical problem solvers
- To learn to communicate mathematically
- To learn to reason mathematically

LESSON PLAN

TITLE: COLLECTING DATA, ANALYZING, REPRESENTING, AND MODIFYING FOOD CHOICES

Age Range: Early elementary, later elementary, and middle school

Time: One hour (to several weeks)

Content Areas:

 Mathematics

Health/Nutrition

Materials: Computer

Software: word processor, graphing package, spreadsheet

Calculators

Variety of paper and writing instruments

Model of the "New" Food Guide Pyramid (fig. 15.3)

Personal Food Diary or Spread Sheet for Data

Objectives:
- Students will select and use appropriate print materials to help themselves make healthy food choices.
- Students will analyze, evaluate, and apply information gathered from observations.
- Students will express information and ideas creatively using technology to represent the data collected related to their food choices.
- Students will demonstrate mathematical procedures to interpret and organize information for logical deductions.

- Students will collect, display, analyze, and interpret the data of personal food choices.

- Students will demonstrate skills and self-responsibility in understanding, achieving, and maintaining physical wellness.

- Students will evaluate dietary practices.

- Students will demonstrate decision-making process by making informed decisions about food choices.

- Students will recognize options, gather information, and propose alternative options for selecting healthy food to eat.

Beginning: The teacher and students participate in a discussion about the "new" Food Guide Pyramid. The teacher might ask if they have heard about the "new" Food Guide Pyramid and how it can be used to help students make food choices. The teacher tells the students they will be using this guide to develop a personal food diary form, analyze their food consumption in comparison to the recommendations on the guide, and design a food-consumption report and plan based on the data collected about their food consumption.

Students are given a copy of the Food Guide Pyramid to draft (on the computer or by hand) a personal food diary form to keep records of their food consumption (in servings) for seven consecutive days (USDA's Food Guide Pyramid, 1992, p. 11).

Middle: After drafting the personal food diary form, students use the form for a one-day trial and then revise and edit the form before continuing to record their food consumption data for seven consecutive days.

End: After seven days of data collecting, students analyze seven days of food consumption data comparing the quantity (in servings) of food they have eaten to the recommended number of servings described on the Food Guide Pyramid. Students may represent their findings in any form they choose (using a graph, on a list, or with a data chart) (fig. 15.6).

Students whose food consumption does not match the recommended number of day-by-day servings per category on the Food Guide Pyramid write a plan to modify their food consumption to conform to the number of servings recommended on the Food Guide Pyramid.

**Assessment
of Student
Learning:**

Students continue to record food consumption data for another week using their food consumption plan as a guide. At the end of the week, students will calculate their daily and weekly food consumption data, analyze data collected during the additional data collection week (fig. 15.7), and continue to modify eating habits to conform to the Food Guide Pyramid.

FIGURE 15.6

Food Data Chart

Dates	Sunday	Monday	Tuesday	Wednesday	Thursday	Friday	Saturday	# of Servings Data
								Fats & Oils
								Sweets
								Milk, yogurt, cheese
								Meats
								Eggs
								Nuts
								Vegetables
								Fruits
								Bread
								Cereal
								Rice & Pasta
								TOTAL # of Servings

FIGURE 15.7

Ways to Conceptually and Contextually Use Mathematical Knowledge

- Graphing data
- Using mathematical procedures/operations
- Measuring distance, time, and space
- Matching objects and ideas
- Classifying objects and ideas
- Combining information
- Comparing information
- Analyzing structures and patterns
- Representing geometric structure and spatial dimensions
- Using numbers to describe and compute
- Observing and describing change on patterns and functions

Adapted from Transformations: Kentucky's Curriculum Framework. *(1995), Frankfort, KY: Kentucky Department of Education.*

REFERENCES

Mathematics

Baker, A., & Baker, J. (1990). *Mathematics in process*. Portsmouth. NH: Heinemann.

Baker, D., Semple, C., & Stead, T. (1990). *How big is the moon? Whole math in action*. Portsmouth, NH: Heinemann.

Borasi, R. (1992). *Learning mathematics through inquiry*. Portsmouth, NH: Heinemann.

Countryman, J. (1992). *Writing to learn mathematics: Strategies that work, K–12*. Portsmouth, NH: Heinemann.

Fennema, E., Carpenter, T. P., & Peterson, P. L. (1989). Learning mathematics with understanding: Cognitively guided instruction. In J. E. Brophy (Ed.), *Advances in research on teaching* (Vol. 1). Greenwich, CT: JAI Press.

Fulwiler, T. (1982). Writing: An act of cognition. In C. W. Griffin (Ed.), *New directions for teaching and learning: No. 12. Teaching writing in all disciplines* (pp. 15–26). San Francisco: Jossey-Bass.

Gardner, H. (1993). *Multiple intelligences, the theory in practice: A reader*. New York: Basic Books.

Gelman, R., & Gallistel, C. R. (1978). *The child's understanding of number*. Cambridge, MA: Harvard University Press.

Greenberg, P. (1994). Ideas that work with young children: How and why to teach all aspects of preschool and kindergarten math, part 2. *Young Children, 49*(2), 12–18, +88.

Hendrickson, A. A. (1989). *Meaningful mathematics. Teacher's guide to lesson plans*. Washington, DC: National Science Foundation.

Kamii, C. (1985, September). Leading primary education toward excellence: Beyond worksheets and drill. *Young Children, 39*(6), 3–9.

Kamii, C. (1989). *Young children continue to reinvent arithmetic, 2nd Grade*. New York: Teachers College Press, Columbia University.

Kokoski, T. M., & Downing-Leffler, N. (1995). Boosting your science and math programs in early childhood education: Making the home-school connection. *Young Children, 50*(5), 35–39.

Kopp, J. (1992). *Frog math: Predict, ponder, play*. Berkley, CA: Lawrence Hall of Science, University of California.

Lamphere, P. (Ed.). (1994, November). Investigations. *Teaching Children Mathematics, 27*, 164–169.

Lilburn, P., & Rawson, P. (1994). *Let's talk math: Encouraging children to explore ideas*. Portsmouth, NH: Heinemann.

Math through children's literature: Activities that bring NCTM standards alive. Englewood, CO: Teacher Ideas Press.

National Council of Teachers of Mathematics. (1983). A position statement: Vertical acceleration. Reston, VA: Author.

National Council of Teachers of Mathematics. (1989). Curriculum standards for grades K–4. In *Curriculum and evaluation standards for school mathematics* (pp. 15–64). Reston, VA: Author.

Pappas, C. C., Kiefer, B. Z., & Levstik, L. S. (1995). *An integrated language perspective in the elementary school: Theory into action* (2nd ed.) (pp. 97–105, 181–185). White Plains, New York: Longman Publishers, Inc.

Piaget, J. (1953). How children form mathematics concepts. *Scientific American, 189*, 74–79.

Price, G. G. (1989). Research in review: Mathematics in early childhood. *Young Children, 44*(4), 53–58.

Riley, M. S., Greeno, J. G., & Heller, J. I. (1983). Development of children's problem solving ability in arithmetic. In H. Ginsburg (Ed.), *The development of mathematical thinking* (pp. 153–196). New York: Academic Press.

Rowan, T., & Bourne, B. (1994). *Thinking like mathematicians: Putting NCTM standards into practice*. Portsmouth, NH: Heinemann.

Siegler, R. S. (1983). Information processing approaches to development. In W. Kessen (Ed.), *Handbook of Child Psychology* (4th ed.) (Vol. 1) (pp. 129–211). New York: Wiley.

Steffe, L. P., & Cobb, P. (1988). *Construction of arithmetical meanings and strategies*. New York: Springer-Verlag.

Tharp, R. C., & Gallimore, R. (1988). *Rousing minds to life: Teaching, learning, and schooling in social context*. Cambridge, England: Cambridge University Press.

Van de Walle, J. A., & Holbrook, H. (1987). Patterns, thinking, and problem solving. *Arithmetic Teacher, 34*, 6–12.

Vygotsky, L. S. (1978). *Mind and society: The development of higher psychological processes*. Cambridge, MA: Harvard University Press.

Vygotsky, L. S. (1981). *Thought and language*. Cambridge, MA: MIT Press.

Wang, M. C., Resnick, L. B., & Boozer, R. F. (1971). The sequence of development of some early mathematics behaviors. *Child Development, 42*, 1767–1778.

Whitin, D. J. (1994). Literature and mathematics in preschool and primary: The right connection. *Young Children, 49*(2), 4–11.

Whitin, D. J., Mills, H., & O'Keefe, T. (1990). *Living and learning mathematics: Stories and strategies for supporting mathematical literacy*. Portsmouth, NH: Heinemann.

Zaslavsky, C. (1986). *Preparing young children for math: A book of games*. New York: Schocken Books.

Health/Nutrition

Bianchi, A. (1992, March). Nutrition and fitness. *Creative Classroom, 6*(5), 75–84.

Burns, M. (1978). *Good for me! All about food in 32 bites*. New York: Little Brown & Co.

Contento, I. R. (1980, Summer). Thinking about nutrition education: What to teach, how to teach it, and what to measure. *Teachers College Record, 81*, 422–423.

Contento, I. R. (1988). *Manual for developing a nutrition education curriculum*. Paris: UNESCO Division of Science & Technology & Environments Education.

Contento, I. R. (Ed.). (1995, November-December). Theoretical framework or models for nutrition education. *Journal of Nutrition Education, 27*(6), 287–290.

Evers, C. L. (1995). *How to teach nutrition to kids.* Tigard, OR: 24 Carrot Press.

The food label, the pyramid and you. (1994, September). Home and Garden Bulletin Number 266. Washington, DC: United States Department of Agriculture.

Jones, R. L. (1996, January 3) Diet advice on sugar, fat moderated. *Lexington-Herald Leader*, p. A3.

Lindroth, L. K. (1995, November/December). Internet connections. *Teaching K–8*, 74.

Mapes, M. C., & Thonney, P. (1995). *Nutrition comes alive—Level 3—The Food Peddlers Nutrition Educator's Guide* (rev. ed.). Ithaca, New York: Cornell University Press.

Sandeman, A. (1995). *Eating.* Brookfield, CT: Copper Beech Books.

Sims, L. S. (1987). Nutrition education research: Researching toward the leading edge. *Journal of American Dietetics Association*, 510–518.

USDA's Food Guide Pyramid. (1992, April). Washington, DC: United States Department of Agriculture.

BOOK SUGGESTIONS FOR CHILDREN
Mathematics

Anno, M. (1982). *Anno's counting house.* New York: Philomel.

Anno, M. (1987). *Anno's math games.* New York: Philomel.

Anno, M. (1989). *Anno's math games II.* New York: Philomel.

Anno, M. (1991). *Anno's math games III.* New York: Philomel.

Anno, M., & Anno, M. (1983). *Anno's mysterious multiplying jar.* New York: Philomel.

Clifton, L. (1970). *Some of the days of Everett Anderson.* New York: Holt, Rinehart and Winston.

Conford, E. (1989). *What's cooking, Jenny Archer?* New York: Little, Brown & Co.

dePaola, T. (1982). *Strega Nona's magic lesson.* New York: Harcourt Brace Jovanovich.

Giganti, P., Jr. (1988). *How many sails? A counting book.* New York: Greenwillow.

Hoban, T. (1972). *Count and see.* New York: Macmillan.

Hoberman, M. A. (1978). *A house is a house for me*. New York: Viking-Penguin.

Lobel, A. (1970). *The lost button*. New York: Harper & Row.

McKissack, P. (1993). *A million fish . . . more or less*. New York: Knopf.

McMillan, B. (1986). *Counting wildflowers*. New York: Lothrop, Lee & Shephard.

McMillan, B. (1989). *Time to . . .* New York: Lothrop, Lee & Shephard.

Reid, M. (1990). *The button box*. New York: Dutton.

Roy, R. (1988). *Whose shoes are these?* New York: Clarion.

Russo, M. (1988). *Only six more days*. New York: Greenwillow.

Scieszka, J. (1995). *Math curse*. New York: Viking.

Viorst, J. (1978). *Alexander, who used to be rich last Sunday*. New York: Atheneum.

Weston, M. (1982). *Math for Smarty Pants*. New York: Little, Brown & Co.

Whitin, D. J., & Wilde, S. (1992). *Read any good math lately? Children's books for mathematical learning K–6*. Portsmouth, NH: Heinemann.

Food-Related Topics

Ackerman, K. (1992). *I know a place*. Boston: Houghton Mifflin.

Adoff, A. (1979). *Eats poems*. New York: Lothrop, Lee & Shephard.

Aker, S. (1990). *What comes in 2's, 3's, and 4's*. New York: Simon & Schuster.

Albny, C. L., & Webb, L. S. (1993). *The multicultural cookbook for students*. Phoenix, AZ: Oryx.

Aliki. (1983). *A medieval feast*. New York: Harper Row.

Aliki. (1983). *A medieval wedding*. New York: Crowell.

Barber, J. (1993). *Of cabbages and chemistry*. New York: Dale Seymour.

Barrett, J. (1978). *Cloudy with a chance of meatballs*. New York: Macmillan.

Belton, S. (1993). *May'naise sandwiches and sunshine tea*. New York: Butterfly Children's Books.

Bose, S. S. (1988). *Know your fruits*. Tokyo: Froebel-Kan.

Bose, S. S. (1988). *Know your vegetables*. Tokyo: Froebel-Kan.

Boujon, C. (1987). *Bon appetite, Mr. Rabbit*. New York: M. K. McElderry.

Breckler, R. (1992). *Hoang breaks the lucky teapot*. Boston: Houghton Mifflin.

Bruchac, J. (1993). *The first strawberries: A Cherokee story*. New York: Dial Press.

Busenberg, B. (1995). *Vanilla, chocolate, and strawberry: The story of your favorite flavors*. New York: Lerner.

Carle, E. (1969). *The very hungry caterpillar*. New York: Putnam.

Carle, E. (1993). *Today is Monday*. New York: Philomel Books.

Carrick, D. (1985). *Milk*. New York: Greenwillow.

Catling, P. S. (1981). *The chocolate touch*. New York: Bantam.

Daddona, M. (1980). *Hoe, hoe, hoe, watch my garden grow*. New York: Addison-Wesley.

Darling, B. (1992). *Valerie and the silver pear*. New York: Four Winds Press.

dePaola, T. (1975). *Strega Nona*. New York: Prentice-Hall.

Dunning, S. (1966). *Reflections on a gift of watermelon pickle*. New York: Scott, Foresman.

Ehlert, L. (1987). *Growing vegetable soup*. San Diego, CA: Harcourt Brace Jovanovich.

Ehlert, L. (1989). *Eating the alphabet: Fruit and vegetables from A to Z*. San Diego, CA: Harcourt Brace Jovanovich.

Fox, M. S. (1990). *Possum magic*. San Diego, CA: Harcourt Brace Jovanovich.

Friedman, I. (1984). *How my parents learned to eat*. Boston: Houghton Mifflin.

Gershator, D., & Gershator, P. (1995). *Bread is for the eating*. New York: Holt.

Giblin, J. C. (1987). *From hand to mouth, or how we invented knives, forks, spoons and chopsticks and the table manners to go with them*. New York: Crowell.

Goldstein, B. S. (Ed.). (1992). *What's on the menu?* New York: Viking.

Gwynne, F. (1987). *A chocolate mouse for dinner*. New York: Prentice-Hall.

Hall, D. (1979). *Ox-cart man*. New York: Viking.

Howard, T. A., with Howard, S. (1992). *Kids ending hunger: What can we do?* Kansas City, MO: Andrews and McMeel.

Janeczko, P. B. (1987). *This delicious day: 65 poems*. New York: Orchard Books.

Jenness, A. (1978). *The bakery factory*. New York: Crowell.

Jonas, A. (1983). *Round trip*. New York: Greenwillow.

Jordan, H. J. (1960). *How a seed grows*. New York: Harper & Row.

Keller, C. (1980). *Going bananas: Jokes for kids*. Englewood Cliffs, NJ: Prentice-Hall.

Kellogg, S. (1985). *How much is a million?* New York: Lothrop, Lee & Shephard.

Foodworks: An Ontario Science Centre book. (1986). Toronto: Kids Can Press.

Kimmel, E. A. (1994). *Anasi and the talking melon*. New York: Holiday House.

King, E. (1996). *Chile fever: A celebration of peppers*. New York: Dutton.

Lasker, J. (1976). *Merry ever after*. New York: Viking.

Lester, A. (1986). *Clive eats alligators*. Boston: Houghton Mifflin.

Manushkin, F. (1996). *The matzah that Papa brought home*. New York: Scholastic.

McCully, E. (1973). *How to eat fried worms*. New York: F. Watts.

McCunn, R. L. (1983). *Pie biter*. San Francisco, CA: Design Enterprises.

Meitzer, M. (1992). *The amazing potato: A story in which the Incas, conquistadors, Marie Antoinette, Thomas Jefferson, wars, famines, immigrants, and French fries all play a part*. New York: Harper & Row.

Modell, F. (1988). *Ice cream soup*. New York: Greenwillow.

Mollel, T. (1992). *Rhinos for lunch, elephants for supper*. Boston: Houghton Mifflin.

Morris, A. (1989). *Bread, bread, bread*. New York: Mulberry.

Mosel, A. (1975). *The funny little woman*. New York: Dutton.

Ormond, J. (1981). *Sunshine*. New York: Lothrop, Lee & Shepard.

Perl, L. (1977). *Slumps, grunts, and snickerdoodles*. Boston: Houghton Mifflin.

Pittman, H. (1992). *A grain of rice*. New York: Bantam Skylark.

Priceman, M. (1994). *How to make an apple pie and see the world*. New York: Random House.

Rylant, C. (1995). *Mr. Putter and Tabby pick the pears*. San Diego, CA: Harcourt Brace.

Schertle, A. (1996). *Down the road*. New York: Harcourt Brace.

Seed, D. (1993). *The amazing egg book*. Toronto: Kids Can Press.

Sharmat, M. (1987). *Gregory the terrible eater*. New York: Checkerboard Press.

Shelby, A. (1991). *Potluck*. New York: Orchard Books.

Showers, P. (1985). *What happens to showers*. New York: Harper & Row.

Slepian, J., & Seidler, A. (1967). *The hungry thing*. New York: Scholastic.

Smith, R. K. (1978). *Chocolate fever*. New York: Dell.

Soto, G. (1993). *Too many tamales*. New York: Putnam.

Soto, G. (1995). *Chato's kitchen*. New York: Putnam.

Spinner, S. (1994). *Aliens for dinner*. New York: Random House.

Stevens, J. R. (1995). *Carlos and the cornfield/Carlos y la milpa de maiz*. Flagstaff, AZ: Northland.

Thomas, J. C. (1993). *Brown honey in broomwheat tea*. New York: HarperCollins.

Tsutsui, Y. (1987). *Before the picnic*. New York: Philomel.

Walker, B. (1995). *Little house cookbook*. New York: Harper Trophy.

Watson, C. N. (1987). *The little pigs' cookbook*. New York: Little, Brown.

Wiesner, D. (1992). *June 29, 1999*. New York: Clarion.

Williams, V. B. (1986). *Cherries and cherry pits*. New York: Philomel.

Yee, P. (1992). *Roses sing on new snow: A delicious tale*. New York: Macmillan.

LEARNING CENTERS, ACTIVITY CARDS, AND MOVEMENT

KEY IDEAS

■ Learning center activities provide space and time for students to practice skills and rethink concepts introduced during small-group-time workshops.

■ Learning center activities provide opportunities for students to become self-sufficient learners.

■ Learning center activities provide opportunities for students to integrate curriculum, learn complex ideas, and participate in observation tasks.

■ Students observe movement patterns among different groups; for example, transportation planners, dancers, builders, athletes, musicians, visual artists, and sculptors.

- Ideas are expressed through movement.

- Emotions are expressed through movement.

- Observation and analysis of movement provide information for decision making, problem solving, and understanding the role of movement in many life situations.

- "Movement *exploration* provides opportunities for problem solving, discovery, and self-expression" (Pica, 1995, p. 30).

STUDENT-CENTERED ACTIVE LEARNING CENTERS WITH ACTIVITY CARDS

The lesson in this chapter departs from the usual lesson plan format and illustrates a lesson presentation for later elementary learners using a Sample Activity Card format (Wassermann, 1990). The lesson in this chapter, Observing and Representing Movement, is presented on an Activity Card (see fig. 16.1).

To introduce students to Activity Cards as a guide for tasks at learning centers, the teacher may use an Activity Card first with students during a small group workshop. During the workshop, the teacher would present the sample activity and encourage students to choose replay activity suggestions during learning center time. Activity Cards also may be placed in a **learning center** where appropriate and ample materials are available for independent investigation of the sample activity and replay activity suggestions. A pretaped reading of the Activity Card may be made by the teacher, a parent, or a student to provide an audio guide for using the Activity Card. This is an effective way to adapt the activity format for students who are visually impaired or for students who cannot read the Activity Card independently. To provide other support for learners at learning centers, teachers, other adults, and more developed peers may act as observers—participants may offer just enough scaffolding to assist students in the learning process in centers (Katz & Chard, 1991; Vygotsky, 1962). Carefully interjected modeling, perhaps during a small-group workshop, and ongoing guidance provide essential support for learners as they construct knowledge and develop skills in centers.

While Activity Cards for practicing skills and reconsidering concepts presented in small-group-time workshops are appropriate for later elementary students, open-ended, hands-on learning centers that are less teacher directed and task specific are more appropriate for early elementary students. A well-designed **learning environment** for students includes a

FIGURE 16.1

Sample Activity Card
Observing and Representing Movement

Title: Observe and represent "people" movements

Concepts: Movements of the body can be observed and represented in a visual art piece to demonstrate a person's understanding of the way the body moves.

Thinking Operations: Observing, comparing, interpreting data; designing sculptures and other visual arts pieces to represent movements observed.

Materials: Movement situations, e.g., a dance, sporting events, children on a playground, baby moving, musical recital or practice, etc. Clay, Playdoh, knife, scraps of wood, nails, hammer, wire, wire cutters, paper, scissors, glue, tape, camera, film, writing instruments, computer, and drawing program software

Sample Activity:
- Select several situations to observe the way people move, e.g., sports events, dance performances, children on a playground, baby crawling, musician, etc. Make several observations about the way people move.

Sample Debriefing Questions for Assessment of Student Learner:
Asking Students to Reflect on Their Observations
- What observations did you make about how people move?
- What differences did you observe when you watched people moving in the various situations? Sporting event? Dance? Children on the playground? Baby crawling? Musician playing?
- Which was more fluid? Which was more rigid?
- Which required grander gestures? smaller gestures?
- Which movements were simple? more complex?
- Why do you suppose we need to know about movement? What are your ideas?
- How would you position your body in a frozen form to represent a variety of movements you observed in the various situations?

Challenging Students Beyond Their Observations
- When you observed sporting events, you found grander gestures were used than when you watched a baby move. What are some of your ideas about these two ways of moving?
- When you observed children on the playground, you found many types of movements just as when you watched athletes. How would you explain the movements of these two groups of individuals?

Replay Activity Suggestions:
- Use any or all of the art supplies to create a single sculpture that represents a position of one body movement you observed.
- Mime randomly and sequentially movements you observed.

Continued

FIGURE 16.1 *Continued*

- Create a series of sculptures representing movements of people within one situation you observed.
- Create a series of sculptures representing a sequence of movements of people within a situation you observed.
- Sculpt several figures representing a variety of movements of one person you observed.
- Describe a sequence of movement patterns orally and/or in writing.
- Take photographs of people in motion. Use these photographs as references for developing sculptures representing movements observed in the photographs.
- Interview a choreographer to learn the terminology used in dance to describe and record dance movements.
- Repeat the activities above after observing movements of a variety of animals.
- Draw figures representing various movements on the computer.
- Read stories about movement.

variety of learning centers to accommodate both the early and later elementary student (fig. 16.2).

Some learning centers should be stocked with a variety of open-ended raw materials, for example, different types of paper, many kinds of writing instruments, paints, blocks, fasteners, measuring devices, scissors, and other materials students may use independently in a variety of ways. Other centers may include materials to encourage play and replay of predesigned activities such as those suggested on the Sample Activity Card.

When designing learning environments, teachers should consider the organizational features of learning centers as well as types of materials and activities associated with each center (fig. 16.3).

An Activity Card holder may be constructed and used to hold Activity Cards (fig. 16.4).

The holder displays the cards and keeps Activity Cards from getting misplaced or lost among materials used by students to carry out tasks.

Self-sufficiency, a lifelong goal of education, can be nurtured if students have daily opportunities to work independently in active learning environments that include learning centers (Kentucky Department of Education, 1995; Hohmann & Weikart, 1995; Wassermann, 1990). Open-ended, hands-on learning centers and centers guided by Activity Cards should be a part of the daily learning environment. According to Hohmann and Weikart (1995, p. 5), "through active learning—having direct and immediate

---

FIGURE 16.2

Suggested Learning Center

Typical Quadrant Arrangement
Art
Block
House/Family Living
Quiet

Typical Academic-Named Centers
Fine Arts
Language Arts
Mathematics
Practical Living
Science
Social Studies
Vocation Studies

Eclectic Arrangement
All About
Art
Block
Multimedia Center
Construction and Woodworking
Family Living Center
Games
Listening
Math/Science
Music
Reading
Research
Social Studies
Writing

Seven Multiple Intelligence Arrangement (Gardner, 1983; 1995)
Interpersonal
Intrapersonal
Bodily-Kinesthetic
Linguistics
Logicomathematical
Musical
Spatial

Eighth Intelligence
Naturalist (Gardner, 1996)

FIGURE 16.3

Organizational Features of Active Learning Centers

Space
- Ample space to accommodate group size
- Safe
- Aesthetically appealing (Trawick-Smith, 1992)
- Comfortable
- Appropriate social and space density
- Outdoor spaces including playgrounds and natural spaces (Harris, 1991)
- Spaces allowing students to see the world from different vantage points
- Spaces that accommodate various group sizes
- Spaces adapted for special needs children

Materials
- Well organized
- Durable
- Varied by developmental ranges
- Varied to address different interests
- Varied to address different cultures, races, genders, family backgrounds (Derman-Sparks, 1989)
- Varied to address different academic expectations
- Easy for children to access, use, and return
- Well maintained
- Items from the real world
- Places to display finished work
- Places for ongoing projects (Katz, 1991)
- Technology-related hardware and software
- Materials adapted for special needs children

Guidance
- Adult nearby to provide verbal, nonverbal, and environmental support (Hohmann, 1993; Bruner, 1966)
- Playmates/peers (Bruner, 1966)
- Choices encouraged and supported
- Support adapted for special needs children
- Provide trusting and accepting atmosphere

Time
- Enough time to plan, implement, and reflect on work/play
- Enough time for set up and clean up

FIGURE 16.4

Activity Card Holder

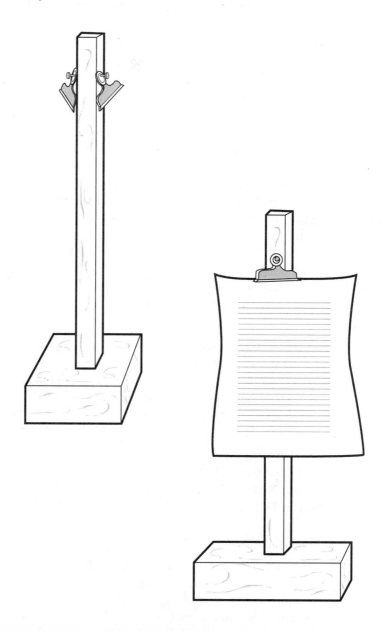

experiences and deriving meaning from them through reflection—young children contract knowledge that helps them make sense of the world." Centers provide an effective means toward achieving this objective. The establishment of an active learning environment takes learners beyond drill and practice activities (Kamii, 1987).

Piaget reminds us that "knowledge arises neither from objects nor the child, but from interactions between the child and those objects" (Kamii, 1987). Therefore, children must have many opportunities for *play-reflect-replay* with materials and ideas (Wassermann, 1990, p. 3). Learning centers provide an ideal environment for students to play and replay activities. In addition to offering multiple opportunities for students to play again with objects, formulate ideas, and practice skills, Activity Cards suggest tasks to call for the generation of ideas, challenge students' thinking, require higher-order thinking, and play with *big ideas*—the important concepts of the curriculum (Wassermann, 1990). Students are supported in their endeavors to construct knowledge in ways that make sense to them by working in the open-ended architecture of the tasks on Activity Cards and in open-ended learning centers. In learning centers and when completing Activity Card tasks, learners create understandings because they are actively talking to each other, working together, laughing, speculating, measuring, experimenting, and sharing ideas (Wassermann, 1990).

To provide learners with opportunities to extract, analyze and synthesize concepts, and use skills, a variety of teaching strategies should be practiced, including discovery learning (Fogarty, 1991). One way to implement discovery learning is for teachers to design and implement learning environments that include materials and investigative tasks in learning centers to encourage students to make sense of ideas and communicate ideas in many ways (fig. 16.5).

Developing and presenting student-centered, active learning centers that include activities like the sample activity and the replay activity suggestions on the Activity Card and open-ended centers provide meaningful and purposeful learning contexts beneficial for learners (fig. 16.6).

MOVEMENT

Confucius said, "What I hear, I forget. What I see, I remember. What I do, I know." Most students acquire understanding of concepts and skills through a combination of modalities, including auditory, visual, tactile, and kinesthetic (Charlesworth, 1992; Reiff, 1992). Gardner (1983, p. 206) defines movement as a *person's capacity to control bodily motions and*

FIGURE 16.5

Ways to Make Sense of Ideas and Communicate Them

- Organize information and materials through development and use of classification rules and systems
- Write using appropriate forms, conventions, and styles to communicate ideas and information to different audiences for different purposes
- Speak using appropriate forms, conventions, and styles to communicate ideas and information to different audiences for different purposes
- Use visual arts to make sense of ideas and communicate ideas
- Use music to make sense of ideas and communicate ideas
- Use movement to make sense of ideas and communicate ideas
- Use computers and other kinds of technology to collect, organize, and communicate information and ideas

Adapted from Transformations: Kentucky's Curriculum Framework. *(1995).*
Kentucky Department of Education, Frankfort, KY.

FIGURE 16.6

Benefits of Student-Centered Active Learning Centers

- Enhance language development
- Encourage children to use language purposefully and meaningfully
- Cultivate higher-order thinking
- Encourage metacognition
- Develop intrinsic motivation
- Develop perseverance
- Cultivate positive disposition toward learning
- Encourage invention and generativity of ideas
- Increase capacity for risk taking
- Provide a setting for students to work through social problems
- Provide situations for students to develop self-sufficiency
- Increase skill level performance
- Improve conceptual understanding and performance
- Provide time and space practice
- Support opportunities for cooperative learning
- Support opportunities for interpersonal development
- Provide intrapersonal development

(Bloom, 1964; Katz, 1991; Hohmann & Weikart, 1995; Wassermann, 1990;
Slavin, 1983; Johnson & Johnson 1989; Gardner 1984).

handle objects skillfully. Learning time, therefore, should be designed and implemented to give students opportunities to include and integrate these four learning modalities. Movement is essential to every learning experience (Hohmann & Weikart, 1995, p. 411).

Unfortunately, teachers often eliminate or reduce the amount of time for bodily kinesthetic activities or movement to accommodate academic learning time, despite documented observations that movement development and bodily expression are related to acquisition of subsequent knowledge and mental function (Piaget, 1952; Montessori, 1949). In some schools teachers inappropriately eliminate recess, gym, or outdoor time as a punishment for students who do not complete their "real" school work. According to Phyllis Weikart, movement experiences are needed but neglected (1991). Garnet (1982) reminds us of the ways movement is part of life.

Gardner (1983) and others (Campbell, Campbell, & Dickinson, 1992; Lazear, 1991) stress the inclusion of kinesthetic activities in the daily routine and standard curriculum because many learners need movement to successfully express and make sense of their ideas using the movement mode (1983). Other studies and groups support the role of movement in abstract learning (Coghill, 1929; Jersild, 1954; Jaques-Dalcrose, 1931; National Dance Association, 1990; Taras, 1992).

Movement exploration encourages students to experience, discover, and "construct meaning from and/or communicate ideas and emotions through movement" (Kentucky Department of Education, 1993, p. 42). Additionally, kinesthetic knowledge and performance is supported more effectively by teachers who give students opportunities to "solve problems, invent their own solutions to challenges, and make abstract concrete" (Pica, 1995, p. 23). A guided discovery or exploration approach, rather than a "demonstration and imitation" approach, provides a more interesting and effective environment for learning to communicate ideas and emotions through movement. Further, kinesthetic activities included in the standard curriculum have the potential to support cross-cultural learning and cross-curricular learning (Derman-Sparks, 1989). Two other areas of development are also enhanced by regular inclusion of movement in the curriculum: creativity (Torrance & Goff, 1989) and cooperation (Slavin, 1983; Johnson, Johnson, & Smith, 1991; Johnson & Johnson, 1988).

Activities can combine locomotor, nonlocomotor, manipulative, and gymnastic skills (fig. 16.7).

Regardless of the framework a teacher selects to serve as a guide for activity development (figs. 16.8 and 16.9), activities can be developed to

---

FIGURE 16.7

Movement Skills

Nonlocomotor Skills
Stretching
Bending
Sitting
Shaking
Turning
Rocking
Swaying
Swinging
Twisting
Dodging
Falling
Dancing

Locomotor Skills
Crawling
Creeping
Walking
Running
Jumping
Leaping
Galloping
Hopping
Sliding
Skipping
Step-hopping

Manipulative Skills
Pulling
Pushing
Lifting
Striking
Throwing
Kicking
Ball rolling
Volleying
Bouncing
Catching
Striking
Dribbling

Gymnastic Skills
Rolling
Transferring weight
Balancing
Climbing
Hanging and swinging

Adapted from Pica, R. (1995). **Experiences in movement with music activities and theory.** *Albany, NY: Delmar Publishers.*

---

include opportunities for students to incorporate many forms of movement exploration and expression as ways of demonstrating their understanding of movement concepts and skills.

In student-centered classrooms, teachers and students often collaborate to design learning centers by (1) initiating center activities that grow from personal interests and intentions; (2) choosing materials to carry out the activity; and (3) deciding what to do with the materials, where to work, with whom to work, and how long to work (Hohmann & Weikart, 1995, p. 40). In this type of learning environment, individuals have many opportunities

---

FIGURE 16.8

Key Movement Experiences

- Moving in nonlocomotor ways
- Moving in locomotor ways
- Moving with objects
- Expressing creativity in movement
- Describing movement
- Acting upon movement directions
- Feeling and expressing a steady beat
- Moving in sequences to a common beat

FIGURE 16.9

Movement Demonstrators

- DEMONSTRATE locomotor and nonlocomotor movement elements combined and separately to express ideas or emotions
- EXPRESS ideas/emotions through movement, e.g., body awareness, space awareness, time, force, technique, relationship
- ANALYZE ideas or emotions expressed in movement sequence using basic terms
- CREATE a movement sequence with a beginning, middle, and end
- ANALYZE the similarities and differences of a variety of dance forms (e.g., ballet, modern, jazz, ethnic, folk, social, and square) among diverse cultures
- CHOREOGRAPH a movement sequence that expresses ideas or emotions
- CREATE and evaluate a dance performance using appropriate technical, performance, and thematic elements

Adapted from Transformations: Kentucky Curriculum Framework. *(1995).*
Kentucky Department of Education, Frankfort, KY.

---

to connect school and life learning through investigative activities (Dewey, 1933) while maintaining enthusiasm for learning.

Dewey (1933, p. 34) instructs the educator "to protect the *spirit of inquiry*, to keep it from becoming blasé from over-excitement, wooden from routine, fossilized through dogmatic instruction, or dissipated by random exercise upon trivial things." One way to foster everlasting love for learning is for teachers to include key actions of teachers throughout the daily routine to establish and maintain active learning centers (fig. 16.10).

Center activities in this lesson plan are designed to encourage exploration to increase self-sufficiency, love of learning, understanding of complex

---

FIGURE 16.10

Key Actions of Teachers to Establish and Maintain Active Learning Centers

- Provide aesthetically pleasing work space, e.g., consider color, texture, lighting, landscape
- Provide a variety of work spaces, i.e., individual, small group, large group, large and small, high and low, private and open
- Provide interesting and varied materials
- Make materials accessible
- Develop a system for organizing materials, i.e., according to difficulty level, academic concepts, or core content areas
- Include opportunities for students to develop plans for their work/play
- Allot a minimum of forty-five minutes per day for investigative work/play
- Seek out students' intentions
- Converse with students
- Focus on actions of students
- Encourage students to solve their own problems
- Listen for students' thinking
- Ask questions to encourage students' thinking
- Offer choices
- Allow students' to adjust or change their plans
- Provide ways for students to work cooperatively and interactively
- Include opportunities for students to reflect and revise
- Provide opportunities for students to use "replay" activities
- Give students opportunities to use the same materials in different ways
- Assist instruction, as needed
- Design ways to assess students' center work/play, e.g., teacher observation and anecdotal recording, photograph work, video- or audiotape work, portfolio file, self-assessment journals or cards
- Develop a process that includes a combination of the students' improvised ideas and suggestions, given with light input by the teacher
- Accommodate special needs children (Knight & Wadsworth, 1993; Loovis, 1990)

(Bloom, 1972; Vygotsky, 1968; Crosser, 1990; Trawick-Smith, 1992; Hohmann & Weikart, 1995; Wassermann, 1990.)

---

ideas, and improvement of fundamental skills. Additionally, the activities suggested on the Sample Activity Card develop confidence and poise; encourage students' taking responsibility for their own work; help develop patience with oneself and one's peers; and lead to students' planning, implementing, and reflecting upon their own ideas and the ideas of others (Bloom, 1964; Vygotsky, 1962; Crosser, 1992; Trawick-Smith, 1992; Hohmann & Weikart, 1995; Wassermann, 1990).

REFERENCES

Armstrong, T. (1993). *Seven kinds of smart*. New York: Penguin.

Bloom, B. (1964). *A taxonomy of educational objectives*. New York: McKay.

Bruner, J. (1966). *On knowing*. Cambridge, MA: Belknap Press.

Campbell, L., Campbell, B., & Dickinson, D. (1992). *Teaching and learning through the multiple intelligences*. Seattle, WA: New Horizons for Learning.

Charlesworth, R. (1992). *Understanding child development*. Albany, NY: Delmar.

Coghill, G. E. (1929). *Anatomy and the problem of behavior*. Cambridge, England: Cambridge University Press.

Crosser, S. (1992). Managing the early childhood classroom. *Young Children, 47*(2), 23–29.

Derman-Sparks, L. (1989). *Anti-bias curriculum: Tools for empowering young children*. Washington, DC: National Association for the Education of Young Children.

Dewey, J. (1916). *Democracy and education*. New York: Macmillan.

Dewey, J. (1933). How we think: A restatement of the relation of reflective thinking to the educative process. Boston: Heath.

Dewey, J. (1938/1968). *Education and experience*. New York: Macmillan. (Reprinted).

Fauth, B. (1990). Linking the visual arts with drama, movement, and dance for young children. In W. J. Stinson (Ed.), *Moving and learning for the young child* (pp. 159–187). Reston, VA: American Alliance for Health, Physical Education, Recreation, and Dance.

Fogarty, R. (1991). *The mindful school: How to integrate the curricula*. Palatine, IL: Skylight Publishing.

Gabbard, C. P. (1992). *Lifelong motor development*. Dubuque, IA: Wm. C. Brown.

Gardner, H. (1983). *Frames of mind: The theory of multiple intelligences*. New York: Basic Books.

Gardner, H. (1995). Interview: Howard Gardner on the eighth intelligence: Seeing the world. *Dimensions of Early Childhood, 23*(4), 5–7.

Garnet, E. D. (1982). *Movement in life*. Princeton, NJ: Princeton Book Co.

Harris, V. (1991, March/April). Open-air learning experiences. *High/Scope Extensions, 6*(1), pp. 1–3.

Hohmann, C. (1992). *High/Scope K–3 curriculum series: Learning environment*. Ypsilanti, MI: High/Scope Press.

Hohmann, M., & Weikart, D. (1995). *Educating young children*. Ypsilanti, MI: High/Scope Press.

Jaques-Dalcrose, E. (1931). *Eurhythmics, art, and education* (F. Rothwell, Trans.; C. Cox, Ed.). New York: A. S. Barnes.

Jersild, A. T. (1954). *Child psychology*. Englewood Cliffs, NJ: Prentice-Hall.

Johnson, D., & Johnson, R. (1988). *Cooperation in the classroom*. Edina, MN: Interaction Book Company.

Johnson, D., Johnson, R., & Smith, K. (1991). *Active learning: Cooperation in the college classroom*. Edina, MN: Interaction Book Company.

Kamii, C. (1987). Leading primary toward excellence: Beyond worksheets and drill. *Young Children, 40*(6), 3–9.

Katz, L., & Chard, S. (1991). *Engaging children's minds: A project approach*. Norwood, NJ: Ablex Publishing Corporation.

Kentucky Department of Education. (1993 & 1995). *Transformations: Kentucky's curriculum framework*. Frankfort, KY: Author.

Knight, D., & Wadsworth, D. (1993). Physically challenged students. *Childhood Education, 69*(4), 211–15.

Lazear, D. (1991). *Seven ways of knowing: Teaching for the multiple intelligences*. Palatine, IL: Skylight Publishing.

Loovis, E. M. (1990). Behavioral disabilities. In J. P. Winnick (Ed.), *Adapted physical education and sport* (pp. 195–207). Champaign, IL: Human Kinetics.

Montessori, M. (1949). *The asorbent mind*. Madras, India: Kalakshertra Publications.

Myers, B. K., & Maurer, K. (1987, July). Teaching with less talking: Learning centers in kindergarten. *Young Children, 42*(5), 20–27.

National Dance Association. (1990). *Guide to creative dance for the young child*. Reston, VA: Author.

Piaget, J. (1952). *The origins of intelligence in children*. New York: International Universities Press.

Pica, R. (1990). *Early elementary children moving and learning*. Champaign, IL: Human Kinetics.

Pica, R. (1990). *Preschoolers moving and learning*. Champaign, IL: Human Kinetics.

Pica, R. (1993). *Upper elementary children moving and learning*. Champaign, IL: Human Kinetics.

Pica, R. (1995). *Experiences in movement with music activities and theory*. Albany, NY: Delmar Publishers, p. 129.

Reiff, J. C. (1992). *Learning styles: What research says to the teacher series*. Washington, DC: National Education Association.

Schweinhart, L., Weikart, D., & Larner, M. B. (1986, March). Consequences of three preschool curriculum models through age 15. *Early Childhood Research Quarterly, 1*(1), 15–45.

Shipley, D. (1993). *Empowering children: Play-based curriculum for lifelong learning*. Scarborough, Ontario: Nelson Canada.

Slavin, R. (1983). *Student team learning*. Washington, DC: National Education Association.

Taras, H. L. (1992). *Physical activity of young children in relation to physical and mental health*. In C. M. Hendricks (Ed.), *Young children on the grow: Health, activity, and education in the preschool setting* (pp. 33–44). Washington, DC: Eric Clearing House.

Torrance, E. P., & Goff, K. (1989). A quiet revolution. *Journal of Creative Behavior, 23*(2), 136–145.

Trawick-Smith, J. (1992). The classroom environment affects children's play and development. *Dimensions of Early Childhood, 20*(3), 27–30.

Vygotsky, L. S. (1962). *Thought and language* (E. Huffmann and G. Vaker, Eds. and Trans.). Cambridge, MA: MIT Press.

Vygotsky, L. S. (1978). *Mind in society: The development of higher psychological processes* (M. Cole, V. John-Steiner, S. Scribner, and E. Souberman, Eds.). Cambridge, MA: Harvard University Press.

Vygotsky, L. S. (1981). The genesis of higher mental functions. In J. V. Wertsch (Ed.), *The concept of activity* (pp. 144–188). Armonk, NY: Sharpe.

Wassermann, S. (1990). *Serious players in the primary classroom: Empowering children through active learning experiences*. New York: Teachers College Press.

Weikart, P. S. (1987). *Round the circle: Key experiences in movement for children*. Ypsilanti, MI: High/Scope Press.

Weikart, P. S., & Carlton, E. (1995). *Foundations in elementary education: Movement*. Ypsilanti, MI: High/Scope Press.

BOOK SUGGESTIONS FOR CHILDREN

Movement/Dance

Akerman, K. (1988). *Song and dance man*. New York: Knopf.

Barboza, S. (1992). *I feel like dancing: A year with Jacque d'Amboise and the National Dance Institute*. New York: Crown.

dePaola, T. (1979). *Oliver Button is a sissy*. San Diego, CA: Harcourt Brace Jovanovich.

Fox, P. (1982). *The slave dancer*. New York: Bradbury.

Grimm, Brothers (1978). *The twelve dancing princesses*. New York: Viking.

Hermes, P. (1991). *Mama, let's dance*. Boston: Little, Brown.

Hoff, S. (1994). *Duncan the dancing duck*. New York: Clarion.

Hurd, E. T. (1982). *I dance in my red pajamas*. New York: Harper & Row.

Ichikawa, S. (1989). *Dance, Tanya*. New York: Philomel.

Lawler, A. (1977). *The substitute*. New York: Parents' Magazine Press.

Lowery, L. (1996). *Twist with a burger, jitter with a bug*. Boston: Houghton Mifflin.

Monroe, J. G., & Williamson, R. A. (1987). *They dance in the sky: Native American star myths*. Boston: Houghton Mifflin.

Patrick, D. L. (1993). *Red dancing shoes*. New York: Tambourine Books.

Paulson, G. (1983). *Dancing Carl*. New York: Bradbury.

Rodanas, K. (1994). *Dance of the sacred circle: A Native American tale*. Boston: Little, Brown.

Shannon, G. (1982). *Dance away*. New York: Greenwillow.

Sneve, V. D. H. (Ed.). (1989). *Dancing teepees: Poems of American youth*. New York: Holiday House.

VanLaan, N. (1993). (Retold). *Buffalo dance: A Blackfoot legend*. Boston: Little, Brown.

Walker, B. K. (1990). (Retold). *The dancing palm tree: And other Nigerian folktales*. Lubbock, TX: Texas Tech University Press.

Wallace, I. (1984). *Chin Chiang and the dragon's dance*. New York: Atheneum.

Waters, K., & Slovenz-Low, M. (1990). *Lion dancer: Ernie Wan's Chinese new year*. New York: Scholastic.

Wood, D. (1991). *Piggies*. San Diego, CA: Harcourt Brace Jovanovich.

Zeitlin, P. (1982). *A song is a rainbow: Music, movement and rhythm*. Chicago: Scott Foresman.

Zelinsky, P. (1991). *The wheels on the bus*. New York: Dutton.

CURRICULUM GUIDELINES FOR PROFESSIONAL ORGANIZATIONS

This appendix contains standards that have been prepared by professional organizations. Some organizations do not have recently formulated guidelines. Referring to the American Federation of Teachers, Gandal (1995) states that standards should:

1. Focus on academics

2. Be grounded in the core disciplines

3. Be specific enough to assure development of a common core curriculum

4. Be manageable given the constraints of time

5. Be rigorous and world class

6. Evaluate performance

7. Include multiple performance levels

8. Combine knowledge and skills

9. Not dictate how the material should be taught

10. Be written clearly

GOALS 2000

Congress passed legislation called Goals 2000: Educate America Act in the early months of 1994. The act calls for every child in the United States to receive a world-class education through strengthened curriculum, raised academic and skill standards, improved teacher training, and increased cooperation and partnerships among parents, schools, and communities. By the year 2000, all students will leave grades four, eight, and twelve having demonstrated competency over challenging subject matter, including English, mathematics, science, arts, foreign languages, civics, government, economics, history, and geography.

United States Department of Education
Office of Educational Research & Improvement
555 New Jersey Avenue NW, Room 522
Washington, DC 20208-3026
1-202-401-3026

FOREIGN LANGUAGE

The *Standards for Foreign Language Education: Preparing for the 21st Century* is a collaborative project of the American council on the Teaching of Foreign Languages, the American Association of Teachers of French, the American Association of Teachers of German, and the American Association of Teachers of Spanish and Portuguese. Believing that everyone needs competence in more than one language and culture, foreign language groups have prepared standards in five categories. Students should learn to:

1. Communicate in languages other than English

2. Gain knowledge and understanding of other cultures

3. Connect with other disciplines and acquire information

4. Develop insight into the nature of language and culture

5. Participate in multilingual communities at home and around the world

National Standards in Foreign Language Education
c/o ACTFL
6 Executive Plaza
Yonkers, NY 10701-6801
914-963-8830
Fax: 914-963-1275

MATHEMATICS

The NCTM publishes *Curriculum and Evaluation Standards for School Mathematics*, which establishes standards for mathematical literacy. The standards, published in 1989, recommend a curriculum for grades K–12. The key points of the standards feature the importance of

1. A rich variety of mathematics topics and problem situations

2. Active student learning

3. Creating environments that support learning

4. Assessment that is ongoing and based on multiple sources of evidence

National Council of Teachers of Mathematics
1906 Association Drive
Reston, VA 22091-1593
703-620-9840
Fax: 703-476-2970

THE ARTS

Dance, Music, Theatre, Visual Arts: What Every Young American Should Know and Be Able to Do in the Arts is a publication developed in 1994 by the Consortium of National Arts Education Associations. The consortium consists of the following groups: American Alliance for Theatre and Education; Music Educators National Conference; National Art Education Association; and the National Dance Association. The standards ask that students should know and be able to do the following by the time they have completed secondary school: (1) communicate at a basic level in the four arts disciplines of dance, music, theater, and the visual arts, (2) communicate proficiently in at least one art form, (3) develop and present basic analyses of works of art, (4) have an informed acquaintance with exemplary works of art from a variety of cultures and historical periods, and (5) relate various types of arts knowledge and skills within and across the arts disciplines.

MENC Publication Sales
1806 Robert Fulton Drive
Reston, VA 22091
1-800-828-0229

SCIENCE

As a result of Project 2061, the publication *Benchmarks for Science Literacy* was published in 1993 in order to rethink the K–12 science curriculum. *Benchmarks* advocates a common core of learning that connects science, mathematics, and technology. Rather than specify average performance, thresholds are presented.

American Association for the Advancement of Science
1333 H Street NW
Washington, DC 20005
202-326-6624

SOCIAL STUDIES

The NCSS has developed a book entitled *Curriculum Standards for Social Studies: Expectations of Excellence*, which was published in 1994. This book focuses on ten themes that form organizing strands for the various social science disciplines: (1) culture; (2) time, continuity, and change; (3) people, places, and environments; (4) individual development and identity; (5) individuals, groups, and institutions; (6) power, authority, and governance; (7) production, distribution, and consumption; (8) science, technology, and society; (9) global connections; and (10) civic ideals and practices.

National Council for the Social Studies
3501 Newark Street NW
Washington, DC 20016
202-966-7840

CIVICS AND GOVERNMENT

National Standards for Civics and Government is a 1994 publication that addresses K–12. It focuses on five areas: (1) What is civic life, politics, and government? (2) What are the basic foundations of the American political system? (3) How does the government established by the Constitution embody the purposes, values, and principles of American democracy? (4) What is the relationship of the United States to other nations and to world affairs? and (5) What are the roles of the citizen in American democracy?

Center for Civic Education
5146 Douglas Fir Road
Calabasas, CA 91302-1467
1-800-350-4223
Fax: 818-591-9330

GEOGRAPHY

Geography for Life: National Geography Standards 1994 is a publication that specifies what K–12 students in American schools should learn and be able to do. There are six essential categories for the eighteen standards: (1) the world in spatial terms, (2) places and regions, (3) physical systems, (4) human systems, (5) environment and society, and (6) the uses of geography.

National Geographic Society
PO Box 1640
Washington, DC 20013-1640
1-800-368-2728

HISTORY

There were three publications issued in 1994 that deal with history standards for grades K–12: *National Standards for United States History: Exploring the American Experience, National Standards for World History: Exploring Paths to the Present*, and *National Standards for History for Grades K–4*. All three were created in response to state and national mandates to ensure that students demonstrate competency over challenging subject matter. The three volumes identify the important content areas and thinking skills that students should acquire concerning the history of the United states, the history of the world, and the history of people who have contributed to the development of their communities, state, nation, and the world.

University of California, Los Angeles
10880 Wilshire Boulevard, Suite 761
Los Angeles, CA 90024-4108
310-825-4702
Fax: 310-825-4723

READING AND LANGUAGE ARTS

The National Council of Teachers of English and the International Reading Association are jointly working on NIELAST (NCTE/IRA English Language Arts Standards Project). When published, these standards will indicate what students should know and do as a result of instruction in grades K–12. They address writing, speaking, literature, language, and media. A standard is stated, followed by an elaboration (an explanation). Next, classroom vignettes show how the standard can be applied in a class setting. Finally, accomplishments, or evidence of work toward the standard, are given as a more complete description of the content, process, and classroom experiences involved in fulfilling the standard.

National Council of Teachers of English
1111 W. Kenyon Road
Urbana, IL 61801-1096
217-328-3870

International Reading Association
800 Barksdale Road
PO Box 8139
Newark, DE 19714-8139
1-800-336-READ
Fax: 302-731-1057

PHYSICAL EDUCATION

In 1995 standards for physical education were released: *Moving into the Future: The National Physical Education Standards*. These standards define what a student should know and be able to do to become a physically educated person. The document also provides guidelines for teachers to assess the progress of students in meeting the standards.

National Association for Sport and Physical Education
1900 Association Drive
Reston, VA 22091
1-800-321-0789

HEALTH

A publication, "National Health Education Standards: Achieving Health Literacy," was released in 1995. It was prepared by a number of organizations: the American Cancer Society; the Association for the Advancement of Health Education; the American Public Health Association; the American School Health Association; and the Society of State Directors of Health, Physical Education and Recreation. The seven standards, stated very broadly, are directed toward both the elementary and secondary levels of schools.

American Cancer Society
1599 Clifton Road NE
Atlanta, GA 30329-4251
1-800-ACS-2345

EARLY CHILDHOOD

The National Association for the Education of Young Children published a book in 1986 entitled *Developmentally Appropriate Practice in Early Childhood Programs Serving Children from Birth through Age Eight.* The NAEYC feels that (1) curriculum should be integrated; (2) learning activities and materials should be concrete, real, and relevant in the lives of young children; (3) parents and other adults should play an important part in the child's education; and (4) multicultural and nonsexist experiences, materials, and equipment should be provided for children of all ages. The book contains much more information on such topics as evaluation, social-emotional development, grouping and staffing, and teaching strategies.

National Association for the Education of Young Children
1834 Connecticut Avenue NW
Washington, DC 20009-5786
1-800-424-2460

NATIONAL MIDDLE SCHOOL ASSOCIATION

In *This We Believe*, the National Middle School Association supplies a rationale for middle schools, gives characteristics of young adolescents, and defines a middle school. Published in 1982, and reprinted in 1992, this booklet attempts to give direction to the middle school movement.

National Middle School Association
4807 Evanswood Drive
Columbus, OH 43229-6292
614-848-8211
Fax: 614-848-4301

CRITICAL THINKING

The Center for Critical Thinking at Sonoma State University believes critical thinking is intended to help people live "examined lives." Some of its recommendations for teachers are to:

1. Design coverage so that students grasp more

2. Speak less so that students think more

3. Focus on fundamental and powerful concepts with high generalizability

4. Present concepts in the context of their use as functional tools for the solution of real problems and the analysis of significant issues

5. Let students observe the teacher "thinking aloud"

6. Question students socratically

7. Call frequently on students who don't have their hands up

8. Use concrete examples to illustrate abstract concepts and thinking

9. Require regular writing

10. Break the class frequently down into small groups of twos, threes, and fours

The Center for and Foundation for Critical Thinking
4655 Sonoma Mountain Road
Santa Rosa, CA 95404
E-mail: CCT@sonoma.edu
Web site: http://www.sonoma.edu/cthink/

VOCATIONAL STUDIES

The Mid-Continent Regional Education Laboratory has prepared some guidelines for what students should be able to do. Following are the statements in the area of vocational studies:

1. Makes effective use of basic tools

2. Manages money wisely

3. Pursues specific jobs

4. Makes general preparation for entering the work force

5. Makes effective use of basic life skills

6. Displays reliability and a basic work ethic

7. Operates effectively within organizations

Mid-Continent Regional Education Laboratory
2550 S. Parker Road, Suite 500
Aurora, CO 80014
Fax: 303-337-3005

There are several other organizations that are connected with vocational studies. Two of them are:

American Home Economics Association
1555 King Street
Alexandria, VA 22314
703-706-4600
Fax: 703-706-HOME

American Vocational Association
1410 King Street
Alexandria, VA 22314
703-683-3111
Fax: 703-683-7424

TECHNOLOGY

The Association for Educational Communications and Technology represents the interests of professionals involved in the field of instructional technology. It promotes the effective application of technology in the teaching/learning process. In 1994 the AECT issued a final report for a Vision 2000 Strategic Plan, which states the following:

1. The AECT will be a dynamaic professional organization anticipating and planning for the forces of change affecting members and the field.

2. The AECT will provide a fluid structure for interaction on the application of instructional technology.

3. The AECT is committed to the continual professional development and personal growth for its members throughout their careers.

4. The AECT, through its membership, will be recognized as a leader in the field of instructional technology.

Association for Educational Communications and Technology
1025 Vermont Avenue NW, Suite 820
Washington, DC 20005
Fax: 202-347-7839

REFERENCES

Gandal, M. (1995, March). Not all standards are created equal. *Educational Leadership, 52*(6), 16–21.

DIRECTORY OF RESOURCES

The following names and locations of resources should be helpful for those who want to obtain materials related to ideas discussed in this book.

Alarion Press, Inc.
PO Box 1882
Boulder, CO 80306-1882
1-800-523-9177
(CD-ROM, posters, and audiovisual materials on history, art, and architecture)

The American Forum for Global Education
120 Wall Street, Suite 2600
New York, NY 10005
212-742-8232
Fax: 212-742-8752
E-mail: globed@igc.org
(Printed materials on international education)

Apple Computer
20525 Marianni Avenue
Cupertino, CA 95014
1-800-282-2732
http://www.info.apple.com/education
(Provides computer materials)

Art Visuals
PO Box 925
Orem, UT 84059-0925
Phone and Fax: 1-801-226-6115
(Publishes visual aids for visual arts)

Bantam Doubleday Dell
School & Library Marketing Dept.
1540 Broadway
New York, NY 10036
1-800-323-9872
(Supplies books for young people)

Broderbund Software
17 Paul Drive
San Rafael, CA 94903
E-mail: webmaster@broderbund.com
(Supplies computer software programs)

Charles Clark Company
170 Keyland Court
Bohemia, NY 11716
1-800-247-7009
Fax: 516-589-6131
(Handles educational videocassettes and videodiscs)

Children's Press
PO Box 1331
Danbury, CT 06813-1331
1-800-621-1115
Fax: 1-800-374-4329
(Books in a variety of curriculum areas)

Corwin Press
2455 Teller Road
Thousand Oaks, CA 91320-2218
1-805-499-9734
Fax: 1-805-499-0871
E-mail: webmaster@sagepub.com
(Distributes Kraus Teacher Resource Handbooks in various curriculum areas)

CRADLE
Wake Forest University School of Law
2714 Henning Drive
Winston-Salem, NC 27106-4502
1-800-437-1054   910-721-3355
Fax: 910-721-3353
(The Center has lesson plans and materials for law-related education)

George F. Cram, Co., Inc.
PO Box 426
Indianapolis, IN 46206
1-800-227-4199
Fax: 317-635-2720
(Supplier of maps and globes)

Creative Publications
5623 West 115th Street
Worth, IL 60482-9931
1-800-624-0822
Fax: 1-800-624-0821
(Handles K–12 math and integrated resources)

Creative Teaching Press
10701 Holder Street
Cypress, CA 90630
(Has books and other materials for classroom use)

Crystal Productions
Box 2159
Glenview, IL 60025
1-800-644-3432
(Posters showing works of art and elements of art design)

Cuisenaire Company of America, Inc.
PO Box 5026
White Plains, NY 10602-5026
1-800-237-0338
Fax: 800-551-RODS
(Materials for learning mathematics and science)

Curriculum Associates, Inc.
5 Esquire Road
PO Box 2001
N. Billerica, MA 01862-0901
1-800-225-0248
Fax: 508-667-5706
E-mail: curricasso@aol.com
(Suppliers of audiovisual materials and print material)

Davis Publications, Inc.
50 Portland Street
Worcester, MA 01608
1-800-533-2847
(Textbooks, resource books, and audiovisual materials on the topic of art)

Educational Resources
1550 Executive Drive
PO Box 1900
Elgin, IL 60121-1900
1-800-624-2926
(Educational software and technology)

ETA
620 Lakeview Parkway
Vernon Hills, IL 60061
1-800-445-5985
Fax: 1-800-ETA-9326
(Has catalog listing of math manipulatives)

Facts on File, Inc.
11 Penn Plaza
New York, NY 10001-2006
1-800-322-8755
Fax: 1-800-678-3633
(Reference materials on people and places)

Folk & Traditional Arts Program
National Endowment for the Arts
1100 Pennsylvania Avenue NW
Washington, DC 20506
(Provides information concerning efforts to support folk art programs in communities throughout the US)

Good Apple
4350 Equity Drive
PO Box 2649
Columbus, OH 43216
1-800-321-3106
Fax: 1-614-771-7362
(Has a catalog of teaching aids and materials in many curriculum areas)

Hammond Inc.
515 Valley Street
Maplewood, NJ 07040
1-800-526-4953
Fax: 1-201-763-7658
(Supplier of maps and globes)

Health EDCO
PO Box 21207
Waco, TX 76702-1207
1-800-299-3366
Fax: 817-751-0221
(Distributes materials for health education)

Heinemann
361 Hanover Street
Portsmouth, NH 03801-3912
1-800-541-2086
Fax: 1-800-847-0938
(Provides books on reading and other curriculum areas)

High/Scope Press
600 N. River Street
Ypsilanti, MI 48198
1-800-40PRESS
Fax: 1-800-442-4FAX
(Provides information on early childhood programs)

IBM Corporation
PO Box 1328-W
Boca Raton, FL 33429-1328
1-800-IBM-3333
E-mail: askibm@info.ibm.com
(Supplier of computer hardware and software)

International Food Information Council
1100 Connecticut Avenue NW, Suite 430
Washington, DC 20036
E-mail: foodinfo@ific.health.org
(Offers publications for elementary, middle, and senior high grades on nutrition, food safety, labeling, etc.)

IRI/Skylight
200 East Wood Street, Suite 274
Palatine, IL 60067
1-800-348-4474
Fax: 847-991-6420
E-mail: irisky@xnet.com
(Books, videos, and training programs for elementary through high school)

The Lerner Group
241 First Avenue North
Minneapolis, MN 55401
1-800-328-4929
Fax: 1-800-332-1132
(Supplies books by Lerner Publications, Carolrhoda Books, Runestone Press, and First Avenue Editions)

Magazines for Kids and Teens
International Reading Association
800 Barksdale Road
PO Box 8139
Newark, DE 19714-8139
1-800-336-READ Ext. 266
(Contains descriptions of 249 magazines for ages 2–18)

Lakeshore Learning Materials
2695 East Dominguez Street
PO Box 6261
Carson, CA 90749
1-800-421-5354
Fax: 310-537-5403
(Carries general educational materials)

Microsoft Corporation
1 Microsoft Way
PO Box 97017
Redmond, WA 98052
1-800-426-9400
(Computer software and information)

Millbrook Press
2 Old New Milford Road
Brookfield, CT 06804-0335
1-800-462-4703
Fax: 203-740-2526
(Publishes books for children and young adults; also distributes Copper
Beech Books)

National Geographic Society
Educational Services
1145 17th Street NW
Washington, DC 20036-4688
1-800-368-2728
Fax: 1-301-921-1575
(NGS provides materials on maps, globes, multimedia, educational
technology, magazines for children, and a pen pal network)

National School Products
101 East Broadway
Maryville, TN 37801
1-800-251-9124
Fax: 1-800-289-3960
(Carries CD-ROM software)

Nystrom
3333 Elston Avenue
Chicago, IL 60618-5898
1-800-621-8086
Fax: 312-463-0515
(Supplier of maps and globes)

Penguin USA
375 Hudson Street
New York, NY 10014-3657
212-366-2000
Fax: 212-366-2666
(Carries books under the names of Viking, Allen Lane, Dutton/Signet,
Signet, Mentor, Onyx, Plume, Meridian, Meridian Classic)

The Peoples Publishing Group, Inc.
PO Box 70
Rochelle Park, NJ 07662
1-800-822-1080
Fax: 201-712-0045
(For students with reading and learning problems)

Personalizing the Past
52 Molino Avenue
Mill Valley, CA 94941
415-388-9351
(Provides artifact kits)

Pleasant Company Publications
PO Box 620991
Middleton, WI 53562-0991
1-800-350-6555
(Features the American Girls Collection books plus activity materials on
theater, paper dolls, crafts, and food)

President's Council on Physical Fitness & Sports
Washington, DC 20001
202-272-3421
(Has a wide range of booklets, medals, and record-keeping charts)

Procter & Gamble Company
Public Affairs Division
1 Procter & Gamble Plaza
Cincinnati, OH 45202-3315
(Has an educational services division for materials used in schools)

PRO-ED
8700 Shoal Creek Boulevard

Austin, TX 78757-6897
1-800-397-7633
Fax: 1-800-FXPROED
(Has materials for speech, language, and hearing)

Raintree/Steck-Vaughn Publishers
PO Box 26015
Austin, TX 78755
1-800-531-5015
(Distributes books by Larousse, Kingfisher, Chambers, and Abdo)

Rand McNally & Company
Educational Publishing Division
PO Box 1906
Skokie, IL 60076-9714
1-800-678-7263
Fax: 1-800-934-3479
(Supplier of maps and globes)

Sax Arts & Crafts Catalog
PO Box 51710
New Berlin, WI 53151-0710
414-784-6880
Fax: 414-784-1176
(Materials, tools, and equipment for art education)

Scholastic Inc.
2931 East McCarty Street
Jefferson City, MO 65101
1-800-246-2986
Web site: http://www.scholastic.com/
(Provides books and computer software in various curriculum areas)

School Arts
50 Portland Street
PO Box 15015
Worcester, MA 01615-9959
1-800-533-2847
(Published nine times per year on the topic of art in schools)

Silver Moon Press
126 Fifth Avenue, Suite 803
New York, NY 10011
1-800-874-3320
Fax: 212-242-6799
(Markets books to schools through Phoenix Learning Resources)

Sportime
One Sportime Way
Atlanta, GA 30340
1-800-283-5700
Fax: 1-800-845-1535
(Materials for physical education, recreation, athletics, aquatics, dance,
and health)

Stenhouse
PO Box 360
York, ME 03909
1-800-988-9812
Fax: 1-614-487-2272

Sunburst
101 Castleton Street
PO Box 100
Pleasantville, NY 10570
1-800-321-7511
Fax: 914-747-4109
(Multimedia materials)

Teacher Created Materials
PO Box 1040
Huntington Beach, CA 92647
1-800-662-4321
Fax: 800-525-1254
(A variety of curriculum products for the classroom)

Teaching and Learning Center
1205 Buchanon
Carthage, IL 62321
(Books and other materials for classroom use)

Thomson Learning
One Penn Plaza, 41st Floor
New York, NY 10119
212-594-8211
Fax: 212-594-8544
(Reference/information books for students)

Tom Snyder Productions
80 Cooledge Hill Road
Watertown, MA 02172-2817
1-800-342-0236
Fax: 617-926-6222
(Computer materials)

Troll Associates
100 Corporate Drive
Mahwah, NJ 07430
1-800-929-TROLL
Fax: 1-800-979-TROLL
(Has paperback book club for students)

UNICEF
Division of Communication
3 UN Plaza
New York, NY 10017
212-326-7344
1-800-252-KIDS
Fax: 212-326-7768
(The United Nations Children's Fund sponsors activities and programs and
supplies curriculum materials of an international nature.)

U.S. Consumer Information Center
Pueblo, CO 81009
719-948-4000
(The Consumer Information Catalog lists an assortment of free and
low-cost government publications on such topics as children, health,
and food.)

U.S. Department of Agriculture
Office of Governmental Affairs/Public Information
3101 Park Center Drive, Room 805
Alexandria, VA 22302-1594
1-800-535-4555
703-305-2039
Fax: 703-305-2312
(The Food & Consumer Service has informatin on food nutrition and
safety.)

U.S. Map and Book Company
103 Commerce Street #120
PO Box 950366
Lake Mary, FL 32795-0366
1-800-458-2306
Fax: 407-333-2496
(Maps and globes in various media)

Weekly Reader
3001 Cindel Drive
PO Box 8996
Delran, NJ 08370-8996
1-800-446-3355
(Current events and news publications)

The Wright Group
19201 120th Avenue NE
Bothell, WA 98011-9512
(Materials on reading and language arts)

Writers Press
5278 Chinden
Boise, ID 83714
208-327-0566
Fax: 208-327-3477
(Books for children that deal with the topic of inclusion)

Zaner-Bloser
2200 West Fifth Avenue
PO Box 16764

Columbus, OH 43216-6764
1-800-421-3018
Fax: 614-487-2699
(Materials for spelling and writing)

Zero Population Growth
1400 16th Street NW, Suite 320
Washington, DC 20036
202-332-2200
Fax: 202-332-2302
(ZPG has an education program on environmental impacts of growth)

APPENDIX

C

MATRIX FOR LESSON PLANS (CONTENT AREA)

The check marks indicate that an area is addressed in a chapter lesson plan.

Area	Chapter												
	3	4	5	6	7	8	9	10	11	12	13	14	15
Language Arts	✔	✔	✔			✔		✔	✔	✔			
Writing				✔			✔						
Social Studies	✔		✔		✔	✔	✔	✔					
Geography		✔									✔	✔	
Mathematics	✔			✔		✔							✔
Arts & Architecture												✔	
Reading	✔		✔	✔	✔		✔						
History		✔										✔	
Science				✔							✔	✔	
Anthropology				✔			✔			✔			
Physical Education & Movement											✔		
Health								✔					✔
Music										✔			
Visual Arts										✔			
Art			✔			✔							
Vocational Studies & Practical Living							✔	✔					
Industrial Technology												✔	

MATRIX FOR LESSON PLANS (GRADE LEVEL)

The check marks indicate the grade levels addressed in the chapter.

	Chapter												
Grade Level	3	4	5	6	7	8	9	10	11	12	13	14	15
Early Elementary Grades			✔	✔	✔	✔					✔		✔
Later Elementary Grades	✔	✔	✔	✔	✔	✔			✔	✔	✔	✔	✔
Middle School		✔	✔	✔	✔	✔	✔	✔	✔	✔	✔	✔	✔

GLOSSARY

Activity card: A written format by which a task at a learning center (or in a small group setting) is described (chap. 16).

Alta Vista: A computer search engine (chap. 10).

Anecdotal records: Carefully documented accounts of a learner's progress (chap. 1).

Anthropology: The study of the culture of a people (chap. 9).

Anti-bias curriculum: A course of study that does not discriminate with respect to age, sex, religion, race, or ethnicity (chap. 3).

Architectural elements: Characteristics of building design including such items as the arch, dome, lintel, post, and buttress (chap. 14).

Architecture: Designing and building structures (chap. 14).

Art: Aesthetically created objects that convey the producer's feelings and ideas (chap. 11).

Artifacts: Objects made by human skill or work (chap. 3).

Assessment: The procedures used to find out what students have learned from a sequence of instruction (chap. 1).

Axis: Lines that go from side to side or up and down on a bar, line, or picture graph (chap. 7).

Block courses: Teacher education courses that are linked and taken concurrently (chap. 1).

CD-ROM: A small computer disk storing vast amounts of data, images, and sound. Stands for Compact Disc-Read Only Memory (chap. 10).

Collaboration: One or more persons working together to attain a goal or objective (chap. 1).

Collage: A collection of pieces of paper or other objects pasted on a flat surface, sometimes with additions of paint to make a composition, especially an abstract or surrealistic composition (chap. 1).

Concept: An idea or mental image that is expressed as a word or phrase (chap. 6).

Conflict resolution: An attempt to come to some settlement when there is a disagreement over issues, attitudes, emotions, ideas, etc. (chap. 5).

Constructivist approach: A child-oriented learning theory supporting the exercise of moral and intellectual autonomy, decentering and coordination of perspectives, and the exercise of initiative in purposeful activities that inspire new cognitive constructions (chap. 1).

Cooperative learning: n instructional method in which students are divided into small groups or partners to achieve a common goal, objective, or task (chap. 1).

Creativity: The act of producing something through imaginative skill (chap. 16).

Culminating performance: A comprehensive and engaging presentation demonstrating the use of knowledge and skills by students (chap. 1).

Curriculum: A process that continually defines and redefines the experiences students have in learning situations (chap. 1).

Curriculum planning map: A schematic guide that shows the composition of a unit (chap. 1).

DBAE: Decision-based art education; a curriculum approach to arts in education calling for students to receive experiences in art making, art history, art criticism, and aesthetics (chap. 11).

Debriefing: Questions that require students to engage in reflection and high-level thinking (chap. 2).

Early elementary: The beginning years of elementary school, usually considered as grades K–4 (preface).

Electronic mail [e-mail]: A convenient way to electronically send messages to or communicate worldwide with people or organizations (chap. 10).

Elementary grades: The years of schooling before a student enters middle school or junior high (preface).

Equity: Fairness or justice (chap. 3).

Field experiences: The activities a college student performs that take place in an elementary or middle school classroom (chap. 1).

Food Guide Pyramid: A model of food groups that should be consumed for good health (chap. 15).

Games: Activities engaged in for amusement or diversion (chap. 13).

Geography: The study of the earth and how people relate to it (chap. 9).

Geometry: A branch of mathematics that deals with the measurement, properties, and relationships of points, lines, angles, surfaces, and solids (chap. 9).

Gopher: A software tool enabling someone to search for items using a menu on a computer screen (chap. 10).

Graffiti wall: A free-form space for brainstorming or communicating key words, phrases, or ideas on a topic (chap. 5).

Graphs: Visual or pictorial representations to show data (chap. 7).

Health: The condition of being sound in body, mind, or spirit (chap. 15).

Horizontal relevance: Learning that equips the learner to solve current problems within and outside the classroom (chap. 1).

http: Hypertext transfer protocol (chap. 10).

Integrated curriculum: An organizational approach to teaching and learning so that various content areas are related, rather than addressed separately (chap. 1).

Internet: A worldwide computer hookup, delivered through telephone lines (chap. 10).

Junior high: The block of time between elementary school and high school (preface).

K-W-L: This is a teaching technique that asks the students to tell what they *know* about a topic, what they *want* to know about the topic, and what they *learned* at the conclusion of study. Sometimes referred to as K-W-H-L when the phrase is added "How will I learn this?" (chap. 1).

Language arts: The area of the curriculum that includes reading, speaking, writing, and listening (chap. 2).

Later elementary: The years following the early elementary years, usually somewhere between grades three through six (preface).

Learning center: A specific location in a classroom, with related materials, where students can go to learn about and participate in curriculum activities (chap. 16).

Learning environment: The milieu in which a child encounters experiences for learning, to include physical social, emotional, and cognitive aspects (chap. 16).

Learning modalities: The way a student learns: auditorially, visually, kinesthetically (chap. 16).

Lesson plan: Detailed suggestions for classroom instruction that covers a short period of time (chap. 2).

Listserv: A program that facilitates discussion groups over computer networks (chap. 10).

Map: A selective view of a geographic area that contains such elements as scale, legend, and grid (chap. 8).

Mathematics: The science of numbers and their operations, interrelations, combinations, generalizations, and abstractions (chap. 15).

McKinley: A computer search engine (chap. 10).

Methods courses: Teacher education courses that provide the college student with direction on how to teach subject matter (chap. 1).

Middle school: The years of schooling after a student leaves the elementary grades, typically beginning with grades five or six and ending with grade eight (preface).

Mock trial: A classroom enactment of a courtroom case (chap. 5).

Movement education: The exploration of space and how one's body can move in space (chap. 13).

Multicultural education: Interdisciplinary, cross-curricular education which prepares students to live, learn, and work together with a culturally diverse world (chap. 3).

Multiculturalism: Encompasses learning about people in the world—near and far. It encompasses age, gender, ethnicity, religion, and lifestyle (chap. 3).

Multiple intelligences: A theory of intelligence that proposes individuals from all cultures possess at least seven domains of intelligence (or ways of knowing): bodily kinesthetic, interpersonal, intrapersonal, linguistic, spatial, logico-mathematical, and musical (chap. 16).

Music: The production of vocal or instrumental sounds to create an aesthetic product having unity and continuity (chap. 12).

Narrative: Anecdotal information (chap. 1).

Norm: A standard for a certain group (chap. 1).

Notes: Interpretations of anecdotal information (chap. 1).

Nutrition education: A set of learning experiences designed to facilitate voluntary adoption of eating and other nutrition-related behaviors (chap. 15).

Objectives: Statements of what a teacher intends for the student to learn from instructional activities (chap. 2).

On-line: Information available on the computer, accessible to a user through a computer system (chap. 10).

Oral response: A form of oral communication with students conveying their reaction verbally (chap. 4).

Parallelogram: A four-sided plain figure whose opposite sides are parallel and equal, as a rectangle or diamond (chap. 9).

Performance based assessment: Assessment done whereby actual products and performances of students are evaluated (chap. 1).

Persuasive speech: A formal talk to convince others to change an idea or try a particular product (chap. 12).

Physical education: Developing the individual through planned movement, physical activity, or exercise (chap. 13).

Play: Activities not consciously performed for the sake of any result beyond themselves (chap. 13).

Portfolio: A collection of student work, the contents showing the progress of a student over time (chap. 1).

Practical living: Area of study that integrates across the disciplines and includes physical, health and wellness education, home economics, family life education, resource and consumer management, social skill development, substance and violence prevention, stress management, and conflict resolution (chap. 10).

Primary grades: The early years of schooling for children, typically from kindergarten through grade three (preface).

Probability: The quality or fact of being likely or probable (chap. 7).

Project approach: An extended study over time by individuals, small groups, or large groups (chap. 1).

Search engine: A utility that enables a person to search for information on a computer data base (chap. 10).

Self-evaluation: Assessing one's own performance or learning (chap. 1).

Self-sufficiency: Being able to take care of one's needs (chap. 16).

Server: A supplier of resources on a terminal screen (chap. 10).

Skill: The ability to do something (chap. 6).

Social mathematics: The study and use of statistics and probability applied to the social world (chap. 7).

Social studies: The area of the curriculum that includes geography, anthropology, economics, political science, sociology, and history (chap. 2).

Special classes: Classes often taught by specialists, such as art, music, physical education, and library (chap. 1).

Statistics: Numeral facts or data about people, the weather, business conditions, and other areas (chap. 7).

Symbol: Something that stands for or represents an idea, quality, condition, and other abstractions (chap. 8).

Teach-reflect-reteach: A process that includes three steps of instruction, thinking about modifications to the instruction, and implementing the revised instructional plan (chap. 1).

Theme: A focus applied to a sequence of instruction (chap. 1).

Thematic teaching unit: A collection of materials, activities, and techniques that is organized around a topic, theme, or concept (chap. 1).

Time line: A representation depicting a sequence of events that occurred during a specific period of time, often placed on a horizontal line (chap. 4).

Unit: The general term indicating instruction on a broad topic (chap. 1).

Venn diagram: A graphic organizer consisting of overlapping circles, each circle containing information unique to the label ascribed to the circle (chap. 1).

Vertical relevance: Instruction that prepares the learner for the next level of instruction (chap. 1).

Visual arts: The graphic arts consisting of painting, sculpture, drawing, photography (chap. 11).

Webcrawler: A computer search engine (chap. 10).

Webbing: A schematic representation of terms arranged on a sheet of paper so that connections among the various terms can be seen (chap. 2).

World Wide Web: A network of sites on the Internet that can be accessed with hypertext (chap. 10).

Yahoo: A computer search engine (chap. 10).

Whole language: An interdependent communication philosophy based on a theory about how people learn and think in meaningful social contexts (chap. 1).

Writing process: A series of writing stages that includes prewriting, drafting, revising, editing, and publishing (chap. 12).

AUTHOR CITATIONS

Lindquist, T.   96

Little, J.   1

Locklege, A.   74

Loovis, E.   235

Madden, W.   75

Mayher, J.   152

McCracken, J.   38, 40

Miller, L.   97

Mitchell, C.   97

Monroe, J.   176

Montessori, M.   232

Mounkhall, T.   190

Nelson, W.   182, 183

Newman, G.   152, 157

Nickell, P.   176, 183

Norton, D.   86

Norton, J.   57

Pahnos, M.   175

Pappas, C.   10, 56, 131, 134, 211

Parker, F.   2

Petty, D.   44

Petty, W.   44

Piaget, J.   232

Pica, R.   224, 232, 233

Piersma, M.   2

Potter, B.   59

Pradl, G.   152

Prelutsky, J.   17

Price, G.   210

Pritchard, S.   46

Reiff, J.   230

Remnant, M.   158

Renga, S.   97

Riley, R.   118

Roberts, P.   16

Salzer, R.   44

Shanahan, T.   14

Sims, L. S.   208

Slavin, R.   231, 232

Smith, K.   232

Steffe, L.   211

Stopsky, F.   86

Strickland, J.   97

Sunal, C.   64, 65

Taras, H.   232

Tharp, R.   211

Thornton, S.   44

Tiene, D.   106

Torrance, E.   232

Trawick-Smith, J.   228, 235

Van de Walle, J.   97

Vukelich, R.   44

Vygotsky, L.   176, 224, 235

Wassermann, S.   224, 230, 231, 235

Weikart, D.   18, 226, 231, 232, 233, 235

Weikart, P.   232

Whitin, D.   74, 97

Whitmore, E.   106

Young, P.   158

Zaccaria, M.   44

INDEX